Evaluation and Social Research

Evaluation and Social Research

Introducing Small-Scale Practice

Irene Hall and David Hall

Consultant Editor: Jo Campling

First published 2004 by
PALGRAVE MACMILLAN
Houndmills, Basingstoke, Hampshire RG21 6XS and
175 Fifth Avenue, New York, N.Y. 10010
Companies and representatives throughout the world

PALGRAVE MACMILLAN is the global academic imprint of the Palgrave
Macmillan division of St. Martin's Press, LLC and of Palgrave Macmillan Ltd.
Macmillan® is a registered trademark in the United States, United Kingdom
and other countries. Palgrave is a registered trademark in the European
Union and other countries.

ISBN 0–333–93095–9

This book is printed on paper suitable for recycling and made from fully
managed and sustained forest sources.

A catalogue record for this book is available from the British Library.

A catalog record for this book is available from the Library of Congress.

10 9 8 7 6 5 4 3 2 1
13 12 11 10 09 08 07 06 05 04

Printed in China

Contents

List of Tables   xi

List of Figures   xii

Preface and Acknowledgements   xiii

1 Introduction   1
What is this book about?   1
Where does this book fit in the growing literature on
  evaluation?   3
How is the book structured?   4
Evaluation and research   5
  What is social research?   5
  What is evaluation?   6
Introducing the model of small-scale evaluation   7
Defining 'small-scale': restriction or strength?   8
Principles of small-scale evaluation   9
  Partnering   9
  Evaluator's role   9
  Evaluation for development   9
  Evaluation for use   10
  Ethics   10
  Scale   10
  Resources   10
  Rights to the report   10
  Experiential learning   11
  Students   11
Small-scale evaluation: some issues and considerations   11
  Students as evaluators   11
  Negotiation   13
  Agreement   15
  Health and safety   17
  Assessment   17
  Access and ethics   18
  Resources and research design considerations   18

Are the findings of small-scale evaluation ever used?   20
   Diversity of use   20
   Consultation and contact   22
   Timing of evaluation   23
   Managerial willingness to act on evaluation   23

2 Understanding Evaluation   **26**
Summary   26
Overview of evaluation issues   27
Evaluation as everyday activity   27
Defining evaluation   28
Formative and summative evaluation   29
Evaluation history: public programs and the 'classic'
   evaluation model   30
Emergence of different kinds of evaluation   31
   Three major approaches to evaluation   31
The role of the evaluator   34
Roles of other evaluation participants   37
   Commissioners of evaluation   37
   Sponsors and gatekeepers   38
   Other Stakeholders   39
Timing of evaluation in relation to program activity   41
The link between evaluation and policy   42
Models of evaluation practice   *44*
Models which emphasize accountability   44
   Impact assessment/outcome evaluation (the 'classic'
      model)   44
   Goal-free evaluation   45
Models which emphasize development/process   46
   Process evaluation   46
   Illuminative evaluation   47
   Responsive evaluation   48
   Utilization-focused evaluation   49
   Participatory evaluation   49
   Empowerment evaluation   51
Theorizing evaluation   *52*
Fourth-generation evaluation   52
Theory-driven evaluation   54
Realistic evaluation   55
Revisiting the small-scale evaluation model   *57*
Student projects   58

3   Evaluation and Ethics   **60**
   Summary   60
   Introduction   61
   Models of evaluation and the treatment of ethics   61
   How can evaluation be seen as fair judgement?   *63*
   Evidence and response: presenting critical findings   64
      Evidence-based evaluation: ethical issues   67
      Being seen to be independent: ethical issues   71
      Student evaluators and independence   74
   Independence and justice: codes and dilemmas   75
      Key principles   76
      Codes   76
      Dilemmas: justice and care   87

4   Planning Research   **92**
   Summary   92
   Planning evaluation research   *92*
   Setting the evaluation questions   92
   Negotiating the research design   95
   Criteria for research design   97
   Combining multiple methods   98
   Research plan checklist   101
   Research activities and methods   *102*
   Epistemology and the role of the researcher   102
   Methods of experiencing   104
      Observation   104
   Methods of enquiring   110
      The survey   110
      Qualitative interviews   117
      Notifying subjects   122
   Recording the information   122
   Research with children   124
   Research with and by disabled people   125
   Methods of examining   126
      Local area statistics   126
      Organizational records   127
      Personal records   128
   Sampling   *128*
   Selection of participants in the research   128
   Probability samples   129

Non-probability samples   131
    Quota sampling   131
    Theoretical sampling   132
    Snowball sampling   133
    Samples of convenience   133
Suggestions for further reading   134

5 Analysing the Data   **136**
Summary   136
Quantitative or structured data   *137*
Data and the rules of measurement   137
    Organizing quantitative data for analysis   139
Using computers with quantitative data   142
    Checking the information for consistency
        and errors   142
    Reducing and summarizing the information   143
    Looking for patterns in the data   145
    Testing hypotheses or constructing explanations   147
Recognizing associations   149
Qualitative or naturalistic data   *150*
Analysing recorded interviews   151
Transcription   152
    Accuracy in transcription   152
Thematic analysis   153
Coding data   155
    Applying codes   155
    Categorizing codes, reducing information and
        developing explanations   156
Narrative   157
Oral history   159
Representation in qualitative analysis   161
Suggestions for further reading   162

**6 Reporting on Evaluation: Communicating to
    Audiences**   **163**
Summary   163
The final report – structure and audiences   164
Style and language   165
Using language sensitively   166
Constructing the text   167
Presenting criticisms   172

Beginning the written report   174
Structure of the written report   175
   Title   175
   Contents list   175
   Acknowledgements   176
   Executive summary   176
   Introduction and background information   178
   Purpose of evaluation and methods chosen   179
   Results and findings   180
   Conclusions and recommendations   181
   Appendices   184
Presentation   184
Length   185
Making the report accessible to readers and
  writers with dyslexia   186
Dissemination   187

7 Reflecting on Evaluation   **189**
Summary   189
Thinking about reflexivity and reflection   *190*
Reflexivity   191
   Position of the researcher   192
Reflection   194
Experiential learning   196
Developing reflexivity and reflection in evaluation
  practice   *197*
Research diary   198
   Structure   198
Reflective account   204
Assessing the process of evaluation: the role of
  reflection   214
Reflection within the evaluation report?   214

8 Case-studies of Small-Scale Evaluation   **216**
Summary   216
Charington Hostel   216
   Executive summary   217
   Research methods   218
   Limitations of the sample   219
   Negotiating the role of evaluator   220
   The findings   221

Meaning of 'home'   223
Conclusions and recommendations   225
Response of the client   226
Comment   226
Oriel Day and Resource Centre   227
Executive summary   228
Research methods   229
The findings   229
Conclusions and recommendations   232
Response of the client   232
Comment   233

Appendix 1: Evaluation Agreement   235

Appendix 2: Risk Assessment   237

Appendix 3: Health and Safety Questionnaire   239

Bibliography   242

Index   252

List of Tables

1.1 Use of evaluation reports   21
5.1 Case by variable data matrix   140
5.2 Descriptive statistics for scales of measurement   144
5.3 Example of a frequency table for political preference   144
5.4 Views on safety by evening activity   148
5.5 Preference for coffee shop by evening activity   148
6.1 Areas of volunteering beneficial for nurse training   181
8.1 Residents' opinions of the staff   222
8.2 Staff opinions of their relationship with residents   222

List of Figures

2.1 Systems diagram   33
5.1 Example of a bar chart for political preference   144
5.2 Schematic of explanatory causal model   146

Preface and Acknowledgements

This book has developed from our working with students conducting evaluation research with voluntary and welfare organizations in the city where they were studying. Through the years, we have seen how they have responded to the challenge of conducting research designed to be of use, providing benefit to organizations and their clients through feedback on service provision, and how they have been able to develop recommendations for future action as a result of their investigations.

Our previous book, **Practical Social Research**, was designed to support those wishing to engage in applied social research, as well as to show through examples how this can be achieved by student projects. Over the years, it has been noticeable that a good many of the requests for projects coming from small and medium voluntary sector organizations are for evaluations of one kind or another. So the idea emerged to write another book, this time making the evaluation process accessible to students.

It has been heartening to see how engaged students have become with the work of small-scale evaluation, and the high quality of their reports has been acknowledged by external examiners. It has also been rewarding to note the increasing awareness by the organizations that the evaluations are valuable for their progress – in making them reassess the way they operate and in making them think about options and potential for future development. For some organizations, the evaluation reports have become an evidence-base for funding applications.

These small-scale evaluations have had long-term impact on the careers of students, because of the skills and experiences they gained working in the community. When interviewed long after their projects were completed, it was noticeable how many felt their evaluation work was the highlight of their degree. Ainé Wolstenholme, the assistant transcribing the interviews, commented on the warmth and enthusiasm which entered their voices when students were asked to recall what they remembered as being important about their experiences, and what they were now applying in their jobs. This research is referred to at the end of the first chapter, but the tables do not capture the feeling or really sum up what the achievement meant to those participating – students and supervisors.

The long term effects on organizations are also noted – how findings have been applied to make the organization more effective, or used with success as evidence of effectiveness to back proposals to funding agencies for their work to continue or expand. Small-scale evaluation, originally part of the teaching of final year undergraduate students, is now also central to the Masters degree programme with which the authors are involved. The reports being produced by students at this level are finding recognition in conferences and publications, as well as in direct use by community groups (and of course, by students as part of assessment for their degrees). This book tries to encapsulate the learning from all these projects, and the authors recognize the central importance of the students' work and the community partnering in developing and extending the model of small-scale evaluation – which is continually being refined with each unique evaluation activity.

Engagement with the community is now being promoted as part of the 'third mission' of universities in the UK (in addition to the traditional academic pursuits of teaching and research). However, to date, much of the engagement with the world outside academia has been with the business world, and involves scientific and technological know-how being shared and developed, rather than social scientific knowledge being made available to those who can benefit from it (and who, in turn, can contribute their own expertise to the discourse with academia).

There are signs, however, that community engagement is becoming more significant for higher education in the UK, and that opportunities for small-scale evaluation will increase. There are converging movements in Europe and North America, for instance, which indicate that the 'third mission' should be understood as part of a wider trend. In Europe, from its origins in the Netherlands, the 'science shop' movement (www.scienceshops.org/) has developed in order to help open up universities to their surrounding communities and their needs for information – to democratize knowledge through scientific/social scientific applied research conducted by students. The authors have been involved with this movement for some time, and as partners in the INTERACTS European Union funded project, are comparing science shop activity across seven nations, in order to develop policy recommendations at the European level to expand science shop activity, where science shops already feature in the European Science and Society dialogue.

In the United States, the 'service-learning' movement has become widely established through Campus Compact (www. compact.org) to enable students in higher education to apply their learning through service to surrounding community groups. While such 'service' may not involve research or evaluation, it does support a major theme of this book – that knowledge, skills, time and commitment can be applied to the benefit of student and organization – and can energize the teaching experience of supervisors. High quality service learning involves the encouragement (and assessment) of reflection by student volunteers. The importance of reflection is also stressed in this book – as an essential part of being an effective evaluator. Working with community groups for research and evaluation means there is plenty to reflect upon – skills are developed, academic learning or theorizing is tested against real-life experience and commitment and enthusiasm can yield results which surprise the participants.

This book is written against this wider backdrop of rethinking the role of universities in their communities. It develops a specific way of negotiating partnership between academia and community organizations through evaluation conducted by students as part of their degree programmes. The book provides guidelines and advice based on many years of practice, and is intended to make a contribution to the literature which is now beginning to emerge for evaluators whose work is not part of national large scale programs, but small scale and local to one agency.

We would like to thank all the organizations who agreed to their reports being used and would like to thank them for their willingness to allow the students to develop their research and evaluation skills in a real life setting. Managers and mentors within these organizations were often very generous in their time and support, in spite of the pressures they were facing as people who work hard in an under-resourced sector.

We are also indebted to the students who responded to the opportunity to do evaluation research, and whose hard work and xvi

PREFACE AND ACKNOWLEDGEMENTS

energy produced so many valuable reports. Their work has helped to develop and improve the small scale model and provided continuous learning for their supervisors. We would like to thank all the students who have participated, and in particular the following whose ideas and experiences are referred to in the text: Anne Aitken, Julie Anderson, Jamie Arnold, Kathryn Bird, Martin Chamberlain, Laura Cockram, Annemarie Cronin, Shirley Fong, Vicky Foster, Julie Gornell, Kate Hayes, Jeremy Iankov, Pat Jones, Jackson Li, John Kavanagh, Kathryn Brady Kean, Andrew Kirkcaldy, Christina Lawrence, Jessie McCulloch, Susan Molesworth, Diane Ogden, Anne Payler, Fiona Quarrie, Joanna Rice, Janine Richmond, Tina Sadler, Aileen Scott, Lucy Senior, Janis Stanton, Katie Sullivan, Julie Thompson, Catherine Thorpe, Hameera Waheed, Elizabeth Walker, Claire Whitworth.

Especial thanks are also due to Sharon Lockley, for her co-ordination of the Liverpool science shop, Interchange (www.liv.ac.uk/sspsw/interchange/) and for her commitment to supporting students, staff and community organizations with patience and with wisdom. Other colleagues who have been supportive of this work include Chris Jones of Liverpool University, John Annette of Middlesex University, Geoff Sparks of Huddersfield University, Pat Green and Andy Cameron of Wolverhampton University and Caspar de Bok of the Science Shop for Biology at the University of Utrecht as well as the Interchange management team.

We are grateful to ARVAC for giving permission to quote from its resource pack for community groups, 'Community Research: Getting Started', to Jo Campling our Consultant Editor, and to Catherine Gray and Kate Wallis at Palgrave Macmillan. There are many others, whose names are not mentioned here, whose support and encouragement has been so helpful. You know who you are. Thank you all. We hope you will find this book useful.

IRENE HALL
DAVID HALL

CHAPTER 1

Introduction

What is this book about?

This book is about applying social research to the evaluation of programs or activities within organizations, and considering how such evaluation can produce usable findings. It discusses how to apply the principles and practice of evaluation to local circumstances where resources for evaluation are limited. Such evaluation is therefore on a small scale and those conducting the evaluation are unlikely to be professional evaluators. A model of small-scale evaluation is detailed in the second half of this chapter. The rest of the book shows how the model has been developed and how it can be applied.

We have three main audiences in mind. First, there are students who are learning evaluation practice through applied research and wish to conduct an evaluation of an organization as part of their degree studies, at undergraduate or postgraduate level. Many of the examples in this book are taken from undergraduate and postgraduate student projects, and show what can be achieved on a small scale. It is hoped that students will take encouragement from these examples and use this book to begin their own evaluations.

Second, the book is also aimed at learners in a wider sense, especially those working for organizations which require evaluation or are subject to it. For these learners, this is a practical guide to evaluation, which aims to help them understand the varieties of practice and competing models of evaluation, to enhance their ability to negotiate and commission an evaluation to be conducted by others.

Third, there are increasing demands within organizations for self-evaluation, to review activities and propose changes in the light of systematic feedback from customers, clients and fellow staff members. Practitioners within organizations looking for help with undertaking evaluation on limited resources should also find this book useful in encouraging them to undertake studies of their own.

The dividing line between practitioners in organizations and students in higher education need not be a hard-and-fast boundary. It can usefully be blurred by engagement in evaluation. This book argues that crossing the boundary brings advantages to both parties. Students gain experience of working in a non-academic setting and learn the priorities and demands of the workplace. Practitioners, who engage in evaluation with students or with work colleagues, learn the issues of evaluation – including research methodology and the clarification of the aims and possible uses of the work. For both, such learning involves a strong reflective element, which is part of the process of producing results that can be implemented.

Evaluation can also be an enjoyable experience. Students confirm it is hard work and demanding – but also rewarding because of the satisfaction of producing work with the potential to improve life for others. For many, it is an introduction to an area or activity which brings new experiences and awareness. Through grappling with the task of evaluation, they have to quickly familiarize themselves with new issues and new people, an experience quite different from learning in the library. These are some of the things students said:

> [The highlight was] to see these women...their experiences...doing something positive for their community.
>
>   I felt I was doing something worthwhile, there was a point, they were appreciative.
>
> (Hall and Hall, 2000a)

Managers of programs can also value the opportunity of having an evaluator to provide feedback, and students are capable of the sensitivity required to work professionally with a small organization. A manager explained:

> Well, one of the unspoken objectives I had...was getting the organisation used to the idea of evaluation and the culture needed to change, and I think that happened, the idea that an outsider can come and probe the work of the organisation. She did that in a gentle way, she wasn't abrasive.
>
> (Hall et al., 2000)

In sum, student engagement with evaluation for a local organization takes learning out of the classroom and into practice. For organizations, evaluation is an opportunity to shape that learning around their needs and to examine their own programs and service delivery. For those wishing to examine their own organization, student experience is equally relevant – it shows the complexities of evaluation within real-life situations. For all these learners, small-scale evaluation provides an opportunity to have the satisfaction of helping to improve organizational practice, and specifically to improve the experience of those using as well as providing its services.

Where does this book fit in the growing literature on evaluation?

There are a good number of books aimed at professional evaluators, concerned with developing theoretical issues within paradigms of evaluation derived mainly from large-scale initiatives (programs at city, regional or national level, for instance). As large-scale evaluation has flourished in the United States from the 1960s onwards, the books have generally been American (until recently), with 'program evaluation' being a favoured term to refer to the evaluation of the activities of organizations which aim to improve services across a wide field of educational, health, development and social welfare initiatives. Such initiatives have tended to be analysed at a fairly abstract level, albeit with examples to illustrate.

This literature, summarized in Chapter 2 and referred to throughout the book, is stimulating and raises issues which all evaluators need to think through. However, it has to be admitted that it is not always readily accessible reading for the beginner – even those with a social science background will find much that is unfamiliar.

Recently, there has been a welcome development in books which cover small-scale evaluation, rather than national programs, and more is being written outside the North American context. This volume is intended to complement such books by providing a more detailed set of 'how to' suggestions. In this way it aims to make evaluation accessible to learners, though without losing awareness of the theoretical and difficult issues which surround it, which cannot always be resolved by a 'quick fix'. This book

advocates, therefore, a thoughtful approach to the problems and
a continuing stress on the need for reflection by a thoughtful
evaluator.

How is the book structured?

This first chapter aims to introduce some of the key issues which
confront the evaluator working within a model of small-scale evaluation. The model is put into the context of other evaluation
approaches, and its main principles are set out. Practical information is provided on how such evaluation can be negotiated, and
dilemmas and problems are also discussed.

The model of small-scale evaluation is then developed further,
with examples derived from practice. These examples are from
student projects that have been conducted in the non-profit or
voluntary sector. This does not mean that the ideas in the book are
restricted to this field – it is simply that the authors' own experiences have come from supervising and conducting applied
research in this setting. For this reason, the examples refer to
'program users' or 'service users' (rather than customers or clients)
and to volunteers as well as (paid) staff and management, all of
whom are stakeholders whose views may need to be accounted for
in an evaluation of a service or initiative or program. (The US
spelling of 'program' is used throughout the book, as this is current
in evaluation literature generally.) In addition to short examples,
there are two lengthier examples in Chapter 8 which give a fuller
picture of evaluation experiences.

In Chapter 2, there is a discussion of various models of evaluation, which aims to help the reader understand the issues which
evaluators face and the different solutions they have developed.
This discussion is designed to enable those unfamiliar with the
literature to make their way through what is a complicated and
demanding field, but which has implications for how they will
conduct their own evaluations.

Chapter 3 focuses on a discussion of ethics and moral dilemmas
and considers the role of professional codes in resolving the problems which arise in evaluation. These problems encompass both
the research activity, with such ethical issues as consent and protection of participants' anonymity, and the evaluation activity
which involves making a judgement on a program. Placing this

discussion before the chapters on research methods is intended to highlight the importance of ethical decision-making as well as its implications for the way the study is conducted.

Chapters 4 and 5 cover the planning of research and the analysis of findings. Examples are presented to illustrate different research methods and to raise problematic issues – to look at the lessons which can be drawn. As there is a substantial literature on research methodology, these chapters should be seen as introductory, and references are provided to enable the reader to follow up the methods in more detail.

The production of the evaluation report is dealt with in Chapter 6, which looks at structure, content and presentation, covers what needs to be considered in the construction of an evaluation text and gives a suggested layout.

The practice of reflection is not usually stressed in evaluation literature, although many organizations (including those in the health field) are increasingly grappling with the need to under-stand more about 'reflective practice'. In social research metho-dology, by contrast, researchers are encouraged to be reflective, to consider their role in the research process, and to understand both how data are created and the subjective elements intrinsic to the process. Chapter 7 focuses on reflection, both because evaluation is primarily a social research task, and also because of the value of discussing how evaluation research is actually carried out as well as looking at the story, the issues and the events behind the final report.

Full examples of evaluation experiences form the content of Chapter 8, the final chapter, and the reader can choose to read these either first, as concrete examples of what evaluation on the small scale is about, or at the end as a summary.

Evaluation and research

The title of this book links evaluation and social research – so what is the relationship between these two activities?

What is social research?

Social research can be described as the purposeful and systematic acquisition and presentation of information about social issues.

It aims not simply at description, but rather at analysis to develop explanations of social life and organization that go beyond the obvious and commonplace, and stand up to critical examination. In doing so, research connects with theory in terms of generalized propositions applicable to the specific and unique encounters and interactions of the researcher with the researched. In the social sciences, research is often distinguished as being about either theory testing or theory building. Theory testing is associated more with quantitative methods, such as the survey based on questionnaire administration, while theory building tends to use less structured techniques, such as in-depth interviews and observation and produces qualitative data (Rose, 1982: 10).

Layder (1993: 3) points out that not all pieces of research fall clearly into these categories: 'they may simply be investigating a social problem or describing some sociologically interesting area'. Nevertheless, theory testing and theory building are the basis of two major traditions in social research. The former tradition uses deductive logic, deriving hypotheses from more general theory, which are tested out against the collection of data. In the light of the findings, the theory can be confirmed or modified. The second tradition argues inductively, through what is called 'grounded theory' (Strauss and Corbin, 1990) – data are created and compared and generalizations emerge from the researcher's engagement with emerging evidence.

Yet both these formulations give social research the appearance of being more structured and rule-bound than it may be in practice. Gherardi and Turner (2002: 86) draw attention to the process of research involving

> the use of judgement, craft skills and what Polanyi (1959) calls tacit knowledge, that it frequently does not follow a preordained path and that the intelligence needed to pursue research is not wholly rational-deductive.

What is evaluation?

Evaluation can be seen as a specific type of research activity, which is closely related to applied research. The emphasis is less on theoretical development than on practical implications. Usually (although as Chapter 2 shows, not always), evaluation focuses on the aims of a program and investigates to what extent the intentions of the program providers are being realized. An evaluation report will comment on the effects of program provision on those involved in receiving or delivering it and usually indicate potential future directions. Evaluation thus implies a judgement of the worth or value of a program.

Because of this judgemental role of evaluation, the standpoint of the researcher and an appreciation of the socio-political context of the evaluation becomes even more salient than it is for social research in general. As will be seen later, the relationship between the evaluator and the evaluees is critical, and gives rise to different models of evaluation, from external and independent to participatory and emancipatory.

All evaluation involves the use of social research, and for some writers there is no real distinction between the terms 'evaluation' and 'evaluation research' (Rossi and Freeman, 1993: 5). This means that sometimes the reader will find the term 'researcher' used (especially when investigative techniques are being discussed). Otherwise the term 'evaluator' will be used – the difference being whether the role emphasizes investigation (research) or judgement (evaluation).

This book aims to trace the relationship between research and evaluation, by reviewing the emergence and development of different patterns of evaluation, and provides a brief guide to the methods of social research that can be used within evaluation designs. Yet its chief focus is on how evaluation can be put into practice on a small-scale, with few resources and by those who may not have attempted evaluation before. It is the authors' conviction that this can be done, with benefit to the evaluator and the program practitioners. This view is based on experience with small-scale evaluation through student projects, as shown in the examples in the chapters and the extended case-studies in Chapter 8.

INTRODUCING THE MODEL OF SMALL-SCALE EVALUATION

The model on which this book is based draws upon many of the ideas, debates and items of good practice found in the evaluation literature discussed in the following chapter. The model is developed, however, from small-scale, locally based projects which are

negotiated between partners – academic researchers (often students) and service providers (usually from local welfare agencies
which are usually not-for-profit agencies). Small-scale evaluation is
a *collaboration* between students and practitioners in service agencies and is a learning experience for both sets of parties.

Defining 'small-scale': restriction or strength?

The assumptions are that those using this model will have limited
resources, that there will be little or no external funding available
for a large-scale research study, that one or maybe two or three
individuals at most will conduct the evaluation on a part-time basis,
that the time frame for the evaluation will usually not be much
more than a few months, and that the evaluation will normally
relate to one particular program or aspect of service provision in
one organization.

These assumptions match pretty well the definition Robson
(2000: 3) provides of 'small-scale evaluation'. He characterizes
such evaluation as being

- restricted in place to one locality rather than being regional or
  national;
- restricted in scope to one or at most two sites and programs;
- restricted in time to less than six months;
- restricted in personnel to one evaluator or at most a small team;
- restricted in funding and resources.

Such restrictions have an impact on the research design that the
researcher is able to employ, so 'small-scale' evaluation is different
in many ways from large-scale program evaluation where resources
are less limited.

However, what have been characterized by Robson as 'restrictions'
can actually prove to be *strengths*. A small team of evaluators working
with one service manager can develop close relationships and work
can be negotiated throughout the project with greater ease than
might be the case with a more formal and larger organization. The
evaluation is likely to focus on the delivery of very specific local
services, which mean that recommendations for improvement
have a greater chance of implementation, as the costs involved will
not be as great as those involved in changing a regional or national
program.

Principles of small-scale evaluation

Evaluation research on the small scale with limited resources works well through a model of partnership with the service provider. How that partnership is worked out in practice leaves room for negotiation and for applying different models of collaboration and participation in the evaluation. However, certain key principles can be elucidated as guidelines for the process under the following headings:

- partnering;
- evaluator's role;
- evaluation for development;
- evaluation for use;
- ethics;
- scale;
- resources;
- rights to the report;
- experiential learning;
- students.

Partnering

The evaluation is based on collaborative research between equals – researchers and organization members. The relationship is one of mutual benefit. The evaluation is conducted by negotiation, with respect being given to organizational goals and ethos and to the needs of the researchers and the researched.

Evaluator's role

The evaluator's role is largely that of an independent consultant, but with the flexibility to become a participant when the study requires this. The role involves collaboration with stakeholders to ensure that their interests and priorities are covered within the study.

Evaluation for development

Because of its limited scale, small-scale evaluation is less concerned with impact according to quantitative/monetary standards, and more concerned with service improvement through recommendations for manageable change.

Evaluation for use

The evaluation is designed to be used by an organization to change its practice. It is not primarily evaluation for theory and it is not research which exploits an organization for data collection for academic publication without benefit to the organization.

Ethics

The evaluation should involve ethical decision-making through all its stages, with due adherence to professional codes and guidelines, and sensitivity to the resolving of dilemmas.

Scale

The evaluation is small-scale and conducted usually in one or two locations, often with a small team of researchers providing feedback on the experience of a program, from the viewpoint of stakeholders. Feasibility studies in local neighbourhoods can also be conducted to help with service development. The evaluation will be conducted over the course of a few months, usually by part-time evaluators.

Resources

Monetary resources from organizations are likely to be limited to expenses (where students or volunteers are involved) along with the provision in kind of office space, computer access and photocopying or printing facilities, where these are available. The evaluators provide research expertise and communication input.

Rights to the report

The details of rights to the report need to be covered in the negotiation, but broadly the organization would normally receive the report with the right to disseminate it in full or in part (with acknowledgement of authorship). Evaluators and student supervisors should retain publication rights, which may include a proviso for informed consent from the organization.

Experiential learning

The evaluation should be a learning experience for all partners, with researchers acknowledging the expertise and wisdom of organizational members, and organizational members respecting the competence and knowledge of the evaluators. The evaluation should be part of a reflective process, with evaluators conducting their work with self-awareness and through regular contact with the people sponsoring the study.

Students

Where the evaluation is being conducted by students, it will be assessed through clear criteria which have been made available at the start of the project. Students will have a right to regular supervision from their university and to support from the organization. Students will be acting as representatives of the university in the community, and will conduct themselves appropriately. Students also have the right to a safe environment.

Small-scale evaluation: some issues and considerations

The principles outlined above have proved to be a practical and realistic guide to evaluation in action. However, they are not unproblematic – other evaluation models differ, for instance in the role of the evaluator or in the primacy accorded to 'partnering'. Some of these issues are discussed below and are expanded upon in the following chapter.

Students as evaluators

Two possible misconceptions can arise. The first is that the work can be done by student evaluators without any extra involvement on the part of the program manager (who may be overworked already – hence the attractiveness of the offer of external and low-cost evaluation). In reality the student evaluators will need to learn from practitioners about what is likely to be a new field of study and practice, in order to make sense of this activity and design their research questions.

For example, one manager of a program to develop services for hard of hearing people was asked to reflect on the negotiation of a local evaluation project, being conducted by a student, Laura:

> I would say it's been a positive experience, it's been a learning experience. In the beginning I was thinking that the student would be able to do all the work. I have had to learn that you just can't expect someone else to do it. You have the knowledge of hard of hearing people, the student has the knowledge about research and we need to put the two together and make a good partnership and that's how it really took off and began to work.
>
> (Hall and Hall, 2000b: 14)

For her part, Laura, the student, noted that the relationship with the program manager involved frequent contact and collaboration (which meant that the misconception of leaving her as a student to get on with the work was fully dealt with):

> We speak to each other, I think on a weekly basis, just to check on what's going on and how far I have got with this, you know, and how far I've got with that. She's very friendly, and always willing to listen if I've got a problem, and if she wants to have an input into something, the questionnaires for instance, then she's more than happy to say, you know, 'here, I think you should be using different language'.
>
> (Hall and Hall, 2000b: 15)

This relationship worked out happily, but sometimes students have to learn to be insistent on asking for appointments or pressing for decisions, especially when they are feeling frustrated with progress, and time is running out. Working with a researcher is a new experience for many organization members and they do not always appreciate the time scales and needs of the researcher. When one manager of a local agency was asked about the advantages of student evaluation, she began with this issue of learning to work with a researcher:

> Having a student coming in and doing this kind of research is good for voluntary organisations, because it teaches them to manage a researcher;
> it's cheap;

it saves a lot of time;
and very often work that they would like to do but cannot see any way of
getting done, can be done.
And they also feel that they are helping the students.

(Hall and Hall, 2000b: 34)

A second and less frequent misconception can be that the program manager acts as an academic supervisor and can determine
what student evaluators do and how they do it. It needs to be
explained during the negotiation (probably at a meeting when the
supervisor is present) that only the academic supervisor has
enough knowledge of the student's degree to judge what it is
possible for the student to do within reason as part of their academic assessment. Support from the organization, with a named
individual for regular contact, is needed. Academic supervision is
separate from this (and listed in the agreement, see below) and
ensures not only that the student will produce enough work of
good quality to provide a useful service – but will also ensure that
the student is not subject to unreasonable demands.

Negotiation

The early meetings between the prospective evaluator and the
organization practitioners help to clarify objectives in the light of
resources available, and to define a research process, which is likely
to have outcomes favourable to each, as the basis for a partnership.
The evaluator brings to the table a generalized knowledge and
experience of methods in research and evaluation (or at least in the
case of students, the ability to access such information, and supervisory support), while organizational practitioners have a specialized
knowledge and experience of their program and its service users.

These initial meetings are also important in establishing trust,
and for the evaluator to learn about the ethos and values of the
organization, and about its history. This is the context for making
sense of the goals which are being pursued, and against which
activity and service provision will be understood and compared.
Negotiation is not always formal – it takes place sometimes in passing
comments or at the coffee machine – and it continues throughout
the length of the study, not just at the initial stages – though those
stages do set the scene and form the parameters for what follows
and will be formalized in an evaluation agreement.

Checklist

- **The organization's range of activities**: are these local, regional, national or international, and how many members of staff are there, and how many clients?
- **Background**: what is the organization's origin and history, and current direction?
- **Ethos and values**: is there a mission statement or guiding philosophy for the organization?
- **The funding basis**: is the organization financed through donations, grants or commercial means, and is funding a problem?
- **Identification of a project**: is the proposed project a priority area, and are there deadlines involved?
- **Details of the proposed project**: who will be involved, stakeholders, local residents, past or present service users, staff, volunteers, management?
- **What kind of data are required**: quantitative, in-depth, case-studies?
- **The audience for the report**: will it include all stakeholders, local staff, senior management at a regional or national level, funding bodies?
- **How the report will be used**: to make changes in local practice, policy recommendations at a higher level, funding applications?
- **Resources available**: are there expenses, or office facilities?
- **Contacts within the organization**: main contact during the study, who will receive the report initially, key secretarial and administrative staff?
- **Ethical concerns**: are there vulnerable stakeholders, or issues of confidentiality and privacy?
- **Health and safety issues**: how should a risk assessment be completed?

Before this stage is reached, students have found it useful to take a checklist of questions to ask in their first meetings with an agency. They need to feel confident that they have something to say, but also need to come out of the meeting with some pointers for the next stage of the study. The questions can be summarized as shown in the box.

The evaluator, in turn, can offer information about themself which relates to the study:

1. The evaluator's interests and background – how these relate to the organization's work.
2. How much time is available – during the week, and the time span involved: when the draft and final reports can be expected.
3. The research skills or previous experience which are being offered, including report writing skills.

4   For students, how the project relates to the degree program and
    what support the university department will be offering.

Agreement

A formal agreement needs to be made and signed up to by all the
parties, so that the research aims and purposes are clear. This can
be produced initially in draft form and used as the basis for
clearing up any issues about the study. An example of such an
agreement based on the authors' practice but using fictitious
names is given in the box. To aid those wishing to adapt this
agreement for their own use, a blank copy of the agreement is
included in Appendix 1 to this volume.

Evaluation Agreement
Kirkton University

The following is the outcome of a meeting on 12 September 2004 between
Janet Owen, School of Social Science, the University of Kirkton, Kirktonfield
(Tel: 0961 123 6789, e-mail owenj@kirk.ac.uk) and Martin Fox, student in
the School of Social Science, and Anne Adjani, Director, Children Come First,
42 Brent Drive, Kirktonfield (Tel: 0961 444 3268, email child1@charnet.org).
   *All parties may comment of the agreement and if any section needs to be
altered a fresh agreement will be issued. Please contact Janet Owen, the academic supervisor, with comments at the above address.*

1. **Project agreement**: between Janet Owen and Martin Fox, from the
    School of Social Science, The University of Kirkton, and Anne Adjani of
    Children Come First.
2. **Duration of the project**: the project will run from September 2004 to
    Easter 2005: fieldwork will be completed by January 2005.
3. **About the organization**: Children Come First has been operating
    since 1994, initially through funding from the Children our Future Trust,
    and since 1996 it has been funded by Kirktonfield City Council and a
    variety of charities. The programme aims to support children who face
    multiple challenges, particularly those children who have a parent in
    prison. Facilities include an after school club, play days, family support
    workers and child-centred counselling.
4. **Issues identified**: the programme is facing a five-year review and needs
    to be evaluated in order to secure funding.
5. **Proposed project**: Martin Fox will evaluate the services provided by
    Children Come First, focusing particularly on the after school club and
    family support activities.

He will interview a sample of parents and children, as well as staff and volunteers, in three stages:

   (i)   Focus groups will be held with children who use the after school club.
   (ii) Parents will be interviewed concerning the support they receive from the support service.
   (iii) Volunteers and staff will be interviewed about their perceptions of the service, although self-completion surveys may be used if time runs out for face-to-face interviewing.
   (iv) If time permits, Martin will also collect case-studies which show the effectiveness of the service from the viewpoint of individual families/children.

All participants will be initially approached by Anne Adjani to ensure that they consent to the research and subsequently the data will be recorded anonymously.

 6. **Project outcome**: Martin Fox will produce a written report which will be available in draft form by Easter and in its final form by June to Children Come First. He will also provide feedback to Children Come First during the course of the project, as appropriate.

 7. **Permission to reproduce the report**: Martin Fox and Janet Owen will have the right to use the report for academic publication, provided Children Come First is first consulted and has no objections.

 8. **Attendance**: Martin Fox will commit the equivalent of one day a week in the first semester for field work and a similar amount of time in the second semester for analysis and for writing reports.

 9. **Expenses**: the payment of travel expenses will be paid by the Families Care Project. Martin Fox will be responsible for providing a typed copy of his report to the University of Kirkton as part submission for his degree.

10. **Policy issues**: Martin Fox will abide by and be covered by the health and safety, equal opportunities and confidentiality procedures of Children Come First. Both he and Children Come First will complete a risk assessment form as required by the University of Kirkton.

11. **Supervision**: Janet Owen will be available for regular supervision throughout the study.

12. **Confidentiality**: Martin Fox will work to the British Sociological Association guidelines on ethics and will respect the confidentiality of the information given. Due attention will be given to anonymity, and the research will be conducted in a sensitive manner.

13. **Assessment**: Martin Fox will submit the client report and a separate reflective report to the School of Social Science and these together will comprise his dissertation.

14. **Acknowledgements**: At any time when the report or any part of it is used, proper acknowledgement should be made to Martin Fox, to Janet Owen, and to the University of Kirkton.

Signed:

Dated:

Several issues arise from this agreement which need some further elaboration – health and safety, assessment, access and ethics, and resources and research design.

Health and safety

The health and safety of students on fieldwork placements is a worry to many academic staff, who are concerned about risks to students, not to mention possible litigation which might ensue. Student/evaluator safety is paramount, of course, though sometimes students do need to be reminded of this, especially if they are tempted (in the interests of their research) to undertake something which could be risky. Also, the students – and all evaluators – have the right to feel safe. For students, their own academic institutions will have procedures which the supervisor needs to understand and follow. For British universities, the Quality Assurance Agency for Higher Education (QAA) has issued a code of practice on placement learning, which can be accessed from its website (www.qaa.ac.uk/public/cop/COPplacementFinal/precepts.htm). The main aim is to ensure that the responsibilities of institutions, placement providers, students and staff are clearly defined and understood, and that students have appropriate support before, during and after their placements.

When working off university premises student evaluators will need induction into the local organization's policy and practice, and when conducting fieldwork there needs to be an assessment of risk, with agreed measures to reduce any risk to personal safety. Generally, risk assessment needs to cover awareness of potential hazards and safety procedures as well as information about the insurance cover for those working on behalf of the organization. (Copies of a risk assessment form for use with students, and a health and safety questionnaire for use with placement providers are included in Appendices 2 and 3 to this volume.)

Assessment

Models can be developed where the organization manager has an input into the student's assessment. However, although it is attractive to give an organizational partner more scope for judging the evaluation, at the end of the day the student has to meet criteria which conform to approved academic practice and be examined through an institutional process with examiners who legally have to meet the institutional regulations. Students whose relationships with managers have not gone smoothly might be penalized, as might students who, through no fault of their own, were unable to gain access to all the participants hoped for (so the data are not as substantial as they should have been), or whose conclusions or recommendations conflict with those of the manager. For all these reasons, it is safer to keep the supervisory and assessment roles separate from organizational support and management roles.

Access and ethics

Creating the trust to make the partnership work will in most cases mean information will be accessible from those associated with the program. It will not always be plain sailing – organizations which run projects for clients and service users who are vulnerable by reason of age or disability, for instance, may be cautious about allowing free access to their clients and to membership lists, and it will be up to the researcher to bring to the negotiating table their commitment to good ethical practice in research, with the evidence of adherence to professional guidelines, and (as applicable) a case history of previous research in order to reassure the partner. (Further guidance to ethics can be found in Chapter 3.)

Resources and research design considerations

Working with limited resources does not imply that the evaluation cannot be valid or useful. But it does mean working in a different way from large funded research studies. Weiss, for instance, writing of independent program evaluation commissioned by a funding body with adequate funding, notes the paramount importance of upholding 'the conventions of scientific research, with special emphasis upon good data, sound analysis, and candid reporting' (1998: 98).

The same criteria of good data, sound analysis and candid reporting also apply where funding on the large scale is not available, and where evaluation is limited by the time, personnel and resources available. The study still requires systematically collected data, the incorporation of the main stakeholders, and the answering of the research questions. The analysis should accurately draw findings from the information collected, and note any contradictory or conflicting evidence. The reporting should be independent, without bias either for or against the program, but an honest reflection of what has been discovered.

However, for many organizations, when they think of conducting research, they think of a large-scale survey. In many cases they will already be experienced with questionnaires, either as originators or as respondents, and large numbers of responses are impressive in themselves to non-statistical audiences, as considerations of bias in the selection are not well understood.

So when the request for a survey is made (and resources are restricted and limited) it's well worth the evaluator and the organization together considering two things:

- Will the survey provide the information required at a cost that is acceptable?
- Are there other ways of collecting information that will address the organization's needs?

Chapter 4 discusses different ways in which data can be collected, which take into account the costs involved, such as telephone surveys, focus groups and face-to-face interviewing. The chapter also covers sampling issues, such as the problem of getting information from 'hard-to-contact' groups, or of sampling from a population whose size is unknown. Alternative strategies are suggested, such as going back to the research question to consider creatively whether small samples, case-studies and qualitative explorative methodology may be as helpful to organizations in devising policy as the large-scale survey they may have envisaged originally (or even more so).

To summarize, there is a tension in local evaluation research between

- what the evaluator would like to do;
- what can be done within the limits of resources and access;
- what the organization needs in order to be able to review its programs.

Are the findings of small-scale evaluation ever used?

The evidence from studies completed by students and others working within the limitations of local, small-scale evaluation is encouraging in terms of usage. Such evaluations have been found to provide useful feedback to organizations, and they have helped in making improvements in services, and in contributing to the success of organizations in attracting funding to develop their programs.

Robson goes so far as to argue that small-scale evaluations probably stand a better chance of their findings being used than do grander initiatives.

> They tend to be closer to the program and the people who make decisions about implementation. The questions to which they seek answers are usually relatively modest and the short timescale of small local evaluations helps to ensure relevant information is available in time for it to be useful.
>
> (2000: 125)

However, as with all evaluation, usage cannot be guaranteed. Reports can be used in ways which were not envisaged – or may not be used at all – and this can be for reasons unrelated to the merit of the report itself. The short discussion which follows looks at some of the factors which influence evaluation usage.

Diversity of use

When projects are negotiated, program managers tend to have expectations that the evaluation will give 'answers' to very specific aspects of program practice which may be problematic, or at least needing to be reviewed. In the event, the 'answers' (findings) of the report may be more general than envisaged, or have implications which go beyond the program itself. This means the reports will be used in ways other than putting right the way the program is done.

Three surveys were conducted by the authors with organizations where small-scale evaluation studies had been carried out by students between two and five years previously (Hall and Hall, 1998).

Table 1.1 Use of evaluation reports

Usage	Direct	Indirect
Internal	To improve the service along the lines of the report's recommendations	To raise awareness among staff of service users' feelings or to promote staff development
External	To provide evidence to support funding applications	To raise local awareness of the service

There was a high level of usage, though the use was not always what had been expected when the evaluation was being negotiated.

There was a broad distinction between internal and external use of reports. Internal use referred to the report being read and distributed within the organization, and external to use by outside agencies. In addition, reports were used directly or indirectly, as summarized in Table 1.1. Direct usage, both internal and external, was the outcome most expected by students and supervisors. Examples of both were given by respondents, but the survey showed that usage was rarely a straightforward response to recommendations – it could be indirect and implementation was most likely when the organization had already perceived certain action as necessary, and the report justified or backed up these views.

Responses from managers on internal direct use included:

the ideas they came up with, actually looking at group structures and things we did…we've changed things significantly since then.

Internal indirect use happened when the report was circularized for awareness purposes:

It was mainly sort of internal with the management committee and, you know, the groups internally, volunteers and staff, they all read it.

External indirect use was when materials based on the report were used for publicity in the local press. External direct use occurred when the report was used to improve the standing of the organization:

But it definitely helped with other agencies, as we found out. Now, because of establishing the young person's services, so many other agencies are working with us and referring young people.

These findings show that evaluation can be used for purposes other than changing organizational practice – for information and enlightenment, or for raising the program's profile.

Consultation and contact

The first of the three surveys concluded that:

> Organisations do make use of the reports, in a variety of ways related to their current needs and priorities, but they felt this usage would be enhanced through more extensive consultation with organisations. This might involve more emphasis on students becoming familiarised early with the issues involved; a longer process of negotiating the project; and better feedback before the final report is submitted through drafts of work in progress.
>
> (Hall and Hall, 1998: 15)

This response from organizations became incorporated into the students' evaluation practice, and the second survey found greater satisfaction with the process and consequently greater usage of the reports. This supports Patton's view that 'what happens from the very beginning of a study will determine its eventual impact long *before a final report is produced*' (1997: 20; his italics).

Patton argues that informal networks are part of the social setting in which the evaluation takes place, and are part of the means by which findings can be communicated effectively. He describes how a study of federal health evaluations showed that much of the important reporting was interpersonal and informal in 'hallway conversations, in rest rooms, over coffee, before and after meetings, over the telephone, and through informal networks' (1997: 329). In other words, oral communication was not just a precursor of the written report, but an essential element of the totality of communication which allowed the participants access to findings and the opportunity to discuss and comment on them.

Patton argues that evaluation conducted in this way will be more likely to be used. While the pros and cons of such interaction (instead of detachment) between evaluator and program participants are discussed in Chapter 3 – the experience of student projects has certainly been that improved communication has produced a more usable end product.

Timing of evaluation

The timing of an evaluation is also important – is it being conducted at a time which is 'opportune' in terms of resources and
organizational support to effect change?

One faith-based organization commented on the evaluation
which had been conducted to help them develop programs with
homeless people in the city:

> [The] report on the involvement of the ... church with housing and
> homelessness in [the city] was received just after Easter, and in time for
> a twenty-four hour Conference ... to review its present and future work
> relating to housing and homelessness in the diocese. The report thus
> came at a most opportune time, and helped us in our general review of
> the current situation. The report has now led us to establish a Working
> Group to review housing and homelessness issues within the diocese in
> greater detail and Christina's report will provide an important spring-
> board for that work.
>
> (Response to the evaluation of the student project by
> the manager of the Homelessness Church Project)

In this case, the evaluation (which was for information and
enlightenment) came when policy was being reviewed and a
working party being set up to take the policy forward.

Managerial willingness to act on evaluation

Whether managers are open or closed to evaluation findings can
be linked to their own values and strategies within the organization. Donald Schön's work on reflective practitioners can be
adapted to this issue.

With a colleague at Massachusetts Institute of Technology, Chris
Argyris, Schön has conducted seminars with professionals from a
wide array of disciplines – industrial managers, school administrators, lawyers, architects, counsellors and so on. This work has
developed a theory of competent interpersonal practice and a
practicum in skills acquisition:

> We have distinguished two levels at which theories of action operate: There
> are espoused theories that we use to explain or justify our behaviour.
> Managers, for example, often espouse openness and freedom of expression,
> especially about negative information – as in 'my door is always open' or 'I
> want no "yes men" around here; managers in this company are expected

to say what they think'. But there are also theories-in-use implicit in our patterns of spontaneous behaviour with others ... Often we are unable to describe them, and we are surprised to discover, when we do construct them by reflecting on the directly observable data of our actual interpersonal practice, that they are incongruent with the theories of action we espouse.

(Schön, 1987: 255)

So, a manager who has expressed willingness at the negotiation stage of an evaluation to take on board whatever the findings reveal, may find that they do not feel so open if faced with a negative report. If the manager is what Argyris and Schön term 'Model 1', that is they strive to be rational (to achieve their purposes as they see them and to be in control), then this type of theories-in-use contributes

to the creation of behavioural worlds that are win/lose, closed, and defensive. It is difficult in Model 1 worlds to reveal one's private dilemmas or make a public test of one's most important assumptions.

(Schön, 1987: 256)

This is interesting, as it implies that even managers who define themselves as rational beings may not act rationally when faced with information they don't like, despite the fact that the information is 'evidence-based', good-quality evaluation. The seminars with professionals are designed to develop Model 2, 'where people can exchange valid information, even about difficult and sensitive matters, subject private dilemmas to shared enquiry, and make public tests of negative attributions that Model 1 keeps private and undiscussable' (Schön, 1987: 259). Part of the coaching for Model 2 appears to be working with professionals so that they can accept failure, or partial success and build on this through improving their interpersonal skills.

One conclusion for evaluators might be to seek out those program managers who have progressed to Model 2! More practically, the reflective practitioner approach underlines that understanding how evaluation gets used, relates to the context of the research – to organizational structure and roles, to the way the aims of the organization are theorized, and to the manager's feelings about the findings. How the results were produced and presented may in turn help decide whether the report which has some negative feedback results in defensiveness and an unwillingness to change, or whether the results are accepted as constructive comment, which, if recommendations are implemented, will be supportive of the organization and its development.

We conclude this chapter with an example of a project where the student evaluator never discovered that her evaluation had been used by the organization. It is not uncommon for evaluators to leave the field before the findings get implemented. In this case it seemed the evaluation had sunk without trace, so the example is included to encourage other evaluators: good work can surface in the future and have an impact but you might just not hear about it!

Example 1.1 Families in stress project

A manager came into post to run a small local office of a national program where volunteers offer friendship, practical help and support to families under stress. In a filing cabinet she found a report that her predecessor had never used. This was an evaluation of the volunteer scheme, which had been conducted with an aim of improving the service.

The research had involved the student visiting families on the program with the organizer, getting to know them and then spending time with them on her own and with the volunteers. The research methods used were in-depth interviews and observations. The report had received a first-class mark, as an excellent piece of research, but it had never been used.

The new manager used the report as evidence for two consecutive funding applications, and it was crucial in helping to keep her organization financially afloat:

> When we're writing funding applications, very often the funders want to know, not just the facts and figures of what we do, but also some of the human interest behind it. Because very often large trusts actually want to know what's real about it, rather than just the accountancy report. And we use the quotations and the stories that Liz gave us.

In addition to this direct external usage, the report was used for indirect external usage, to raise awareness of the service (both to recruit volunteers and to contact potential clients):

> We've recently had a window full of quotes from volunteers and families in one of the shops [locally], and we're looking at repeating that exercise in some of the community centres.

There was also direct internal use for training purposes:

> In training, the project has been very useful in giving potential volunteers a good idea of what's expected of them, because there are very detailed descriptions of the families' circumstances and the volunteers' responses to the family, and the sort of diversity of work that the volunteers do for the family.

(Hall and Hall, 2000b: 33)

CHAPTER 2

Understanding Evaluation

Summary

This chapter explains and expands the context for the model of small-scale evaluation introduced in the previous chapter. It discusses the various strategies used by evaluators as well as the differing theoretical approaches which can be taken. The chapter finishes by examining the specific ideas which the small-scale model has adopted and explaining why these are relevant to the model.

The challenge is how to treat so complex a subject. There are so many ways in which evaluation can be done. As evaluation practice has expanded, different methodologies have developed, often in response to what have been perceived as inadequacies in the previous approaches. For instance, early evaluation concentrated on the *impact* of a program while later approaches have emphasized the need to study the *processes* in program delivery, not just the outcomes.

The first section of the chapter gives an overview of key issues which face evaluators. The second section outlines the different solutions program evaluators have devised, indicating where models have emerged either to develop and refine existing models or else to challenge them. The models which are relevant to small-scale evaluation (those which take a developmental approach) are explored in greater depth.

The third section provides a short discussion of developments in evaluation theory – that is the more abstract way of connecting various models through an overarching set of ideas. While this goes beyond the scope of evaluation of a single program (which is what most evaluators are involved in), it is helpful to envisage the kind of future developments that are possible – and which are opened up by the breadth and depth of theoretical thinking.

The chapter provides guidance for those embarking on evaluation research by explaining the basis for the choices which evaluators face – in ethical decision-making, research and report writing (all issues which are treated in depth in succeeding chapters). For instance, the role that the evaluator adopts – whether to be detached and objective or participatory and involved – will be determined by choices taken according to the model of evaluation which is being used. This chapter, therefore, is not just of theoretical interest, but provides information to guide practice, with the concluding section pulling together the threads which run through the small-scale evaluation approach.

OVERVIEW OF EVALUATION ISSUES

Evaluation as everyday activity

Evaluation, in the sense of gathering information and making judgements and decisions about certain courses of action, is something that people do everyday in their own personal choices and decision-making, for example as consumers choosing the best product to meet their needs at a price they can afford. Students, deciding on which course modules to choose, weigh up their choices using the information provided by tutors and feedback from other students, as well as their own interests and long-term career plans.

Evaluating organizational programs is different from this particular example. It is still concerned with judgements about the outcomes of activity and its effectiveness and about resources. But in addition to drawing on everyday understandings and judgements it constitutes a distinctive approach where evidence is systematically assessed through rigorous research.

Patton, for instance, states that evaluation includes

> any effort to increase human effectiveness through systematic data-based enquiry ... When one examines and judges accomplishments and effectiveness, one is engaged in evaluation.

(1990: 11)

Defining evaluation

A number of definitions have been offered by writers on evaluation. Clarke (1999: 3–4), in reviewing the definitions provided by the evaluation literature argues against the possibility of giving one simple definition of evaluation. Nevertheless he comes up with a general statement, echoing Scriven (1997: 490) and others, to the effect that

> Evaluation is primarily concerned with determining the merit, worth or value of an established policy or a planned intervention.

Weiss offers as a 'provisional definition' that:

> Evaluation is the *systematic assessment* of the *operation* and/or the *outcomes* of a program or policy, compared to a set of *explicit* or *implicit standards*, as a means of contributing to the *improvement* of the policy or program. (Italics in the original)
>
> (1998: 4)

These definitions reinforce the assumption that essential features of evaluation are:

- a *systematic* collection of information distinguished from casual observation and biased reporting (or family loyalty), which leads to
- a *judgement* about the value of the program being evaluated.

Other criteria can be added – at whatever stage evaluation is done, before, during, or after a program runs, in each case there is an aim of *improvement*, to ensure that the program meets needs, operates effectively, and applies or has applied resources efficiently. Evaluation produces research results which are intended to be *used*, which makes it distinct from other kinds of research which are analytical or theoretical but are not essentially designed to be applied.

In so far as organized programs are aimed at ameliorating 'social problems', then evaluation is (or aims to be) beneficial to society at large as well as to the recipients of social interventions in particular, through the more efficient use of resources. The Guiding Principles for Evaluators of the American Evaluation Association (Shadish *et al.*, 1995) accept responsibilities for general and public welfare, and encompass the public good as a concern of evaluation.

Formative and summative evaluation

A useful and much-quoted distinction has been drawn by Scriven (1967) between 'formative' and 'summative' evaluations. These terms can be explained most easily by reference to educational processes of testing, where a similar distinction is made between formative and summative assessment. Formative assessment gives the student feedback for continuing improvement, while summative assessment provides a grade or mark at the end of a course to sum up overall performance. These assessments provide different types of feedback, have different purposes within education, and convey different meanings to the student. They are also likely to be performed differently by the teachers/assessors. Providing a mark and writing comments are different activities.

Summative assessment is a judgement on the student. It represents a measure of their learning following exposure to a program of instruction. It may be on a simple pass/fail basis (like a driving test) or may be graded (like most exams). It is often regarded as an objective measure of performance, though in practice it is derived from the student's performance on a particular day in response to a particular set of questions under testing conditions. How the student learned, studied and revised for the assessment is not a consideration, though the assumption is that those with higher grades achieved this through greater effort and better learning strategies, and by drawing on a greater stock of knowledge.

Formative assessment is feedback to help people learn better. It may or may not be graded, but it should offer comment as to how the student performed the task, or answered the question. The intention is not simply to assess knowledge and performance but also to reward good achievement and to identify weaknesses that can be improved upon. The assessor is likely to be interested in the student's learning processes and development, and to make suggestions for improvement.

Within a system of education, both formative and summative assessments are used. There may be some conflict between the two types of assessment, especially if one and the same assessor takes on both roles. Public examinations, therefore, like the driving test, use examiners who are different from those involved in teaching and formative assessment.

When it comes to evaluations, much the same reasoning applies. Formative and summative evaluations do different things, and are in principle quite distinct. Formative evaluation applies to programs that may be improved through timely feedback, while summative evaluation is concerned with the impact and effectiveness of a program. Summative evaluation offers a judgement on a program at the end of a period of evaluation research. How well did the program meet its objectives? In order to study the effects of the program, the summative evaluator has to keep at arm's length from the program itself, so as not to contaminate the findings by providing feedback that changes the program's operation. Formative evaluation, on the other hand, positively uses interim feedback from the evaluator to redirect and improve the program, so the aim is more on understanding and refining the processes of program delivery.

Evaluation history: public programs and the 'classic' evaluation model

The distinction between summative and formative evaluation arose historically. The huge expansion in evaluation (and in the literature on evaluation) since the 1960s came from the growth in government funding, both in the UK and elsewhere, for educational, health, social and welfare programs aimed at remedying social problems. Many commentators have noted that the big federally funded programs in the USA in this period led to the development of evaluation as a separate field of research activity. There was concern that government funds were spent wisely, that the programs could be deemed effective, and that they gave value for money. So government action became the spur to much evaluation which was summative, with external agents being engaged as evaluators to investigate program impact, and with evaluation becoming mandatory for the receipt and auditing of funding.

In this process, evaluators used the 'classic model' of positivist social science research, based on the collection of empirical data through experimentation with the use of control and experimental groups, before and after studies and probability sampling in order to show causality in terms of programs and their effects. These quantitative methods were intended to answer questions about whether the programs worked and whether they were good value for money.

Government itself became involved in the elaboration of evaluation design, with the US General Accounting Office publishing special reports on evaluation, as key texts in the field (USGAO, 1991). Evaluation of this kind began with concerns about summative issues such as *impact* (did the program have the effects it set out to produce?) and *efficiency* (could the benefit have been delivered to more people or at lower cost?). The people who wanted the evaluation were those providing the funds for the program, and they wanted to know if the money was well spent or not. But later even government accepted that process approaches and qualitative research had important things to offer evaluation.

Commenting on this period, Pawson and Tilley note:

> For us, the experimental paradigm constitutes a heroic failure, promising so much and yet ending up in ironic anticlimax. The underlying logic... seems meticulous, clear-headed and militarily precise, and yet findings seem to emerge in a typically non-cumulative, low-impact, prone-to-equivocation sort of way.
>
> (1997: 8)

Emergence of different kinds of evaluation

Three major approaches to evaluation

As evaluation of large public programs developed, and the experimental approach failed to show what had worked and why, evaluators' aims became more mixed – they were still concerned with ensuring accountability and reporting back to funding agencies, but they were also concerned with finding out how the programs operated – in other words formative evaluation began to develop alongside summative evaluation. Writers such as Chen (1990), Clarke (1999) and Robson (2000) have noted how impact studies have usually included formative issues such as a description and understanding of how the outcomes have been – or have not been – produced. In turn, studies of process have also dealt with summative factors such as program effectiveness.

Chelimsky and Shadish (1997: 10) link these developments with the different *purposes* which evaluations serve, ranging, for example, from measuring and accounting for the results of public policies and programs to gaining explanatory insights or increasing agency responsiveness to the needs and expectations of service users. They argue that these different purposes fall into three general perspectives:

• evaluation for accountability;
• evaluation for development;
• evaluation for knowledge.

Accountability refers to the provision of information to decision-makers, who are usually external to the organization, such as government sponsors, funding bodies or private donors. Accountability is about whether there is clear evidence that the program or policy has 'caused' any discernible effects or changes in outcomes (such as a reduction of poverty through an assistance scheme).

The accountability approach has its roots in the application of systems theory and cybernetics to organizations. Such theories see organizations as complex systems for achieving stated goals, with the need for a control system to manage the transformation of inputs (raw materials and labour) to outputs (products and goals). What happens inside the box is taken for granted, and attention is paid instead to the control mechanism which keeps the outputs as specified. For the system to be self-regulating, information on how well the organization is performing at any given time is fed back through the control system so that action can be taken to vary the inputs if the goals are not being achieved.

An organization producing a social intervention (a program) is a 'black box' with certain inputs and outputs that can be identified through evaluation (Figure 2.1). So, when the outputs of the system diverge from the desired state, information has to be fed back through the control mechanism of the system to modify the inputs (resources and/or goals) in order to bring the system back into its designed state (or move it into a newly designed position). Evaluation is then part and parcel of a rational system of control of a process, designed to have an effect on output – program delivery.

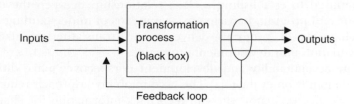

Feedback loop

Figure 2.1   Systems diagram

As Posavac and Carey explain:

> The rational processes of assessing needs, measuring the implementa-
> tion of programs to meet those needs, evaluating the achievement of
> carefully formed goals and objectives, and comparing the degree of
> achievement and the costs involved with those of similar programs serves
> to improve the use of human and material resources in organizations.
>   (1989: 15)

An alternative *developmental* model of evaluation is preferred by
writers such as Everitt (1996), who rejects the systems-based
accountability perspective as being too abstract, impersonal and
technocratic and instead advocates one based on an understanding
of programs as human systems. Human systems develop their own
cultures and styles of interaction, and, in such a system, evaluation
can bring change, development and emancipation only by a
thorough understanding of the particular culture concerned, and
the social constraints under which it is transmitted.

The development perspective stresses that the process of program delivery (what goes on inside the black box) should be the
main focus for evaluation. Programs are delivered not through an
abstract enumeration of inputs and outputs but through human
interactions. Development perspectives therefore stress process
rather than outcome, and developmental evaluators see building
evaluation capacity among program staff as a key function of
evaluation.

This may involve improving the design of projects, for instance,
or finding out how beneficiaries feel about an agency and its service provision. Or it may mean helping to enhance program staff's
skills in developing and strengthening program delivery. In contrast to the accountability perspective, development evaluation is

committed to establishing a close relationship between the evaluator and program participants as a means of understanding the
mechanisms of program delivery, and translating evaluation
information into developmental practice.

The accountability and development perspectives make different demands on evaluators. The accountability approach requires
an objective evaluator who can feed back information for change
and decision-making. So long as the information is reliable and
free from bias, how the program is delivered is no part of the brief.
The developmental model, on the other hand, needs an evaluator
who is alert to understanding the process, and who is prepared to
work with the program practitioners to enhance their performance
and that of the program itself.

Evaluation for *knowledge* is about generating understanding and
explanation. It therefore seeks to unravel complex interactions of
causality, to explore the issues underlying social problems and to
examine the appropriateness of program provision in dealing with
these problems.

Evaluating the results of a set of evaluation studies in a particular
field, or *meta-evaluation*, is one approach to reaching a synthesis of
different evaluation research studies in a particular area. The aim
is to develop a robust understanding of program effects through
pooling the best-attested findings. There are complex issues of
judgement involved in terms of how to compare different studies
with different objectives and methods, and what should be considered for inclusion as a well-conducted and trustworthy study.
Meta-evaluation (or meta-analysis; see Rossi and Freeman, 1993:
127; Weiss, 1998: 236), and its sibling, knowledge-based practice,
tends to favour experimental and quantitative methods over
observational and qualitative studies.

The role of the evaluator

None of the above perspectives is trouble-free, and for all of them
the part played by the evaluator is critical. This relates both to how
the evaluation is conducted and also to how the results are likely to
be accepted by the program staff. Accountability evaluation, which
operates on the basis of the separation of evaluator from evaluees,
reporting back to external agencies who have the power to
determine the continuation or otherwise of a program, has been

frequently criticized for its negative impact on program staff. Writing from a developmental perspective, Rubin argues that this 'traditional' approach to evaluation by non-governmental organizations (NGOs) has failed to deliver what it claims to do:

> [O]ver the years they [evaluations] have often been found inappropriate in terms of scale, cost, and the underlying technocratic view of development. Resistance to evaluation has built up in response to inappropriate use of these methods.
>
> (Rubin, 1995: 20)

When organizations have had evaluation imposed on them by external evaluators feeding back the results to a distant decision-making authority, the result for the organization has often been one of insecurity and non-cooperation. Rubin suggests instead that an alternative approach – as in Chelimsky and Shadish's developmental perspective – will be more fruitful. If evaluation is in essence about changing things for the better, then this is more likely to be achieved if evaluation becomes an integral part of the change process rather than an assessment after the fact.

Developmental evaluation has been extended into models which stress empowerment. Fetterman *et al.* (1996) argue for the incorporation of program staff into evaluation design and practice, for cooperation between them and the evaluator, and for the use of reflection on the part of staff to generate strategies for change. The evaluator becomes more of a facilitator than a detached observer.

This shift in emphasis from the evaluator having an external role to adopting a facilitative one can in turn be criticized. If the evaluator's strongest card is that he or she has a professional commitment 'to tell the truth, the whole truth and nothing but the truth', then any close contact with program managers and staff before the final report is delivered may call into question the evaluator's objectivity and expose the report to accusations of bias (Scriven, 1997: 480). Furthermore, if facilitative or developmental evaluation becomes the norm, then there is a danger of the whole profession of evaluation losing the trust of its sponsors – the agencies which promote evaluation in order to keep a check on the operation of social programs.

Yet the strongest feature of external evaluation in providing accountability – its freedom from bias through detachment from the program participants – is also one of its problems. The detached evaluator may be so remote that access to people within the program is hindered, and at the finish staff are critical of the findings of a report with which they have had no involvement. On the other hand, greater involvement through facilitative evaluation may provide evaluators with readier means of access to the internal processes of programs and so help them build up their under-standing of how programs operate (or fail to operate). Such forms of evaluation are also more likely to result in support from prac-titioners to change and adapt their program delivery in the light of evaluation findings.

Participatory forms of evaluation (Fetterman, 2001) take the development approach and the empowerment imperative even further by assisting program staff to become their own evaluators. The aim is to let participants themselves generate the learning which it is hoped will motivate them to reflect on their perfor-mance and develop changes in program delivery and goal attain-ment. But the problem already discussed remains – that greater involvement between evaluators and program staff will produce greater potential for bias, with collusion among participants causing criticism and negative findings to be watered down.

The relationship between the evaluator and the evaluees con-tinues to be a live issue, linked to concerns with the objectivity of evaluation and the development of evaluation as a profession. Scriven (1997: 490) suggests that the solution is to make a dis-tinction between 'evaluators' (who would conduct accountability evaluation) and 'evaluation consultants' (who would conduct developmental evaluations). 'Evaluators' would be external, inde-pendent, clearly distinct from all program staff, and certainly not in their employ or likely to be retained by them in the near future. Distinct from these would be 'evaluation consultants', those who adopt a developmental brief and work with an organization to provide 'evaluation-related services'.

However, many evaluators would reject this distinction, as they wish to retain the professional status of 'evaluator' for the non-accountability evaluation which they support. Patton (1997), for example, argues that for evaluation to be utilized, program staff need to be involved in the collection of evidence, and that evaluators need to understand from close quarters how program staff operate – they need a developmental approach. Those who advocate empowerment evaluation, such as Fetterman, disagree with Scriven even more fundamentally. The evaluator is a facilitator of evaluation activity undertaken by the program participants themselves – this is not fulfilling a 'consultant' role but is a *bona fide* 'evaluator' role. With such different views about the purpose of evaluation, it is hardly surprising there is no unanimity about how evaluators should do their work.

Finally, although the discussion has focused on the accountability *versus* empowerment debate, it should be noted that the knowledge evaluation perspective is also experiencing some challenges. The role of the knowledge evaluator has been seen as being 'critical' and independent. Currently, however, there is some debate about whether this role could move towards one which incorporates a degree of advocacy for a program. There is a suggestion that evaluators with a knowledge perspective should step beyond reporting on individual programs, and contribute more to major policy debates – for instance, by publishing summaries of their findings for a wider public audience (Weiss, 1998: 307).

Roles of other evaluation participants

The evaluator has to interact with other participants as part of the evaluation activity. The key players or stakeholders are:

- those who commission or sponsor evaluation;
- participants (providers and beneficiaries) in the program under evaluation.

Commissioners of evaluation

The evaluator has a responsibility to those who commission and pay for the evaluation. In evaluation for accountability, the commissioners of evaluation are mostly those who provide funding for the program and are distinct from program practitioners. In contrast, in small-scale evaluation for development, those commissioning the evaluation are likely to be – and will certainly include – program practitioners. In the case of students, their responsibility is to those who have sponsored or supported the project placement both in the program and in the academic department.

The actual situation in any evaluation may be more complex than a simple model of one commissioning body. To take an example from community regeneration, evaluation of a program is likely to mean multi-agency involvement and consequently the report will be required to address the issues of a variety of groups. These groups can include local government agencies, private businesses and non-profit voluntary organizations in health, education, employment and social welfare. Reporting back to such a varied consortium with such varied interests and demands can prove taxing for the evaluator, if the agreement for the research is not clearly defined and strictly observed.

The program can additionally have a further level of commissioners – regional, national or even European agencies with requirements on what the evaluation should include. In such circumstances, the evaluator will need not just good research skills, but also good political skills to negotiate a project and manage what could be many competing interests in the evaluation. All parties – the consortium, the funders and the evaluator(s) – need to be realistic about what the budget can cover; not everyone's interests can be paramount.

Sponsors and gatekeepers

'Sponsors' are people who have an interest in promoting the evaluation research. They may provide funding for the study (in which case they are commissioners), or they may lend their prestige to facilitate the study.

'Gatekeepers' are those with the power to open or restrict access to the program organization and to its participants. In practical terms they hold the key to the evaluator/researcher being able to collect relevant information. Their capacity to facilitate or restrict information gathering is thus significant, and how they act may affect the ability of an evaluation to achieve its goals.

How can access be gained? This is a topic that will be considered later under research practice. In the main, there are two models of gaining access, by external mandate or through internal negotiation (though these are not necessarily alternatives). External mandate relies upon a powerful sponsor to urge or compel compliance from internal gatekeepers, as may occur with an evaluation required by an external funding agency. Compliance by the gatekeepers is assured, but may be given grudgingly and with informal resistance.

Internal negotiation may assure more willing acceptance of the evaluator, but possibly at the expense of the acceptance of restrictions on research. For example, the researcher might require access to the names and addresses of all service users in order to draw a random sample. But where a confidential service is provided, gatekeepers might object to releasing such information as contrary to their policy, and propose instead that they select those to be contacted for the evaluation. It is a matter for negotiation as to how far the requirement for generalizable information can be reconciled with organizational values and practice – and also an ethical issue which needs to be resolved. (Ethical considerations around access are further considered in Chapter 3.)

Studies of organizational power (Morgan, 1986; Gabriel *et al.*, 2000) show there is a distinction between organizational authority (power legally and formally exercised on the basis of organizational position) and *de facto* power within organizations (control and influence on the basis of personal characteristics and knowledge). It cannot, therefore, be assumed that permission from the highest gatekeeper in an organization will open all doors – rather, there are many gatekeepers, and many permissions may need to be sought. Also, gaining access is seldom a once-for-all matter, but rather a process that extends over the life of the study as different areas come under scrutiny. However, the fact that access has been granted in one area may predispose to the granting of access in others.

The development of trust is also part of the equation. Evaluators have to bear in mind the need to provide credible evidence of their ability to conduct the evaluation in a professional way, both at the outset and as the work proceeds. As they prove by their actions that they are acting responsibly, they are then likely to be offered further access on more favourable terms.

Other stakeholders

Apart from commissioners and sponsors, there are other interested parties in an evaluation. 'Stakeholder' refers to anyone who holds an interest or stake in the program under discussion. Like the formative/summative distinction, stakeholder is a word that has escaped from evaluation studies into more general use. One reason for this is that stakeholder is seen to offer a neutral or even positive status for those with differing degrees of power and authority in an organization. It is inclusive. It differs from such traditional polarities as management and workers, government and the governed, service providers and service users, with their implications of interests which may conflict, although using a neutral term does not imply that inherent conflicts will disappear!

Stakeholders include the following people who have an obvious and *direct* interest in a program:

- managers of programs;
- program staff;
- volunteers and other service providers;
- service users and beneficiaries of the program;
- those initiating and providing finance for the program.

Stakeholders also include those with a more *indirect* interest,

- other organizations providing or receiving services or clients from the program;
- local and state government (if not directly involved through funding);
- other organizations providing complementary or competing services to the program;
- local residents who may be supportive of the program; and
- local residents who may be negatively affected by the program.

Guba and Lincoln (1989: 51), however, do not share the view that 'stakeholder' is a neutral or positive term. Instead, they categorize stakeholders as 'groups at risk', that is, those who have something to lose (and gain) from an evaluation. They subdivide stakeholders into three broad classes:

- agents, who are active in the development of the program under evaluation;
- beneficiaries, who profit in some way from the program, directly or indirectly; and
- victims, who are negatively affected by the program, by exclusion from its benefits or suffering losses in resources or prestige.
                                                                      (1989: 41)

The idea of including 'victims' as stakeholders forces attention onto the impacts of a program that might otherwise be missed or ignored. This is definitely a useful addition to the concept of stakeholder. However, to take account of all who might have an interest in a program, and to be aware of all unintended consequences which might impact on stakeholders, would be a massive undertaking for evaluation. It is questionable how practical it would be to widen the scope of the evaluation to search for all negative consequences, and there is also the problem of how to weight the different impacts.

Timing of evaluation in relation to program activity

So far, this discussion has assumed that evaluation is concurrent with program activity. But within the field of evaluation can be included activity that is undertaken before and after program delivery, as well as what might be called prospective evaluation, research designed to discover evidence for a future program, either:

- what kind of needs there are for a new program, or
- how much a planned program is likely to be used.

Ex-ante evaluation refers to an evaluation performed before a program starts, in order to 'help to define what is to be done, and provide a baseline from which to measure change' (Rubin, 1995: 33). Before-and-after measures of change, as required by impact assessments, need to collect information to map the area and investigate variables that it is proposed or likely that the program will alter. Sometimes, however, where evaluation is 'tacked on' to a program intervention, time or resources may not have been given to this phase, creating problems for estimating impact.

This pre-program evaluation should be distinguished from *needs assessment*, which is an evaluation undertaken (usually before a related program is implemented) in order to assess the needs of the target group. There is considerable ambiguity around the concept of 'need': who decides what the standard for need is, and how does need differ from want? But in general terms it has been proposed (Roth, 1990) that a need is a discrepancy between a desired and an actual state. Needs assessment is then a systematic research process to acquire information on the extent of need within a given population, and of establishing ways that such needs

could be met. It may result in a set of priorities for a future program to undertake, or a revision of a planned future program if
the proposed program activities are found not to be matched to
local needs.

Another form of evaluation activity prior to an evaluation proper
has been termed *evaluability assessment*. This refers to a formative
process designed to test if a program is ready for formal evaluation. It attempts to clarify program goals and the program theory
which links proposed action with expected outcomes. Often this
can become an end in itself and lead to significant change and
development to the program (Patton, 1990: 108). In so far as this
helps to explicate the intended mechanisms by which change is
produced, it has clear links to the practices of realistic evaluation as
proposed by Pawson and Tilley (1997).

Most evaluation studies have a limited timescale, fixed by
funding and personnel considerations. Yet it is possible that program effects are both short-term and longer-term, and even that
longer-term effects may arise in areas that the evaluators had not
considered; however, with the passage of time, it becomes more
difficult to separate out the influence of a program from other
influences occurring in participants' lives.

Ex-post evaluation is long-term evaluation, conducted some time
(often two years or more) after a project has finished, 'and looking
at impact and sustainability' (Rubin, 1995: 34). Evaluation of this
kind is understandably rare, as funding for this kind of evaluation
is difficult to sustain, and decision-makers usually cannot wait for
information on long-term effects to become available.

The link between evaluation and policy

An evaluation is one input into, rather than a determinant of, policy
decisions. What is regarded as convincing evidence in policy formulation varies from person to person, and from situation to
situation. The reliability accorded to the evidence is in part related
to the methods that were used to obtain it. For some decision-
makers, quantitative research methods have greater credibility
than qualitative ones, though if they don't like the findings, they can
still raise technical methodological issues to question them. For
instance: was the sample size large enough? Was there a control
group? Did the questions really ascertain the sample's true views?

Other people may be more persuaded by the illustrative case story, or a rich description of a social problem and the related program of intervention. Here the critique would be along the lines of: Is this evidence representative or restricted only to the case-studies? Is the case-study unique, and was it chosen because it demonstrated the desired results? The researcher or evaluator, who wishes to be heard and to influence policy decisions, therefore needs to consider what sorts of evidence are going to be most persuasive to the decision-makers, and which are likely to be discounted.

It is here that the factual link between evaluation and decision-making becomes weak. There is no guarantee that a technically excellent evaluation will be acted upon, either by policy-makers or by program staff. Empirical studies of organizations have shown that it cannot be assumed, either, that policy will be reached through rational means. And, as Weiss points out,

> people decide to have a program evaluated for many different reasons, from the eminently rational to the patently political.
>
> (1998: 22)

Evaluations are only one aspect of information in a policy decision; indeed, there is talk of 'pseudo-evaluations', where an evaluation is carried out for form's sake, but the actual decision has already been taken. Weiss (1998: 22) labels this tactic as 'window dressing', part of a wider process of illegitimate use of evaluation as subterfuge. Other forms of subterfuge include situations where evaluations are used to delay decision-making or to avoid decision-making by appearing to give the responsibility for making unpopular recommendations to someone else.

Those specifically concerned with the utilization of evaluation findings argue that one of the reasons for lack of impact may lie in the failure to involve stakeholders in the evaluation process. Not only do program participants contribute to improving quality by asking relevant questions, but they often have a role to play in implementation as well (Patton, 1990). Failure to bring program staff on board can result in action that can hamper research or provide misleading results.

It is obviously frustrating for evaluators if their work, even with high standards of research, is not used in decision-making. But Cook (1997: 38) argues that this concern has been overplayed, and that the impact of evaluations is larger than its critics generally assume. With increasing interest in evidence-based practice, and the use of meta-evaluation to provide an overview of individual evaluations within a particular field of interest, it is likely that evaluations will be increasingly specified for new social programs, and that evaluation findings will enter more strongly into policy decisions.

MODELS OF EVALUATION PRACTICE

In this second section, a summary of the main types of evaluation is given, along with some of the more distinctive alternatives.

Models which emphasize accountability

Impact assessment/outcome evaluation
(the 'classic' model)

Impact assessment is a form of accountability evaluation which has traditionally employed scientific methods of control and comparison to establish the outcomes of programs. Rossi and Freeman (1993: 217) argue that 'all impact assessments are comparative'. That is to say, in order to speak about the effects of a program, the evaluator needs to compare those who have experienced the program with those who have not. Although there are many ways of doing the comparison, the experiment with randomized experimental and control groups is held to offer the strongest proof that the effect observed is due to the difference between the groups – the experimental treatment. Impact assessment seeks to attribute observed effects to a specific program by ruling out other possible causative factors; '[e]stablishing impact essentially amounts to establishing causality' (Rossi and Freeman, 1993: 218).

However, experimental designs with treatment and control groups selected by random assignment are both difficult and costly to achieve. They may also give rise to ethical issues concerning allocation of individuals to treatment groups, and the extent of information given to participants. Where true experimental designs cannot be achieved, then quasi-experimental designs are often used. Here random assignment is replaced by other forms of selection to experimental and control groups. Examples would be the selection of controls to match the experimental group, before-and-after studies with the same participants, or statistical controlling on selected factors for differences between experimental and control groups.

Impact assessments which follow the methodology of the randomized experiment are likely to involve quantitative rather than qualitative data. Although qualitative data are not ruled out, the emphasis upon the reliability of measures of impact makes them unlikely to carry as much conviction. As Rossi and Freeman conclude:

> assessing impact in ways that are scientifically plausible and that yield relatively precise estimates of net effects requires data that are quantifiable and systematically and uniformly collected.
>
> (1993: 254)

Goal-free evaluation

Within the scientific tradition, *goal-free evaluation* seeks to reduce any bias in an evaluation by completely separating the role of evaluator from those of program practitioners. It seeks to ask questions about the effects of a program, without taking the stated goals of the program as the arbiter of what is to be included as impact. Thus it investigates all outcomes, anticipated as well as unintended, attributable to a program. This approach is associated with Scriven (1972), whose concern for the independence of the evaluator and the objectivity of the evaluation data led him to propose that an evaluator should not be in contact with program staff, and should not be influenced or biased by knowledge of the program goals. Instead, goal-free evaluation seeks to gather a wide array of data on the actual effects of a program, and to consider how these meet demonstrated needs.

Scriven argues that the distancing of the evaluator from those being evaluated is consistent with the ideal of objectivity in research, as instanced in the double-blind experimental design. Goal-free evaluation is a way of doing distanced evaluation, where

> the evaluator not only never talks to program staff at all, but never reads the program rationale documents. Heavy interviewing is done,

but only with consumers – and sometimes a selection of stakeholders – and the results of those interviews are combined with observation of process and the analysis of relevant extant data, possibly also with the results of tests.

(1997: 485)

However, critics argue that goal-free evaluation has hardly ever been tried in practice; it sets aside the stated program goals that policy-makers wish to hear about, because recommendations for change will involve them in reassessing these goals. Further, because it has no theory to explain the effects observed, goal-free evaluation raises the possibility of confusing chance differences for program-related ones (Chen, 1990: 173). Responding to such criticisms, Scriven accepts the difficulty of applying goal-free evaluation, but still argues that it could form one part of a multi-strand evaluation, which employs other methods to look at process.

Models which emphasize development/process

Process evaluation

Patton (1990), and others who favour approaches that emphasize the importance of understanding process, criticize a predominant focus on impact or outcomes on the grounds that:

> where outcomes are evaluated without knowledge of implementation, the results seldom provide a direction for action because the decision-maker lacks information on what produced the observed outcomes (or lack of outcomes). Pure pre-post outcomes evaluation is the 'black box' approach to evaluation.

(Patton, 1990: 105)

Process evaluation attempts to unpack the black box of impact evaluation by seeking to understand, and so evaluate, the process by which a program is delivered. Understanding these internal processes is crucial for helping program participants develop successful strategies for program implementation, so the approach is therefore formative rather than summative, with less emphasis on the role of the evaluator being detached than on being committed to working with different sets of stakeholders.

Process evaluation is an alternative strategy to impact evaluation, and its key features can be summarized as follows:

- priority being given to developing a relationship with practitioners;
- the application of formative evaluation;
- the use of qualitative research.

The reason for using qualitative research is to employ the depth and richness of interview and observational data in reaching an understanding of process, of how a program affects individuals, who may be practitioners, service users or other stakeholders. Quantitative methods are attractive in that they can provide standardized information over large samples, but they are limited in terms of how much light they can shed on what program activity actually means to the participants. However, *qualitative evaluation* does not necessarily imply a total rejection of quantitative research methods, as mixed strategies are increasingly common.

Illuminative evaluation

An example of a qualitative approach is that of *illuminative evaluation*. This falls within the tradition of social anthropology rather than the experimental model of 'classical evaluation'. In educational evaluations, Parlett and Hamilton suggest, evaluators need to distinguish between the 'instructional system', the formal plan of how an innovation is supposed to operate, and the 'learning milieu', the network of factors, cultural, social, institutional and psychological, which influence how an innovation is actually delivered, and which illuminative evaluation seeks to understand.

Illuminative evaluation offers an adaptable strategy of three stages; observation, focused enquiry and explanation. The aim is to produce a rich description of the program in action, rather than its theoretical or formal structure, goals and outcomes:

> It becomes imperative to study an innovation through the medium of its performance and to adopt a research style and methodology that is appropriate.
>
> (Parlett and Hamilton, 1972: 31)

Patton (1990), commenting on Parlett and Hamilton (1976), places illuminative evaluation within a 'transactional model' of evaluation, based on the core assumptions of qualitative research:

> The importance of understanding people and programs in context; a commitment to study naturally occurring phenomena without introducing external controls or manipulation; and the assumption that understanding emerges most meaningfully from an inductive analysis of open-ended, detailed, descriptive, and quotational data gathered through direct contact with the program and its participants.
>
> (Patton, 1990: 119)

This approach means that the evaluator moves away from the distant scientific experimenter role of the classic model and closer to collaboration and participation with stakeholders in order to incorporate their perspectives into the evaluation.

Responsive evaluation

One form of evaluation that places the views of stakeholders at the centre of a definition of needs and impacts is *responsive evaluation*. According to Guba and Lincoln its emphasis is that

> all stakeholders put at risk by an evaluation have the right to place their claims, concerns and issues on the table for consideration (response), irrespective of the value system to which they adhere.
>
> (1989: 12)

Evaluation is oriented towards providing stakeholders with an understanding of the program held by others. Evaluation is responsive if it 'responds to audience requirements for information' (Stake, 1980: 77). Based on a descriptive approach and observation of process, interpretation and discussion of reports is undertaken with program practitioners in order to allow practitioners to compare their own personal insights and experiences with the evaluator's observations and thereby develop their understanding. Responsive evaluation uses an external evaluator to develop formative information to improve program practice, which may be done iteratively, in repeated cycles of feedback and practitioner involvement. However, Patton (1997: 54) argues that while the stakeholders are sources of data and an audience in responsive evaluation, they are not real partners in the evaluation.

Utilization-focused evaluation

A strong argument for involving stakeholders, particularly program practitioners, in developmental evaluation is that this is one of the best ways of increasing the use of evaluation reports. *Utilization-focused evaluation* is associated particularly with Michael Quinn Patton (1997), who addresses the question of how evaluations can be designed so that their findings are implemented.

Beginning with the use made of evaluations, Patton enquires what kinds of relationship between evaluator and program practitioners sustain use. He quotes one program director:

> We used the findings to make some changes in our intake process and improvements in the treatment program... But you know, the big change is in our staff's attitude. They're paying more attention to participant reactions on a daily basis. Our staff meetings are more outcomes oriented and reflective... We're more focused. And the fear of evaluation is gone.
>
> (Patton, 1997: 88)

Patton argues that while any evaluation could have this range of effects, 'the process of actively involving intended users increases these kinds of evaluation impacts'. To do this involves a focus on the process of the program under evaluation, and an involvement on the part of program practitioners so that they can learn from the process. So, utilization-focused evaluation is 'inherently participatory and collaborative in actively involving primary intended users in all aspects of the evaluation' (Patton, 1997: 100).

Patton comes down in favour of emphasizing 'stakeholders' needs, program improvement, qualitative methods, and assisting with program decisions' (1997: 88). Where this emphasis on supporting the learning of program practitioners continues into long-term partnering relationships between evaluator and clients, it may lead to what Patton (1994) has called *developmental evaluation*.

Participatory evaluation

As was indicated in Chapter 1, when the evaluator's role in small-scale evaluation was discussed, participatory evaluation can take different forms. Weiss (1998: 99) sees these as ranged on a continuum:

- *Stakeholder* evaluation engages with different stakeholder interests in order to understand their views, concerns and priorities, but keeps the evaluator in charge of the conduct of the evaluation. (This is closest to the model of small-scale evaluation.)
- *Collaborative* evaluation places the evaluator as 'co-investigator' with program staff, where the research skills of the one are allied with the empirical knowledge of the others to take joint responsibility for the evaluation.
- *Empowerment* evaluation gives control of the evaluation to the practitioners, with advice and help from the evaluator. Ownership of the study aims to democratize the evaluation, empower the participants and ensure that the data are relevant to stakeholders' concerns.

As the practice of *participative evaluation* moves from involving stakeholders in the aims and design of the evaluation towards helping program participants use their own knowledge to improve a program, there is an increase in the potential for program participants to share in and learn from evaluation. Participative evaluation at its most participatory treads much the same ground as that covered by *action research*, especially community-based action research.

Action research

Stringer defines the values underlying action research, emphasizing that

- It is *democratic*, enabling the participation of all people.
- It is *equitable*, acknowledging people's equality of worth.
- It is *liberating*, providing freedom from oppressive, debilitating conditions.
- It is *life enhancing*, enabling the expression of people's full human potential.

(1999: 10)

He argues that *community-based action research*

commences with an interest in the problems of a group, a community or an organization ... [and] provides a model for enacting local, action-oriented approaches to inquiry, applying small-scale theorizing to specific problems in specific situations.

(Stringer, 1999: 10)

The role of the action researcher, as with the fully participative evaluator, is not to be an external expert but to act as a facilitator rather than a director, someone who offers expertise but cedes control to the practitioners and stakeholders for the research/ evaluation process.

Action research and participatory evaluation share the 'utilization focus' of process evaluation, because action (to change adverse situations for community groups) is the essential of action research and the goal for program participants. Less important to these models is the generalizing of research and evaluation. Instead priority is given to producing changes in the immediate circumstances of program delivery.

Empowerment evaluation

Within the field of evaluation, these ideas have been developed by David Fetterman (1996, 2001). In *Foundations of Empowerment Evaluation* he argues that people who have ownership of evaluation are more likely to adopt change and to develop as individuals. Empowerment evaluation uses collaborative methods with program participants to enable them to reflect on their activities. A learning organization is created, with evaluation becoming a tool for developing new strategies to achieve the program's goals. As well as the evaluator facilitating practitioner learning and practitioner-led evaluation research, they must ensure that neglected or minority groups have a voice in the developments.

This model of evaluation aims to empower those who are excluded from participation under traditional forms of evaluation, to take control of the evaluation, decide what issues are important, and phrase the research questions in ways that are meaningful to them. Participants are encouraged not just to take on board the agendas of the powerful, but to find their own voice and exert determination over their treatment. This can be emancipatory for groups, often from minorities, who are usually cast merely as users of services determined by others. Instead of being further victimized by an evaluation model which sees them as passive, empowerment evaluation aims to use their active involvement to redirect program aims and to enhance personal growth.

THEORIZING EVALUATION

Fourth-generation evaluation

Guba and Lincoln's *Fourth Generation Evaluation* (1989) has been influential in developing a theoretical approach quite distinct from the early 'scientific' or 'classic' model of evaluation presented at the beginning of the previous section. The key proposition is their rejection of the notion that evaluations can deliver 'facts' about impact, or describe the 'way things really are', and instead they argue that what come from evaluations are one or more 'constructions' shaped by the actors to make sense of their situation. These constructions are the only realities.

Fourth-generation evaluation presumes three prior generations and forms of evaluation. The *first generation* is identified by Guba and Lincoln as the measurement generation, when, particularly in education, testing took off on a large scale. This included IQ tests, and measurement was inextricably linked with evaluation. The effects of measurable evaluation can be seen today in the use of pupil examination successes to rank and evaluate school performance. However, such rankings have been criticized either for ignoring the entry criteria to schools and other contextual elements of school performance (such as socio-economic class), or for attempting to incorporate an over-simplistic system of quantifiable criteria, which gives a false sense of validity to the measures. For these reasons, an alternative to simplistic measures was needed.

The *second generation* which emerged was description evaluation, which focused not just on testing but also on the means for achieving desired outcomes, such as implementation strategies and organizational contexts. It then related these objectives and outcomes to actual practice by describing their strengths and weaknesses. This then was process evaluation as described in the previous section, although there was little judgement made of the value of the process – evaluation of process concentrated on describing rather than developing a critique.

Judgement was the predominant focus of the *third generation*. Enquiry had shifted from the first-generation scientific, value-free research model to one where the subjectivity and values of the investigator could not be denied. However, in response to the inadequacies of merely describing process, many evaluators decided they could make judgements about programs because as professional outsiders they considered they had a greater claim to objectivity than the stakeholders. In doing so they also created the justification for the profession of evaluation which conferred status and credibility to the activity, and reinforced confidence in the evaluators' findings.

Fourth-generation evaluation, however, dismisses the idea of judgement evaluation, that facts can be known with certainty to form the basis for objective judgements. Instead, fourth-generation evaluation adopts a relativistic approach to knowledge, based on individual constructions. Constructivism rejects the notion of a single discoverable truth, and accepts instead that social constructions are generated within specific social and cultural contexts. It is the task of the evaluator to create a discourse with the many different stakeholders in a program, and to reflect back with them on the differing constructions held by participants within the program, in the hope of reducing the number of constructions to one agreed pattern.

The practice of constructivist evaluation is performed through a responsive cycle of operations, where stakeholders are first identified and their concerns uncovered. These concerns are opened to all other stakeholders for comment and clarification. Where unresolved concerns remain, information is collected to throw light on those concerns. Finally, negotiation between stakeholders is facilitated by the evaluator to resolve any remaining concerns, if possible. The evaluator is not an adjudicator on those concerns, but part of the negotiation, which ends when resources of time and money are exhausted, or when outcomes are agreed upon.

Fourth-generation thinking has been useful in providing an antidote to the scientific paradigm, by questioning how evidence is collected and presented and by prioritizing the views and meanings of those concerned with the program. It has influenced the development of participatory models of evaluation, especially those which emphasize that the task of evaluation is to empower participants.

However, critics such as Pawson and Tilley (see below) argue that Guba and Lincoln's approach to constructivism is extreme when they claim that there is no reality beyond what the participants express. By encouraging such a relativistic view of truth, they are in danger of 'throwing the baby out with the bathwater' (Pawson and Tilley, 1997: 18). And Pawson and Tilley believe that Guba and Lincoln's theoretical stance on open-ended evaluation cannot be put into practice, because there is no clear way of deciding which constructions are to be accepted – for example if the participants' or evaluator's constructions conflict, which is to be preferred? They point out that in their own field of expertise, criminology, it is unlikely that one group of 'stakeholders', the criminals, will be able to agree a common view with other stakeholders regarding crime reduction measures.

Theory-driven evaluation

Guba and Lincoln's major contribution was to point out the lack of explicit theory to support evaluation practice. Chen takes up the challenge by providing another critique of much of program evaluation, on the grounds that it has been atheoretical. In his *Theory-Driven Evaluation* (1990) he defines theory as the 'set of interrelated assumptions, principles and/or propositions to explain or guide social action' (Chen, 1990: 40). Where impact evaluations have been based upon an input–output black-box model, these 'underlying assumptions, principles' have not been investigated and so the causal mechanisms producing the effect have not been understood. Without understanding the mechanisms linking cause and effect it is impossible to apply the findings from programs, whether of positive change or of little or no impact, to other programs and situations.

This has clear application to governments trying to implement national policies – they need to know there are generalizable causes of problems, so that there can be generalizable solutions (not just isolated programs which work in one locality and may not have relevance to other localities). Such general applicability needs to be sufficiently certain, with causal links substantial enough to justify funding – for example in prison reform or in changing health provision.

Chen argues that in those (quite frequent) cases where evaluation shows that no great impact has been found through implementing a specific policy, it is unclear whether the poor results are due to a failure of theory (the expected relationships did not work out) or a failure of implementation (the ideas were right, but the program did not in fact operate as planned).

Chen is also critical of the level of debate among evaluators, arguing that the main issues have been methodological, concerned with quantitative versus qualitative data, or scientific experimentation versus naturalistic observation, rather than being concerned with explicating theory. The theory Chen is interested in has to do with how the program works to produce its effects. People who plan a program of service or intervention, and those who deliver the program, also have theories about how the program works, though often such explanations are implicit and unsystematic. The work of the evaluator is to explicate the theory of action, which then may be generalizable to other contexts.

Chen specifies two broad types of program theory – *normative theory* that sets out how the program is believed to work, and can be used to check if the program is being implemented in accordance with the theory, and *causative theory* that details the proposed relationships between variables. Normative theory can be used to improve and develop the structure of a particular program, while causative theory can help in identifying unintended as well as intended consequences.

Realistic evaluation

Pawson and Tilley (1997) use the term 'realistic evaluation' for their theory-based approach, which follows Chen in advocating that evaluators should be developing theoretical models of what works. Their interest is with the middle-range theory of how a change is effected, and like Chen they use the term 'mechanisms' to describe causal factors which need to be understood in order to investigate and interpret program outcomes which can be measured. They advocate a concern with reinvigorating a theory-driven approach to evaluation in order to 'throw light into the black box'.

Pawson and Tilley, like Chen, are critical of the experimental approach to evaluation for its inability to explain why programs have (or have not) an effect. But they are even more critical of the pragmatic turn of 'utilization-focused evaluation' (associated with

Patton), which they see as being at the whim of the policy-maker and too dependent on the evaluator's 'skill' in choice of methods.

Pawson and Tilley also reject the constructivism and relativism of Guba and Lincoln's 'fourth-generation' approach as mistaken and impractical. Instead they argue from a *realist* view of social science research, that is, that researchers can study social objects scientifically while rejecting the positivist view of science (Blaikie, 1993: 59). Instead of the global question, 'What was the effect of the program?', they propose a substitution of the more specific questions, 'Why does a program work, for whom and in what circumstances?' (Pawson and Tilley, 1997: xvi).

Under the realist approach, instead of searching for general laws for explanation, causal patterns of events are seen as 'mechanisms' which connect at a theoretical level. Such mechanisms are not themselves observable ('empirical'), but they are considered to be 'real' structures and processes, that can explain the events that *are* observed. Mechanisms cause regularities or patterns of actions within particular contexts, so that '*outcome = mechanism + context*'. Specifying the context(s) is important in discovering why for some people and some areas a program may have a positive effect, and not for other people and other areas:

> Programs work (have successful 'outcomes') only in so far as they introduce the appropriate ideas and opportunities ('mechanisms') to groups in the appropriate social and cultural conditions ('contexts').
> (Pawson and Tilley, 1997: 57)

This realist view of program outcomes, that some may work in some contexts for some people and not for others, enables a more optimistic view of the frequently reported lack of evidence of positive effect from evaluations. For it is only by investigating carefully the contexts where program mechanisms operate that positive effects can be isolated. These may have been over-shadowed or counterbalanced by lack of effect in different contexts when a global evaluation has been taken over a number of sites.

Pawson and Tilley direct the evaluator's attention, therefore, to the useful task of attempting to specify the various means by which a program is supposed to have an effect ('mechanisms') and the variety of surrounding circumstances and target groups ('contexts') in which and to which a program is delivered. Because the variety of mechanisms and contexts is large, possibly infinite, it follows that they have little use for the 'one-off' evaluation, and call instead for planned programs of testing the different propositions derived from different mechanisms and contexts (Pawson and Tilley, 1997: 57).

Bringing together the evidence of different evaluations is described as 'cumulation'. This is not the additive model of meta-evaluation which for Pawson and Tilley perpetuates the black-box approach to program effects by failing to distinguish what is specific in the mechanism/context relationship in the individual studies that led to the outcomes reported. Rather, they see the aim of cumulation in realist evaluation as abstracting from specific studies middle-level propositions about why programs work in particular contexts that can both increase knowledge and improve practice. Inevitably, this involves fairly large and complex evaluations and the reinterpretation of other evaluations to permit 'cumulation' of evidence to improve understanding of mechanisms, contexts and outcomes.

Such theoretical endeavour is beyond the scope of the small-scale evaluator concerned with single program evaluation, but it does direct attention to different forms of explanation which are at play in the question, 'Was the program a success?'

REVISITING THE SMALL-SCALE EVALUATION MODEL

The emphasis on partnership or collaboration in the small-scale model obviously contrasts with the classic scientific model, where the evaluator is the objective expert and has control of the evaluation – what Weiss (1998) terms the 'evaluator-in-charge model'. The model of evaluation that draws heavily on the principles of partnership and collaboration is developmental, and owes something to ideas of empowerment through its recognition that all participants are equal and should benefit from the evaluation activity.

Fetterman (2001), for instance, advocating empowerment evaluation, draws a distinction between, on the one hand, models of collaboration where the researcher consults with the program practitioners but is largely responsible for the conduct of the research independently (as in small-scale evaluation), and, on the other hand, what he regards as empowerment evaluation, where the research is conducted by the program participants themselves and the evaluator acts as a facilitator of their research and learning.

As noted above, Weiss (1998) similarly describes three approaches to participative evaluation which she ranks along a continuum. 'Empowerment' evaluation, at one extreme, is where organization/community members conduct their own evaluation. In the middle is the 'collaborative' model where the evaluation is a joint enquiry, conducted by the evaluator and practitioner together. Third and 'least radical' is 'stakeholder' evaluation which approximates to the role of the small-scale evaluator:

> She [the evaluator] engages in a structured effort to learn [the stakeholders'] concerns, their assumptions, their questions, their data needs, their intentions for the evaluation. She seeks to shape the evaluation to answer their questions and meet their priorities, but she remains in charge of the technical research work. She reports back frequently to be sure that the study is on target. When the data are analysed, she engages representatives of stakeholders in interpreting the meaning of the data and its implications for program improvements.
>
> (Weiss, 1998: 99)

Weiss points out that within this model the evaluator's role can vary, as the evaluator

> can conceive of herself as partner and helper, or she can maintain the posture that once other participants have determined the kind of study they want, she has responsibility for the design, measurement and analysis phases of the study. It is even possible for her to lay claim to the role of objective outsider insofar as the conduct of the study is concerned, but the press is to collaborate with others all along the way.
>
> (1998: 100)

But why does small-scale evaluation differ from these other models which involve more participation or empowerment than the collaborative approach? If partnership is a good thing, then shouldn't we have more of it? The answers to these questions are less to do with criticisms of the alternative models and more to do with what is feasible and not feasible for student projects.

Student projects

Empowerment and collaborative models can be effective ways for experienced practitioners to develop themselves and the program through action learning, or for an evaluator with a lengthy time frame to work with an agency to create change. But for students on a short timescale, what Weiss terms stakeholder evaluation and what Fetterman refers to as consultant collaboration is a feasible option that works effectively at the local level.

Working within the constraints (and opportunities) of small-scale evaluation, collaboration is still real. The objectives of the study are determined through consultation with organization members, the research questions are checked with the members to make sure that all questions relevant to the organization's interests are included, and the research is carried out by the student evaluator on behalf of the organization. But the key negotiation is likely to be conducted by the student and academic supervisor with the program manager and those members of staff whom she/he wishes to involve.

The consultancy approach of collaborative evaluation also adds a measure of independence to the research and the report, and this is often welcomed by organizations when they come to make use of the findings. For those organizations using the report for fundraising, a criterion in the application process to funding bodies is often that independent research must be provided as evidence of need. And small-scale evaluation is intended for *use* – so there is a strong argument for retaining a collaborative rather than a participatory approach if this means the findings are more likely to be implemented.

However, small-scale evaluation also fits with models of *development* rather than accountability – with the stress on understanding process rather than impact. Examples are given in the following chapter where student evaluators have also acted as participants – as volunteers – and this has enhanced their perception of the program and its effects on the people they work with and serve. Ethical issues are raised by this dual role, and accounts are shared where students found they had to withdraw from participation and stress their research function in order not to mislead staff or program users – and to ensure that clear consent was given to information used in the evaluation report.

CHAPTER 3

Evaluation and Ethics

Summary

Ethics is the practical study of moral choices. Ethics explores the principles we draw upon to deliberate on options; why some options seem right and others do not; the actual choice made; consequences; and personal accountability.

(Porter, 1999: ix)

Ethical issues and dilemmas arise in all forms of research, but they have a particularly critical role when it comes to evaluation. Weiss sums it up as follows:

> Evaluation deals with real people in real programs, often people in serious need of help. The results of the evaluation may have real consequences for these programs and those people. Therefore, evaluation has an obligation to pay even more attention to ethical questions than most other kinds of social science research have to do.
>
> (1998: 92)

Similarly, Robson indicates that these 'real consequences' relate to the political nature of the evaluation. Even a small-scale evaluation

> focusing on some possible change of practice in a work setting concerns the exercise of power which can affect the working life and conditions of those involved.
>
> (2000: 28)

Ethical and political considerations are, therefore, inextricably linked.

This chapter explores the ethical issues in evaluation by reference to case studies of student evaluations, and to guiding principles formulated by professional associations.

Introduction

For those seeking ethical guidance from evaluation texts, there is considerable disparity in the amount of attention given to ethical issues. With some writers, ethics are dealt with in depth, with others direct references are more cursory (although ethical concerns may be embedded in the discussion – particularly when qualitative methods are being discussed). Issues covered can be problems common to social researchers, such as how to deal with confidentiality and consent, or the emphasis can be on professional codes of evaluation practice (such as that of the American Evaluation Association).

What tends to be missing in many standard evaluation texts is a discussion of the kinds of ethical dilemmas which are now widely debated in the literature on social research methodology – particularly the writing on qualitative research. This may be because the 'classic' models of evaluation are derived from the positivist ideals of objectivity and detachment, and ethical issues are discussed in terms of codes of practice. This seems to be the case even when the research methods being advocated are qualitative as well as quantitative.

However, even when the evaluation models are participatory, discussion tends to focus on general ethical principles, rather than on the dilemmas which occur in real-life practice. This is because evaluation reporting is almost exclusively non-reflexive/non-reflective. The opportunities to record and discuss dilemmas is therefore non-existent. A discussion of issues reflexivity and reflection is included in Chapter 7.

Models of evaluation and the treatment of ethics

The way ethics are treated relates directly to the model of evaluation being advocated. This is not surprising, as the model has been derived from its exponent's view of what is the *right* way to act in establishing the value of programs. So Kushner, for example, claims:

> The moral order I tend to operate in – as a practitioner of democratic evaluation – is one where there are mutual obligations to openness, to reflection and information sharing.
>
> (2000: 152)

The model of small-scale evaluation proposed in this book has already been described as collaborative rather than democratic, with an emphasis on partnership. Its ethical stance involves awareness of appropriate professional codes and guidelines, which are seeking to set clear and recognized standards of conduct, as well as awareness that everyday issues involve moral and ethical dilemmas which need to be resolved in the light of the values and commitments of partnership research. These ethical dilemmas relate to the role of researcher as well as to the role of evaluator. In other words, they involve the kind of issues concerning confidentiality or access to sensitive information which social researchers face, as well as dilemmas concerning reporting back to an organization (perhaps with negative findings) or making recommendations for action (the work of evaluation) within a relationship which is designed to foster partnership and mutual benefit. The bottom line in all this remains truth-telling.

Whatever the model of evaluation being pursued, it is not always an easy matter to resolve complex and difficult problems which arise, even when an ethical position appears to have been clearly defined. For example, Kushner, with his 'mutual obligations to openness, to reflection and information sharing' referred to above, includes in his book a lengthy discussion of an occasion when his 'democratic' approach encountered multiple problems. By providing this detailed personal reflection of a case-study, Kushner bravely lays himself on the line for readers to draw their own conclusions.

Kushner's case-study concerns a problematic evaluation where the managers of a hospice disputed his description of their organization in his report which he intended to publish. The evaluation concerned a musical concert in the hospice, when poems by two of the patients were set to music and performed by students as part of a wider program of involving students in the community. It seems some of the students felt distressed about the plight of patients and upset about the negative reaction of hospice staff to their performance (staff felt the material was insensitive).

The specific key dilemma in this example is that the study was intended to be 'democratic evaluation' with stakeholder involvement, but the 'mutual obligations' of all the parties were actually in conflict and apparently irreconcilable. More generally, the example shows that the relation between ethics in theory and in practice is not straightforward and that it is possible to criticize positions, even when those involved felt they were acting ethically. Kushner himself states:

> At no time ... was I acting unethically, in the sense that there was always a reasonable ethic to which I could appeal to justify my actions. But that by no means implies foreclosure or resolution of ethical issues.
>
> (2000: 160)

Kushner's example indicates the complexity of the task when choices have to be made, and when the evaluator has to reconcile their own morality with their professional role:

> Ethics are about how we inhabit our evaluations. In an important sense they are about the balance we strike between our personal values in respect of justice and morality, and the public values we have to acknowledge in our role.
>
> (Kushner, 2000: 172)

Ethical considerations, then, enter into discussions about evaluation in two ways, which are in theory distinct, but which overlap in practice. First, there are considerations arising out of the nature of evaluation itself, where setting a value on an activity or program implies a responsibility to those whose lives can be changed by the findings and so requires a judgement which can be seen to be fair. Second, evaluation proceeds by research activity, and that activity should be justifiable in terms of the standards to which the research community itself is increasingly sensitive. In the discussion which follows both these elements will be considered.

HOW CAN EVALUATION BE SEEN AS FAIR JUDGEMENT?

Evaluation has to be just and fair. Shaw (1999: 128) notes that 'The issues of social justice for evaluation have been addressed patchily, although there is a growing literature.' Shaw mentions the reformist position of House (1993) and constructivist theories of justice as part of this literature. One way into this debate is to begin with the established principles of 'natural justice' of English common law, which contain two key elements:

- Anyone being accused needs to know the *evidence* against them and have an opportunity to defend themselves.

- The person making the judgement must not only be independent but be *seen to be independent* (with the *seen* condition being
  even more important than the independence itself).

In terms of evaluation, this might translate into:

- The importance of *evidence-based findings*, which are valid and
  reliable, and which can therefore support claims and recommendations. For findings which are critical, an opportunity
  should be available for a *response*.
- The value of being *seen to be independent* provides freedom to
  'tell it as it is' – to be honest in presenting evidence, however
  negative it might be. In classic evaluation practice, being
  employed by an agency external to an organization, has been
  held to produce more *seen* independence than if the evaluator is
  directly sponsored by the organization being evaluated (Patton,
  1998).

Both principles raise issues requiring further discussion, and
again, the way these issues are resolved will relate to the model of
evaluation being practised as the 'right' way. A further question
also needs to be considered – should evaluation just be about
fairness – or should it also be about care? So, using case studies, the
discussion below looks at the two 'fair judgement' principles as:

- Evidence and response: presenting critical findings.
- Being seen to be independent: detachment and participation.

Then ethical codes are considered in terms of how these relate to
the 'fair judgement' ethos, and the principles of one particular code
(the American Evaluation Association) are used to guide the discussion. Finally, we address the issue of whether *fairness* is enough,
or whether evaluation should also be about *care*. This is considered
in the context of ethical dilemmas taken from reflective accounts
by student evaluators.

Evidence and response: presenting critical findings

What if findings are critical, and the client organization staff feel
they have to defend themselves from the results and dispute the

recommendations? This is was the situation referred to in the Kushner example above and it is a situation all evaluators have to consider.

The American Evaluation Association (AEA) states in its Guiding Principles that:

> Because justified negative or critical conclusions from an evaluation must be explicitly stated, evaluations sometimes produce results that harm client or stakeholder interests. Under this circumstance, evaluators should seek to maximise the benefits and reduce any unnecessary harms that might occur, provided this will not compromise the integrity of the evaluation findings.
>
> (AEA, 1994: Principles D2)

Weiss comments pungently on this formulation:

> Can't you hear the wrangles in the committee room that went into that carefully worded statement? The point is that the evaluator has to take account of the well-being of the people involved with the program. On the other hand, she can't compromise or soft-pedal or omit information from evaluation reports that shows them in a less than positive light. Her first obligation is the honesty and integrity of her work.
>
> (1998: 110)

In short, the evaluator is someone who not only has to find out the truth, but also has to have the ability to give bad news well. One solution would be to keep all negative criticism under wraps, until the final report is produced. The justification for this would be to avoid bias through the influence of program staff, to complete a job and fulfil an agreement, while for a student their assessment requirements would have been met. It would be time to skip town, but would this be ethical? Natural justice requires the right to a defence and it's also possible that fulfilling an agreement may require adhering to a clause giving the organization some rights concerning publication. So the way a negotiation is completed much earlier in the process is highly relevant to this issue.

Weiss, for instance, recommends that the negotiation agreement should cover whether the evaluator has full control over the report, or whether the client can insist on changes. However, Weiss also advises that the evaluator should listen to the response of the client if they are unhappy with the report, and she suggests different courses of action, in addition to citing research codes to justify the evaluator's right to make negative comment:

> The sponsor or the staff have insights to offer. Perhaps their interpretation should lead to a softening of certain conclusions or a recasting of others. If so, the evaluator can profit from their suggestions. But if she listens and considers and then decides that the changes they want violate the meaning of the data, she should have the right to say no. She can include their objections in an appendix to the report, which may satisfy most of the critics. But autonomy is an important value in evaluation...
> If there is one universal research rule, it is: Do not distort the data.
> (Weiss, 1998: 304)

Weiss's position is based on her commitment to the evaluator having a role which is independent, and not participatory. For those who advocate participatory or empowerment evaluation, the role of evaluator/researcher/participant is combined with that of stakeholder and the way critical findings are handled is consequently different. Some feminist researchers, such as Stanley and Wise (1983), would give the researched the right to rewrite drafts and even prevent publication.

The way to deal with negative findings depends on the approach to evaluation which is being advocated, and specifically on the nature of the evaluator's role. In collaborative, small-scale evaluation, the evaluator is somewhere between a detached observer and an empowering participant. This means that negative findings can be relayed back as the study progresses as part of the collaboration, in order for the client to make a response – which can be further tested out in data collection – through eliciting the views of service users or staff to this response, for instance.

However, it is possible that the evaluator might prefer to withhold the information until the draft stage of the report, or to give a verbal summary of problematic issues after the fieldwork is completed. This may be to protect the anonymity of the participants and to protect against bias from a persuasive manager who feels defensive about a program. More emotively, the evaluator may not want to cause trouble or hurt feelings or embarrassment. The findings are going to be presented to people with whom the evaluator has developed a relationship, and she/he may feel unwilling to risk the pleasantness of the process by producing unwelcome news.

Students do worry about these issues, and good advice is to talk over concerns about negative findings with the manager or person(s) with whom the study has been negotiated. But the findings themselves cannot be compromised – they express the voices of those who have participated and their voices need to be heard in the report, in ways which are authentic (Lilley, 2002). Evaluation is intended to change and improve practice, after all, to generate results which will be used even when evaluation is small-scale and locally based. If everything was perfect, then there would be no need for the study.

Evidence-based evaluation: ethical issues

In the following extended case-study (Benington Hospital Volunteers; Hall and Hall, 2003), a student evaluator produced negative findings in her report. She had confidence in her methodology, with her results confirmed by observations she made as a volunteer worker within the organization. Her volunteer role also meant that other volunteers were candid with her about their views, knowing that she had seen their behaviour and had experienced similar situations.

One ethical issue was whether the volunteers were fully aware their opinions were being treated as confirming data (from the interviews). Another issue was how comfortable they would have been with a report which was negative in its conclusions about an aspect of service they were highly attached to. These issues show how subtle ethical questions can be.

The case-study shows how evidence was collected revealing a gap in the training and awareness of the hospital volunteers and how this negative result had to be presented within the context of a service which was highly respected within the institution and fervently supported by the volunteers themselves.

Example 3.1 Benington Hospital Volunteers

Introduction
Benington Hospital has a highly successful volunteer scheme, with volunteers helping in wards by making tea for relatives, talking to patients, and 'gophering' for staff – delivering mail and so on. The scheme had been the subject of previous evaluations, which had been very positive in terms of

senior management's appreciation of the scheme's input, and in terms of the volunteers' high levels of satisfaction with the way they were being organized, and with the leadership of their dedicated coordinator.

The coordinator was interested in a further study dealing with a specific issue, namely an evaluation of awareness of infection control by the volunteers. Infection control was recognized by the hospital as being of major importance in their service delivery, having implications for training all their staff. To lead their strategy the hospital trust had appointed a nurse manager who was also keen for an evaluation to be done with the volunteer group.

Nationally, infection control was being regarded at this time as a major problem. As the introduction to the evaluation report noted:

> At any one time 9% of patients in hospitals are being treated for an infection they acquired there (Kmietowicz)...Treating such infections is costing the National Health Service as much as £1 billion a year...
> (Waheed, 2002)

National research on the problem had been developing, but the report noted that volunteers (fast becoming an integral part of hospital life) were the least-researched group in the health sector, particularly with regard to infection control.

Aims of the study

The student evaluator negotiated the project with both the nurse manager and the volunteer coordinator (and her supervisor). Initially there was one main objective:

> To evaluate infection control practices by hospital volunteers, focusing particularly on their perception and understanding of their own risks of acquiring and transmitting nosocomial infection.

Two further objectives were added as the research got underway.

   (i)   To identify any fears/concerns the volunteers may have had regarding infection control
   (ii) To identify what they felt they needed regarding infection control

Research methods

It was decided to use semi-structured, in-depth interviews and a self-completion questionnaire-based survey. In the event, the survey was not used in analysis (for a mix of reasons beyond the evaluator's control). The evaluator had to depend more heavily than anticipated on qualitative data to complete the report, although as the nurse consultant preferred this kind of data anyway that was not too problematic.

Participant observation was also used and had an important effect on the results. The student already had experience as a nurse assistant in another hospital, and she wanted to spend time as a volunteer on the wards (not just for research purposes, but to enhance her career prospects in health care).

In the reflective account, she noted how her role as researcher was negotiated. She was initially introduced as a student undertaking research on behalf of the infection control unit:

> I felt [the volunteers] saw me as someone who had expert knowledge of the subject, and was there to judge their knowledge of infection control and practices, which not only made them uncomfortable, it also made me uneasy. However, once I changed my strategy, on the advice of my supervisor, and started introducing myself as a volunteer at the Trust who was interested in learning whether they had similar or different perceptions and/or experiences to myself regarding infection control, this significantly appeared to relax them and helped to break the ice.
>
> (Waheed, 2002)

The student kept a diary of her research and of her volunteering activity. The diary reveals a number of occasions when infection control procedures were not followed by various personnel on the wards, including nurses (these observations were not included in the evaluation report, because the observations had not had ethical approval from the hospital as part of the publishable research). The report did contain the results of interviews with the volunteers which confirmed that they had low awareness of infection control, and little perception that they themselves were at risk, but that, nevertheless, they felt the issue to be an important one. These findings were supported by detailed quotations and analysis, and with relevant references to other research studies which had found that infection control was not felt to be important by hospital staff.

The Hospital Research Ethics Committee

Halfway through the fieldwork, the evaluator was told that permission for the study would be required from the Hospital Research Ethics Committee. Because of a change to regulations, the conditions for gaining ethical approval had been extended and the committee now required all research on hospital grounds to be referred to them for approval (even studies like the evaluation project, which did not involve patients). This approval had not been a requirement when the research began or when the research brief had been submitted and agreed with the sponsors. However, this study and another conducted by a postgraduate student (also concerned with infection control) were required to be approved, and they were the first pieces of research to go before the newly extended committee.

Although this situation was harmoniously resolved, it is a warning to other researchers in a health setting to make sure that the requirements on ethical permission are fully understood, and that any likely changes can be incorporated into the planning. Hospital requirements are becoming increasingly stringent, and lengthy and detailed applications, with appropriate signatories, are often demanded. This can delay or prevent research, and it can be particularly difficult for students on a tight time schedule. As was noted in the reflexive account:

> The research timetable would not have allowed sufficient time, had the project been dependent on securing this permission, and the study would therefore have had to go through a drastic revision or be scratched completely leaving me high and dry.
>
> (Waheed, 2002)

Conclusions and recommendations

The conclusions in the evaluation report noted that there was not enough infection control information and training for the volunteers:

> Worryingly, although not surprisingly, however, given the lack of infection control input, it would seem that volunteers do not perceive there to be an infection control problem at the hospital, as a result of which they do not feel motivated to further their knowledge base or to comply with infection control practices. A review of the literature suggests that there is a general lack of motivation among healthcare workers to comply with infection control procedures due to a low perception of the importance of these measures (Bartzokas, Williams and Slade, 1995).
>
> (Waheed, 2002)

Recommendations were that guidelines to infection control should be in the volunteer induction packs, that infection control should be a central theme of the volunteer orientation program and that the hospital should develop accreditation for training. Annual information updates on this subject were also suggested, while it was noted that ward staff needed to be educated about the role of the volunteers.

The results of the evaluation related to a program where previous evaluation of the volunteer scheme had been very positive. This time the evaluation showed that volunteers themselves felt there was a need for more training. Without the participant observation of the student it is possible that a more rosy picture would have emerged, particularly through the interviews with volunteers who, as the Reflective Account noted, were

> fiercely loyal towards [the coordinator] whom they held in very high regard and were particularly concerned with presenting her and the volunteer service, in general, in the best possible light.

The evaluator assured the volunteers that the coordinator was not under investigation and that their perceptions and opinions could help bring about beneficial changes. But it is clear that the validity of the research was undoubtedly strengthened by her participation as a volunteer:

> [B]ecause I was also a volunteer, as well as a researcher, the informants interviewed were able to be more open with me, and in most cases felt

that I could relate to their responses with regards to infection control, as throughout the interviews, many of them started or ended answers with 'as you well know' or 'you know what it's like'.

(Waheed, 2002)

Use of references to other relevant research findings also provided concurrent validity for this particular local evaluation, and were helpful in 'sugaring the pill' – providing evidence that the poor knowledge of a serious problem by the volunteers was part of a national trend and not a specific failing of their organization.

Response to the evaluation

The response to the research was very positive. Although the findings had revealed a lack of knowledge and awareness, one of the managers who had responsibility for infection control awareness and training in the hospital commented on her evaluation sheet:

I found the report thorough, comprehensive, giving a wealth of data. It is well presented, logically progressed, making useful recommendations for practice ... The findings are useful in establishing a baseline of hospital volunteers' perceptions of infection control which is an important issue. Although a small study, the recommendations for training could be implemented by [Benington].

(Waheed, 2002)

In addition, the comment concerning the student was that 'her attitude and application and enthusiasm for the subject was exemplary'. In this case, an independent and critical study was well received. The evaluator's competence and diligence was accepted, her methodology approved and the validity of the findings accepted with recommendations seen as offering a way to make progress. Negotiation and collaboration throughout the study ensured that problems (such as the Research Ethics Committee's approval) could be resolved.

Even more satisfactory was the decision to incorporate the findings in the training of the volunteers and to include appropriate information in their induction packs. When the scheme received further funding this issue was highlighted and a development worker was given the specific task of ensuring the recommendations in the evaluation report were implemented.

Being seen to be independent: ethical issues

'Being seen to be independent' was the second principle of natural justice to be considered. Whether employed or sponsored by an external agency or directly by an organization, the independence of the evaluator needs to made clear in negotiation unless the evaluation is a participatory one. These ethical considerations suggest that the most defensible position for an evaluator is one that respects participants and engages with them about the purpose and use of the evaluation findings.

Small-scale evaluation takes a midway position between the advocacy of independent external evaluation and a wholly participatory model. However, this role can sometimes become fuzzy when evaluators adopt participant roles in order to facilitate the research, as the case-study above illustrated.

The next extended case-study (Lake View Day Care Club; Hall and Hall, 2003) develops the issue of researcher/participant dilemmas by considering the situation of other student evaluators who also acted as volunteers. In this case the evaluation was positive but one student still had to resolve ethical issues, particularly in relation to her relationship with vulnerable service users.

Example 3.2 Lake View Day Care Club

The organization
Lakeview Hospital is a non-profit organization, providing health and social care for older people in the locality. The day club, which is designed to combat loneliness among a group of socially isolated people, provides recreation and meals for its members who attend once a week. Club members must be mentally alert, though some are physically frail, and transport to and from the club is provided for some members.

The manager's aim for evaluation
The stimulus for the research was a request from the manager, who was looking to back up internal monitoring of services with an independent and external view, but did not have money available to commission an independent commercial research organization. In a subsequent interview he noted:

> But, if we look at ourselves and say, well you know, who we are and what we do, who would be the best the people to give us some thoughts and advice? If you go to someone [in the area], even if you went to somewhere like the Department of Social Services, I doubt they'd have found the time to help us anyway, but they have an agenda. The University by definition from our point of view would not have an agenda. They'd have an overview...
>
> So, we thought... let's ask the University, ring up and see if they'd be interested in doing a project to look at our club...

In this case, it was believed that independence came from the academic role of the university, to provide an external evaluation based on the 'overview' of broad-brush theory and knowledge. In addition the management wanted credibility for the study: 'We felt at the time it made good sense to us to have it looked at by an external body who was seen to be reputable.'

Aims of the evaluation

The main evaluation questions were set by the manager:

- to give a picture of those who used the club and their needs;
- to evaluate the services provided by the club and whether they were meeting the service users' needs.

Research methods

The research methods were decided upon by the students and the manager jointly, and elaborated with the supervisor. All recognized that the standard administration of a questionnaire was unlikely to provide detailed information. In the close and intimate setting of the club, with members interacting in groups at tables, the researchers would not be able to stand around observing activities in a non-participant manner, and they would need to build up familiarity and trust with members in order to gain their confidence to answer questions. In the event, the students used a variety of research methods:

- *participant observation* of the club, through joining in activities, for example handing out lunches, washing up, playing bingo;
- *in-depth interviews* with 24 members, plus 'informal chats' with both members and volunteers;
- *self-completion questionnaires* with 20 members and 16 volunteers;
- *documentary sources* on the history and operation of the centre;
- *case-studies* of 2 members.

The participant volunteer role and the evaluator partner role

Although non-participant observation would have been difficult and intrusive, the reflective account of one of the students shows they were initially keen to establish their identity as researchers and not as any other sort of visitor.

> It was anticipated beforehand that we would be expected to participate in the activities and would be seen as volunteers probably there to amuse the older people. Initially we resented the fact that we were not properly introduced as researchers especially to the members... It was then decided to introduce ourselves in a proper way [through] flyers stating our names and our purpose in the club, and our photos, too.
>
> [However] it did not really matter to the [members] who we were and what we were there for, they were just happy to see new faces... and new people to talk to rather than repeating the same topic to the same group of people over and over again... Consequently we 'did do rather a lot of sympathetic listening to catalogues of problems' (Bresnen, 1988: 44) and sorrows.
>
> (Fong, 2001)

However, 'sympathetic listening' produced some problems, for example whether the information should be relayed to staff or whether other help should be offered. As the student noted,

> Although much as I would have liked to help them out by telling their problems to a member of staff, I was afraid that I would breech the contract of confidentiality.
>
> (Fong, 2001)

For one of the students, this problem of 'sympathetic listening' became acute because of her professional expertise from past training as a nurse.

> [W]hen a service user was feeling sickly and refusing to eat despite several persuasions from the volunteers, ... I volunteered to speak to her... On this occasion, I have no intention of conducting an interview but merely the thought of helping as I have experience of persuading patients to eat. Unknowingly, however, the entire conversation turns out to be a complete interview and I have successfully persuaded her to have a glass of milk. ... My initial reaction was to record every detail and include this conversation in the study. But at the same time I was concerned that it would be unethical on my part, as I did not first ask for her permission. Hence I went back to her explaining my intention and asked if she minded being included. She was very obliging and has given her permission.
>
> (Fong, 2001)

The students remained in a collaborative role, still maintaining their independence, though yet another challenge occurred when they were included in an invitation to a social event, and given 'thank you' gifts.

> We were even invited to the Club Christmas parties and also the Matron's party ... [which] we declined because of the possibility of bias as suggested by Douglas (1976) that 'when one has enjoyed the hospitality of a group it may become harder to offer criticism of their efforts' (Hall and Hall, 1996: 14) This also relates to the gifts we received from Friday's volunteers [which we accepted]. Nevertheless, we returned the appreciation by presenting a gift (an Art and Craft book) to the Club.
>
> (Fong, 2001)

Student evaluators and independence

Participation as 'sympathetic listeners' was essential to produce good data, so it was part of a valid research method. It also allowed the evaluators to be sensitive in the way they conducted the study, and this approach had been negotiated and agreed with the club, whose manager was keen to have an inclusive approach with all stakeholders feeling involved and comfortable with the evaluation process.

(When the report was produced, it was circulated to members, volunteers and staff as well as to the board and outside agencies.)

For students generally, independence does not just relate to their specific research role, but is also complicated by their position within the academic structure as learners who are supervised. Negotiation agreements should include an item which gives the student the right to regular supervision, and gives the tutor responsibility for ensuring that the evaluation is conducted in a way which is responsible and meets the standards of the academic institution. This supervision needs to include opportunities to discuss ethics, with specific help on offer if and when dilemmas arise.

The student is in a political situation, with a balance of power residing with the tutor, who has a strong influence on the research which is for assessment. Students could fear conflict might jeopardize their results, even their degrees, if their opinions on ethical decisions were different from their tutor's. However, tutors are part of the wider political structure of the university, which is likely to include an ethics committee whose approval is requisite for all student and staff research. Staff are constrained by this structure, and also by the ethical codes or guidelines of their discipline.

Grievance procedures would also mean that conflict should be manageable. The point is that independence for the evaluator operates within a structure. For the student being assessed, this structure includes support through supervision, but supervision may also limit their freedom to make ethical choices.

Independence and justice: codes and dilemmas

'Fair judgement', our initial 'jumping-off point' for the discussion, is thus the outcome of complex processes and decisions and reflects the reality of the political relationships governing the evaluator's ethical freedom. Shaw (1999: 30) notes that the constructivist approach to social justice 'pushes us to an empirical concern with "how justice is constructed, communicated and experienced in everyday life"' (Altheide and Johnson, 1994: 184). For this reason, some researchers such as de Laine (2000) prefer to discuss dilemmas and actual experience where emotion and intuition are part of the ethical decision-making process, rather than the application of abstract principles.

Examples of how personal, emotional, gender and political issues are empirically part of resolving the ethical demand for fairness in local evaluation practice are provided in Chapter 7.

Key principles

Writing on qualitative evaluation, Shaw underlines the distinction between the day-to-day process of ethical decision-making and broad ethical principles, and notes that different views have tended to emerge in discussion about the latter arena. So

> Eisner (1991) occupies familiar territory with 3 main principles of informed consent, confidentiality and the right to opt out of research at any time.
>
> (Shaw, 1999: 74)

House has a different Big Three for 'professional evaluation' – mutual respect, non-coercion and non-manipulation, and the upholding of democratic values (House, 1993: chapter 7). Robson's trinity for small-scale evaluation is a variation again – with consent, privacy and confidentiality, and 'risks as related to benefits' being regarded as the main aspects of ethics (Robson, 2000: 29).

Codes

The debate on principles has been developed into ethical codes and guidelines by practitioners who have tried to codify (and thereby systematize) such issues as a guide to professional practice. So, for instance, the American Sociological Association (ASA), the American Psychological Association (APA), the British Psychological Society (BPS) and the British Sociological Association (BSA) have produced ethical guidelines relating to research and professional practice, all accessible from their websites:

www.asanet.org/members/ecoderev.html

www.apa.org/ethics/code2002.html

www.bps.org.uk/documents/Code.pdf

www.britsoc.org.uk/about/ethic.htm

As evaluation has grown as a professional activity, it has had to develop standards to ensure that there can be public confidence in evaluators and their evaluations. Such codes are not only to protect the public – 'to maximise benefits and minimise risks' (Robson, 2000). Codes are also designed to be a protection to evaluators themselves, and could even be used as a defence if clients are unhappy about methods or results ('I was only obeying the code'!).

The code produced by the American Evaluation Association (AEA), which can also be found on their website, www.eval.org/EvaluationDocuments/aeaprin6.html is designed to encourage the professional development of evaluation, by providing documentation on a set of values, commitments and standards which can help produce commonality among the members. There are five Guiding Principles which are 'meant to stimulate discussion and to provide a language for dialogue about the proper practice and application of evaluation among members of the profession, sponsors of evaluation, and others interested in evaluation'.

The five Guiding Principles are

  (i)   Systematic Inquiry;
 (ii)   Competence;
(iii)   Integrity/Honesty;
 (iv)   Respect for People;
  (v)   Responsibilities for General and Public Welfare.

Three of the principles (Systematic Inquiry, Respect for People, Integrity/Honesty) are common to social science endeavour, and it could be argued that at first sight they seem laudable but self-evident – who, for example, would admit to doing unsystematic, disrespectful or dishonest evaluation? Or what evaluator would regard incompetence or irresponsibility as acceptable standards for their work? The 'illustrations' which accompany the code expand on what these principles mean and raise important issues which are not always apparent from the Guiding Principle terminology, although even the 'illustrations' are of necessity succinct, and complex and conflicting aspects cannot be developed. The five Guiding Principles provide the framework for the discussion below.

Systematic Inquiry: facts and values

'Systematic Inquiry' relates not only to rigorous research methods, but also to the way the work is presented. Evaluators should, in presenting their work,

> discuss in a contextually appropriate way those values, assumptions, theories, methods, results, and analyses that *significantly* affect the

interpretation of the evaluative findings. These statements apply to all aspects of the evaluation, from its initial conceptualization to the eventual use of findings.

(AEA, 1994: Principles A3)

This indicates that the evaluator should flag up, from the start, that the findings will not simply be factual – they will be subject to interpretation in the light of the reasoning, purposes or intended uses (or theorizing) of stakeholders in the program. And, of course, different groups of stakeholders may differ in their inter-pretations as a result.

It is interesting that the AEA makes this point, as it might have been expected that their approach would have been more tradi-tionally conceptualized – along the lines that evaluation provides concrete empirical facts on which sound judgements can be based, leading to a rational redistribution of societal resources in favour of those programs which produce the greatest benefits. In fact, the AEA is recognizing the role of fact (empirical data) *and* interpretation.

The emphasis on interpretation of findings has been taken further by House and Howe (1999), who, in a provocative work, argue that attempts within evaluation to disconnect fact from value, or to separ-ate objective data from judgements on those data, are misguided:

In our view there is no hard-and-fast separation of facts, which eva-luation can determine, and values, which it cannot. Because facts and values are not two separate domains, evaluation can help determine conclusions that are blends of both.

(1999: 134)

House and Howe note that evaluations which try to keep out the evaluator's own values, and produce instead simple facts and descriptions, may not be entirely factual. For what on the surface appear to be plain descriptions often foreshadow the report's conclusions by picking out items and issues for comment. There is no such thing as a value-neutral description. However, they also reject the view of radical constructivism, which denies 'the exis-tence of any objective reality' (House and Howe, 1999: 57). Under radical constructivism, as Guba and Lincoln assert,

Views are neither right nor wrong but different according to how the construction is formed, the context in which it is formed, and the values that undergird construction in the first place.

(1999: 59)

Both House and Howe's case for 'deliberative democratic evaluation' (participatory evaluation with stakeholders) and the constructivist model of Guba and Lincoln are very different from what the AEA is advocating, and it may be that the key word underlined in their guidelines – *significantly* – is itself significant. Evaluators can argue, after all, that information or interpretation can be included or withheld according to its 'significance'. But at least the AEA principle shows that this issue needs to be considered for enquiry to be regarded as systematic.

Competence

Assuring stakeholders of the evaluators' competence requires that

> [e]valuators should possess (or, here and elsewhere as appropriate, ensure that the evaluation team possesses) the education, abilities, skills, and experience appropriate to undertake the tasks proposed in evaluation.
>
> (AEA, 1994: Principles B1)

Competence is a protection to the public, but it is also part of defining the boundaries of what evaluation practice is. Evaluation is developing as a profession, and a key distinction of professions is that they establish control over entry requirements (attainment of specific competencies) to let certain people into the profession and to keep other people out (Freidson, 1988). There is a growing demand for evaluation from public bodies, and higher-education institutions are responding to the need somewhat slowly, through graduate training. Competence is also being developed by the increasing numbers of texts on the subject, and by the emergence of evaluation societies in different countries which are developing standards of competency.

Students can feel they are not competent to produce good evaluation. It is necessary that they have had good research training as preparation, that they are well supervised and supported by their institution, and that they are familiar with evaluation texts and guidelines. However, they should have confidence in their ability to offer insights, and to provide a valuable means of feedback with useful recommendations.

Example 3.3   Competence in a medical setting

One social science postgraduate student, evaluating the effectiveness of a training program in a hospital, felt incompetent to comment on what were medical and nursing procedures. But as her study progressed, she discovered through interviews that the reason the program was not being effective was to do with management and organizational factors, rather than with medical reasons. Opposition to the program from those with ward leadership positions had to be overcome by and the student recommended ways in which they could be incorporated more effectively into the program so that it would be implemented by those with 'hands on' responsibility. Understanding organizational practice and culture was something a social science student could appreciate and feel competent in commenting on.

Integrity/Honesty: relating principles to credibility

Access is also relevant to this Guiding Principle, which states that:

> If evaluators determine that certain procedures or activities seem likely to produce misleading evaluative information or conclusions, they have the responsibility to communicate their concerns, and the reasons for them, to the client (the one who funds or requests the evaluation).
>
> (AEA, 1994: Principles C6)

No examples are offered by the AEA of situations in which apparently well-founded procedures producing misleading information might arise, but one can imagine certain possibilities, to do with restrictions on sampling. For instance, one set of stakeholders might control access to the selection of respondents, in order to produce an unreasonably favourable (or unfavourable) evaluation of a program.

An example where misleading information can be produced in this way comes from university teaching quality assessment exercises. It is not unknown for external assessors to be presented with hand-picked and well-coached students as representative of the student experience (Alderman, 2001). Bias also occurs once the criteria for evaluating teaching are known, when it becomes possible to tailor performance in a lecture to those criteria (whether or not this improves the overall program). Those subject to teaching quality assessment learn to play the game so that

> [t]he proportion of departments getting at least 22 points out of [the maximum] 24 has risen from around a third in the 1996–98 round to over two-thirds in 2000–2001.
>
> (Alderman, 2001: 17)

Respect for people: reducing harm, encouraging engagement through reciprocity

Reducing harm has already been considered in the discussion on presenting critical findings, but it also includes harm that might be incurred through the process of research. In medical research the scope for doing harm to patients, through the maladministration of drugs or the misuse of surgery, is obviously much greater than the potential harm to those people who are exposed to questionnaires or interviewing. But questioning can bring to mind painful incidents in a person's life, and the evaluator needs to consider the extent to which people may become upset by being asked questions on sensitive subjects, and whether the risk of disturbance is outweighed by the potential benefits of the research.

So an interesting aspect of the principle of *Respect for People* is that the AEA proposes a view of reciprocity or social equity, such that

> those who give to the evaluation can receive some benefits in return. For example, evaluators should seek to ensure that those who bear the burdens of contributing data and incurring any risks are doing so willingly, and that they have full knowledge of, and maximum feasible opportunity to obtain any benefits that may be produced from the evaluation.
>
> (AEA, 1994: Principles D4)

This is at least a recognition that those participating in an evaluation should get something out of it. Most likely this notion has been a response to criticisms of evaluations, particularly those conducted from an external expert perspective, where information has been gathered from or supplied by participants who don't feel they are getting much benefit from their cooperation. A further issue which this raises is whether participants should be liable to some consideration of their workload and possible compensation if the evaluation has involved them in extra work, for example by taking up their time in collecting information, or by requesting extra forms on program activities to be completed.

The inclusion of *encouraging engagement through reciprocity* indicates the importance of establishing participation in evaluation which is willing rather than grudging – and so more likely to be a valid representation of the participants' views. Etzioni's (1975) threefold classification of organizational compliance is relevant here. Those whose programs are being evaluated can respond to the evaluator's requests from three basic value orientations: normative, calculative or alienative. Under normative compliance, people respond because they associate themselves with the action being undertaken, believing that the evaluation will improve the service on offer. Under the calculative response, they comply with evaluation requests because they are being compensated (perhaps in money terms) for their involvement. Under alienative control, compliance is not a request but a demand that cannot be refused. The consequence in terms of level of compliance can be imagined.

The position held by those within a program is likely to influence their value orientation towards compliance. Senior managers may share normative assumptions about evaluation improving the services provided (although they may have particular concerns about the specific evaluation being proposed), while those towards the lower and less powerful end of the organization might find they have little choice in whether to take part or not, once the program director has approved the research. If external organizations such as government or funding bodies require the evaluation, then it becomes more difficult for the program director to refuse to respond, but compliance, if alienative, may be restricted and information manipulated, distorted or withheld.

The principle of *Respect for People* relates to key ethical issues – *access*, *consent*, and *anonymity/confidentiality* – which apply to all social research.

Access
Access is negotiated at the start of the evaluation, with those who are the 'gatekeepers' of the organization (that is those who control entry). 'Sponsors' may also be involved – those with influence in an organization whose support is crucial if staff and service users are going to be willing to participate.

However, access does not just involve entry through a formal process of sponsor and gatekeeper. Darlington and Scott point out the ethical demands of getting in and getting on.

> It is not sufficient to just 'get in'. The researcher must also be able to 'get on' with research participants. From the perspective of staff, researchers can get in the way of people going about their normal work and are a potential source of interference. Issues related to the degree of access which researchers have in the setting need to be clearly worked out and communicated to all those concerned.

(2002: 32)

Formal and informal access need to negotiated and sensitivity is essential. This is not always easy and unexpected problems can arise for the researcher.

Example 3.4   Access to a program for ex-offenders

The director of the regional office of a national charity for ex-prisoners wanted to hold the initial negotiation for an evaluation project in her office. The project involved a study of one training centre and so, as well as the director (the sponsor), the gatekeepers of the study were also present – the manager of the centre and a key member of his staff, who would provide the hands-on support for the study. Following this initial meeting for access, the project continued with negotiation between the centre staff (the gatekeepers), centre users, the student evaluators and their supervisor.

Example 3.5   Access to Holly Tree Prison

A postgraduate student was asked to evaluate a new program involving liaison between Holly Tree Prison and professionals providing after-care facilities for prisoners with mental health problems about to be released. Access to the prison involved rigorous vetting procedures (including having the evaluation proposal approved by the ethics committee of the hospital providing psychiatric care) and was only permitted through formal negotiation with the professionals who had requested the research on the program.

Even so, access was not straightforward, as the student's reflective report showed.

> Gaining access to the prison was easy... On my first visit what immediately struck me was the necessity of keys. Once past the main gate you need keys to go everywhere, even the toilet... I was intimidated

by the prison environment and felt that if I had keys at least I knew I would be able to get out.

Having given some thought to my 'role' I dressed informally, wearing a pale blue shirt, my trousers an off-blue and no tie... Eventually was given a set of keys for the doors... Interviews were arranged, some interesting comments made... I left feeling confident, everybody seemed interested and wanted to talk to me.

The next day I received a call from [the sponsor, Tony], apparently I had called quite a stir in the prison. Some members of staff who didn't know who I was had wanted to know why an inmate was wandering around with keys opening doors! This was because my clothes were exactly the same as the prisoners... According to [Tony] at one point I was going to be jumped by a couple of warders because I must have been planning to escape. Luckily a prison medical officer had told them who I was.

So, what did this mean? Well, it helped me develop a rapport with the prison staff because it broke the ice with them. The next time I visited, everybody I met laughed about it, even the prison Governor, which was lucky.

(Chamberlain, 1999)

This student managed to 'get in' (and get out!) and he also provided a good example of 'getting on', even though the rapport was created through such accidental circumstances.

Consent

Consent, if it is to be regarded as valid, has to be voluntary and informed, that is, based upon full disclosure of information, including information about any harm that might occur as a result of the research. In almost all cases this requirement rules out a covert study, where the individual does not know they are being studied. The only exceptions would be rare instances where another ethic is accorded priority, for example, if the interests of society in the acquisition of knowledge were held to be of greater importance than the deception of the researched, and there was no other way of gaining the information. This essentially paternalist argument, that the researcher is better able to judge the interests of society than the researched, would be rejected by many ethicists and researchers.

But deception can be harmful, if people find out later they have been tricked or manipulated. Respect for persons, and respect for truth both suggest that subjects should be fully aware of the purpose of the research, and what they are being asked to do. Standard research practice for interviews that will be recorded is to

---

Example 3.6 Special needs youth group video

One evaluation project involved establishing the interests of young people with special needs in order to widen the activities which could be offered by the youth centre they attended. A successful focus group was held and videoed by the researcher, to strengthen the reliability of the data – she did not have a partner to record the participants' views while she acted as group facilitator. She also felt that it would be empowering for the young people to see themselves on video expressing their opinions. But while the young people felt that they were happy to have more group sessions, they did not want videos made – they felt too uncomfortable with this.

---

produce consent forms. Such forms are produced to ensure that involvement is voluntary, that participants know how the information will be used and that guarantees of anonymity/confidentiality will be given as appropriate. Forms are not always a sufficient way of establishing if consent has been given, particularly if participants do not fully understand the form, or when consent has been given by parents or guardians – young people may not be willing to cooperate.

Researchers need to be sensitive as to how far they can go in asking personal questions, and participants need to know they can always refuse to answer, and can terminate an interview at any point. Program stakeholders should always be given the right to refuse to participate in the research. Refusal can be caused, as in the example above, by people feeling uncomfortable about what they are required to do, or fearing an invasion of privacy, or being so alienated from the organization that they just do not want to comply. Or it can be that certain groups feel that they are over-researched and suffering from 'research fatigue', and would prefer solutions or action to even more research.

Anonymity and confidentiality
Researchers sometimes give assurances that the information collected will be treated 'confidentially' and that the individual giving their views will be 'anonymous'. However, these are not the same things – the identity of participants may be kept secret but the information they give is not 'confidential', because it will not stay with the interviewer but be used in producing the report.

Even with anonymity, and the use of pseudonyms, it is possible that people might be identifiable because of characteristics which are described or because their title or role within an organization is used. Consent is needed for this information to be included in the report. However, even with adequate procedures in place concerning consent and anonymity, researchers still have the principle of *'not harming'* to consider, and in practice many researchers and evaluators have taken decisions to exclude material because of concerns that it could produce damage.

Qualitative data are most likely to produce identifiable information, in the form of quotations or observations. Evaluation reports may also use information about individuals in the form of 'case-studies' or 'case histories', to illustrate how programs impact on individual lives. In-depth data of this type can be influential in making policy-makers realize the human implications of their programs in ways quantitative data do not. Sometimes people prefer a pseudonym to be used, but sometimes they prefer their own name to be used – it is empowering to have their story told directly and their views given through direct quotations. So those being interviewed for case-studies (or for quotation or observation) should be given a choice on how the material is attributed in the report.

However, even before the report stage, protection of the identity of participants needs to be acknowledged throughout the research process, and data should be recorded and stored with code numbers replacing names and with the code kept secure. Video and audio tapes also need to be securely kept, and respondents should be asked if they wish the tapes to be destroyed at the completion of the research.

Responsibilities for General/Public Welfare

The AEA Guiding Principle 5 entitled *Responsibilities for General and Public Welfare* relates to the public role claimed by evaluators in respect of the efficient allocation of resources and the general improvement to social programs from evaluation, and thereby the betterment of society itself. Evaluators are enjoined to consider the 'perspectives and interests of the full range of stakeholders' and not just those of the client, on the basis that 'Evaluators have obligations that encompass the public interest and good.'

There could be instances where a client might want, for example, to suppress an evaluation, or conversely to play up the positive aspects of only a moderately successful pilot program evaluation in order to roll out a full program of activity, in which case the evaluator might feel unease at how the results have been used. Quite how the public interest could be protected in such cases is unclear in the AEA guidelines, although independent publication could be a possibility – but only if this had been negotiated in the agreement.

Dilemmas: justice and care

Codifying ethics in the way the AEA has attempted has its critics. Porter, writing from a feminist perspective, argues that ethics should be understood through grounded experience and real-life examples rather than through abstract rules, rights and principles. She argues:

> Frameworks that present simple options fail to grasp the complexities of life. Perspectives that assume either-or options provoke inclusionary– exclusionary responses. Dualism dictates hierarchically ranked options with traits traditionally associated with men ranked more highly than those associated with women.
>
> (1999: x)

Traditionally, traits associated with men include rationality, intellect, and political awareness while women's ethical judgements are held to be distorted by sensuality, emotions, nature and concentration on personal issues.

Porter argues that feminist ethics are basically about challenging this gendered dualism through integrating the value traditionally associated with women – care – with the value associated with men – justice. Justice is not possible without care and care without justice is oppressive. From this perspective, evaluation which is just or 'fair' would have to include care. Caring evaluation might be expressed in different ways – through the 'mutual respect' principle of House, or through participatory action research which engages with gender issues rather than being 'gender-blind'.

The 'partnering' principle of collaborative evaluation (as in the small-scale model) includes sensitivity, openness, protection for participants in the research and an opportunity for participants to comment on findings. However, while it is one thing to adhere to such values, or to the guiding principles of codes, it is another to apply such values, and to resolve problems which arise when values are in conflict – or when the role of researcher itself produces ethical dilemmas. Here, feelings and emotions come into play, which are not usually recorded in evaluation reporting, and so go unrecognized as part of the process. Where a reflective report (see Chapter 7) accompanies the evaluation report, such dilemmas can be explored and learned from.

In the final two dilemmas reported below, it is important to note that there is no 'right' answer – the reader may disagree with the action and decisions of the evaluator. Indeed, a dilemma exists because no course of action seems satisfactory; 'it exists because there are "good" but contradictory ethical reasons to take conflicting and incompatible courses of action' (de Laine, 2000: 3). However, in the examples, the reasoning behind the decision is given – in both cases the evaluators were concerned with the twin ethics of *justice* and of *care*, and the care ethic was what was particularly problematic for them. As with all researchers facing dilemmas, they chose to do what was nearest to right as they saw it, and for both there was a positive outcome – in terms of what they learned about research – and about themselves.

Example 3.7   Dilemma in trauma and bereavement counselling

A particularly poignant example of a dilemma was contained in a reflective report by a postgraduate student who conducted research with a group of vulnerable service users, relatives of people who had died in an accident and emergency department (ER) and who had been offered befriending and counselling support. The experience of the student and its emotional impact is revealed in his reflective account.

> I felt that in seeking out responses from people concerning traumatic periods in their lives I was approaching what could be termed an 'ethical minefield'. The first thing to consider, when choosing methodology for the purposes of investigating the views of past service users, was the question of how to best obtain information without causing undue distress to those being involved in the research.
>
> (Kirkcaldy, 2000)

The project was designed to evaluate the service, and advice was taken from the manager of the unit who had requested the evaluation and who was also a very experienced counsellor. Her preferred method of contact was to use a postal questionnaire and to direct the evaluation to those whose bereavement had been over 12 months previously. This caused the student and his supervisor some concern, as it seemed to be an impersonal and insensitive means of contact. However, the counsellor felt that a postal questionnaire was less intrusive than any other means of contact, including face-to-face interviewing. If people did not want to participate, then it was easy for them to discard the questionnaire.

The method was approved by the Hospital Research Ethics Committee and it was justified by referring to previous research, including that of Stroebe *et al.* (1993), where it had been found that a large percentage of people are unwilling to give information about past traumatic experiences over the telephone. The only other practical means of contacting past service users in a wide geographical area was therefore through a postal survey.

The questionnaire was accompanied by an explanatory letter with contact details for the service. The survey received a very low response rate (which had been predicted by the supervisor), but the student was also devastated to be shown a letter which complained about the insensitivity of the communication:

> For me, seeing the words of this letter was the 'low' point of the research process. To think that I had been involved in something that might have in some way caused someone a degree of anger and distress was not a pleasant feeling. I approached [the counsellor manager] about this matter and she put my mind at ease, telling me how this is quite common in any postal survey regarding medical matters.
>
> (Kirkcaldy, 2000)

The counsellor was reassuring, took responsibility, and revealed that the negative response had been more than matched by a positive outcome – several past users had resumed contact with the service to continue to use the facilities to help them deal with their bereavement. Nevertheless, the student found the experience difficult to resolve, though it did mark a 'turning point' in his development as a researcher.

> Taking all this into account brought home some of the harsh realities of conducting a piece of social research. No one had ever said it would be easy and I knew that undertaking a piece of work in a health care setting would be a challenge. However, the letter received also marked a turning point for me as a researcher. It seemed to emphasise the importance of the research to me – that people were grieving, that they did need help, and that investigating the views of service users was intended to improve the trauma and bereavement services available. In some ways it brought home to me the reality of what I was researching. I had not been thoughtless or inconsiderate at any stage of the project, but in many ways this letter provided me with more of a picture of people's feelings in times of grief than many of the questionnaires that were received.
>
> (Kirkcaldy, 2000)

Dealing with such a dilemma was a learning experience, which meant more than the classroom discussions of codes and principles had offered.

It gave me insights into the many pitfalls and problems that researchers can face, and emphasised the importance of considering the ethical implications of what is being proposed or carried out – a lesson that will always be remembered and considered crucial in my development as a researcher.

(Kirkcaldy, 2000)

Example 3.8   More dilemmas in Holly Tree Prison

Another example of a dilemma was described in the reflective account of the postgraduate student evaluating a program involving mentally ill prisoners about to be released from prison. He was given access to prisoners' files where he found information which seemed to indicate that one prisoner was being released into a situation which could be difficult or even dangerous for another member of the public. The student was unsure whether this information had been discussed fully by the professionals dealing with the case, and he received advice from his tutor on how to handle the problem – to raise the issue first of all with the manager responsible for the evaluation, and if this was not satisfactory then with the appropriate psychiatrist.

This seemed to deal with the matter, but as the student noted in his reflective account, this situation had been demanding – and made him realize that his own interests as a researcher were involved in his conflicting feelings.

This all preyed on my mind for quite a while. But I realised I needed to tell [the professionals] that I had a problem. I felt nervous. Why? Because I was worried it might affect me, that it might lead into me not being able to complete my research and so get my Masters. I learned a lot about myself in that instant. I realised how the personal interest of a researcher could interfere in ethical situations. I was not a computer programmed to respond to certain situation in a prescribed Manner. Being human meant being attached, involved, and having a personal interest in the project. I decided I needed to talk to my supervisor and tell them my concerns...

My ethical dilemma has taught me more about myself and the political nature underlying research conducted for organisations with set agendas. Also, before I started the project, I was sure I knew what to do when faced with such dilemmas, but I did not quite understand how researchers become attached and personally involved in the research process, which can cause such issues to become even more problematic.

(Chamberlain, 1999)

These dilemmas illustrate the argument that decisions can be guided by codes, but ethical standards cannot simply be set at the start of an evaluation and followed through regardless. Neither can decisions be taken without reference to a wider ethical context. In this context, Plummer (2001) contrasts two positions, the *ethical absolutist* and the *situational relativist*. The former seeks to establish firm principles which should guide all social research, such as risks being outweighed by benefits – principles which are enshrined in codes. The latter suggests the ethical dilemmas of researchers are not special but part of the problems of everyday living.

> Both sides have their weaknesses. If, for instance, as the absolutists usually insist, there should be 'informed consent', it may leave relatively privileged groups under-researched (since they will say 'no') and under-privileged groups over-researched (they will have nothing to lose and say 'yes' in hope) (cf. Duster *et al.*, 1979; Lofland, 1976). If the individual conscience is the guide, as the relativists insist, the door is wide open for the unscrupulous – even the immoral – researcher. But as in so many debates, it may be that this is a false polarity. Individual decision taking around ethical concerns could surely take place within wider frameworks of guidance?
>
> (Plummer, 2001: 227)

So, it is in the working out of the relationship between general principles and day-to-day process that evaluation ethics really need to be understood. Different ethical issues will be embedded in the different stages of a project and will need to be addressed and negotiated. If the evaluator is consciously reflective about her/his practice, then such issues will be thought through as an integral part of the evaluation process.

CHAPTER 4

Planning Research

Summary

In this chapter the emphasis is placed on formulating evaluation questions in an appropriate research design or strategy that will lead to robust and systematic practice in generating data. The choice of research methods is discussed from both quantitative and qualitative perspectives, with examples of how these methods have been used in small-scale evaluations by students.

Within the space of this chapter, it is possible to outline only some of the choices the evaluator has to make, and *emphasis is given to the issues which face those conducting small-scale evaluation*. This means the complexity of methodological issues has been simplified and the reader will need to consult the large and specialized literature on social research methods – for further details of questionnaire construction, interviewing, conducting focus groups, sampling and so on.

PLANNING EVALUATION RESEARCH

Setting the evaluation questions

Owen (1999: 99) describes the research process in evaluation as a three-stage process:

- determination of the evaluation questions;
- assembly of evidence; and
- analysis of evidence.

This is deceptively straightforward – the stages do not necessarily follow in chronological sequence (there can be interaction back and forth between stages) and *report writing* needs to be recognized as part of the research process. (Chapter 6 discusses how the report needs to be incorporated into planning at an early stage).

Owen's third stage – analysis of evidence – is dealt with in Chapter 5, while the present chapter develops the themes of determining evaluation questions and assembling (or creating) data.

By *evaluation questions* we mean, first of all, the main questions that frame the evaluation – the 'who, what, how and why' relating to the program being researched. These evaluation questions set the scope of the research, within which specific questions are then devised.

The selection of research methods to ask these questions can be related to the contrasting models of evaluation research, discussed in Chapter 2:

- evaluation for accountability (e.g., the measurement of results or efficiency)
- evaluation for development (e.g., the provision of evaluative help to strengthen institutions)
- evaluation for knowledge (e.g., the acquisition of a more profound understanding in some specific area of field)

(Chelimsky and Shadish, 1997: 10)

Where the evaluation is summative, and focused around the impact of a program, the *accountability* perspective is likely to be foremost, and *measurement and quantification* will be stressed. The evaluation questions will be phrased around what the program does, what benefits it produces, and whether this is a good (or the best) use of resources.

On the other hand, when the evaluation is formative, and focused around the process of program delivery, the *developmental* perspective is stressed. *Qualitative* questions about the meaning of the program to its stakeholders are emphasized along with questions on whether they are experiencing benefits from the program.

Knowledge questions, about why the program works – or does not work – in one particular context, and how this relates to other examples in other contexts, are also important. However, the larger *comparative study* this implies is likely to be out of the reach of small-scale evaluations.

While these considerations will guide the specification of the evaluation questions, who determines these questions must also be considered. Within the quantitative accountability perspective, it is the evaluator who has the key role as the objective expert in deciding what should be studied. In consultation with the sponsors of the study, the evaluator seeks to devise questions that will operationalize (make concrete) the factors or variables which are likely to provide explanation, through causal relationships which can be statistically tested.

Where a development perspective is used, with participatory methods, program stakeholders are likely to be involved in the discussion of evaluation questions. With empowerment evaluation especially, participants are actively involved all stages of the research, including the formulation of the evaluation questions. They become subjects in their own right rather than mere respondents.

In small-scale evaluation, based on a collaborative stakeholder approach, the evaluation questions stem from the current concerns of participants in the program under evaluation. Evaluators may shape these into researchable questions through their research expertise to meet issues of impact and process, but do not act without reference to the stakeholders.

Example 4.1   Setting the research question: involving disabled youth

One student was asked by the manager of a youth club for disabled young people to evaluate its provision of activities outside the club premises – namely day and evening trips to sports and leisure facilities in the city and surrounding area. The evaluation was also intended to generate fresh ideas for activities, and, following discussion with the manager, the evaluator was also asked to approach local activity centres to explore with managements there whether there were any 'disabling' aspects in their provision which would prevent access for the group. The student decided to hold focus groups with the young people to generate the questions which would be at the heart of the research; these questions became the basis of group discussions and interviews with staff, families and volunteers at the youth club, and with the outside agencies.

The issue of who sets the evaluation questions is important in generating evaluation which will be used, as findings in which stakeholders can take some ownership are more likely to influence action. Patton (1997: 30), an advocate of utilization-focused evaluation, provides an example from his experience.

Example 4.2   Setting the research question: creating ownership

When asked to undertake an evaluation in a large school district in Canada, Patton brought representatives of the different stakeholder groups together (administrators, parents' groups, school principals, teachers' union). Faced with initial hostility about this externally sponsored evaluation, he resisted attempts to frame the discussion around methods and instruments of research (What questions will be in the questionnaire?), and instead asked participants to concentrate first on what *they* wanted to know.

By asking them to work individually and in groups to complete the sentence, 'I would really like to know——about Frontier School Division,' Patton broke through initial hostility to gain their interest, so the group ended up with a series of questions to be asked, and a sense of ownership of the evaluation itself, to such an extent that when external funding for the evaluation was not in the end forthcoming, they decided to pay for it themselves out of local funds.

(Patton, 1997: 30 ff.)

Negotiating the research design

In any evaluation situation, Patton's question, 'What do you really want to know?', is a good way of finding out about people's real interests in the research, what the evaluation questions are, and what the research design should be like.

Within a collaborative model, the negotiation stage is where the major questions for the evaluation are hammered out. Organizations providing (or intending to provide) services may initially approach the evaluator with requests for information that are not openly stated as evaluation, but, on enquiry, there is an evaluation question behind the request.

Example 4.3   Some initial requests

- We would like to know what young people think of their time in this youth club. Why? So that we can say what difference it has made to their lives.
- We would like to know what older people feel about our service. Why? So that we can, if possible, improve our service.
- We would like to know why people don't volunteer to help in this community centre. Why? So that we can improve our recruitment and retention of volunteers.
- We would like to know how many people there are with special needs in this area. Why? So that our service users are truly representative of the local population.

These are all genuine requests that have been made for student projects, and though some are more easily researchable than others, all require the fundamental process of evaluation – collecting information rigorously with a view to forming a judgement on a program, and improving the service. Negotiation with organization managers and staff can clarify what are the main requirements of the research, and what are the main areas under investigation.

Evaluators should also consider that program participants, either explicitly – or more often that not, implicitly – carry around in their heads a *'theory of action'* (Schön: 1987) which explains how a particular program produces its effects. Exploring this theory about why the program is believed to work will help to direct attention to the social processes thought to operate, as well as the particular context of local operation. This should generate questions for the evaluator to check on in the research. Some of this theory in action may be found in the organization's documentation: the aims and objectives of the program, the mission statement, grant applications and so on, which form the 'official view'. However, it is also instructive to talk with program participants about how and why they think the program actually works, and it should not be assumed that all participants will share a common theory of action. Any differences uncovered may point to tensions within the organization that require more detailed examination.

The research design, aimed at answering the evaluation questions, in an orderly and systematic manner, summarizes these initial decisions and acts as a plan for future research activity. The research design also includes consideration of the practicalities of finding answers to the main questions:

• What are the best ways of accessing relevant information?
• Does the information already exist, or will it need to be created?
• Who will need to be asked?
• What are the problems of gaining access?
• How can this fit in the timescale allowed for the research?
• Who will read the report, and how will it be used?

Unlike a research proposal, a *research design* is not usually a public document and may be seen by only a few people close to the researcher.

It is an integrated statement of and justification for the more technical decisions in planning a research project.

(Blaikie, 2000: 21)

The research design, therefore, should clearly justify the choice of research methods to be used in order to answer the research question. The design or plan should also specify the people or groups to be included in the research (the sample), the timing and sequencing of the research methods, and any costs that will have to be met. There should also be thought given to how the data will be analysed, and what the final report is likely to include.

Criteria for research design

Because the research, through its interim and final reports, is aimed at an audience who will be able to use its findings, the research methods need to be understandable and credible. The methods used need to be seen to have high quality and to have produced an authentic account of the program being evaluated. For Cousins and Leithwood (1986) *relevance, credibility* and *quality* are seen as the three factors which most affect the utilization of evaluations. One definition of quality concerns *'fitness of purpose'*. Do the methods provide appropriate evidence concerning the research questions? Are the questions the right ones to allow judgements about the program to be made? Other definitions may be in terms of competent and systematic application of procedures. Was the research carried out to agreed professional standards?

Relevant and credible research needs to be measured against two vital criteria – *validity* and *reliability*. Babbie defines validity as

> [a] term describing a measure that accurately reflects the concept it is intended to measure. For example, your IQ would seem a more valid measure of your intelligence than would the number of hours you spend in the library.

(2004: 143–5)

Babbie also points out that while the ultimate validity of a measure can never be proven, relative validity can be agreed according to a host of judgements – face validity, criterion validity, content validity, construct validity, internal validation and external validation.

Reliability is a different criterion, and relates to whether a particular research instrument, administered repeatedly, would yield the same result each time. Punch (2003: 42) refers to this as 'stability of response' in response to the question, 'Would the same respondents answer the same questions in the same way if they were asked again?'

Qualitative interviewing is highly unlikely to produce the same kind of standardized response produced by structured questioning (and it would be suspect if it did!) and so can be seen as low on the reliability criterion. However, because in-depth interviews allow the respondent to explain and enlarge on answers, qualitative interviewing can be argued to be high on external validity – the results relate to 'real-world' feeling and experience rather than the artificial world of the experiment or the tight control of response required by the questionnaire. The survey, in turn, may score higher in internal validity – the precision with which the concept has been turned into a measurable factor or variable – but it can still be questioned whether a narrowly specified variable really validly represents the wider concept of interest. To use Babbie's example, we might ask, 'Is intelligence really reducible to IQ tests?'

Combining multiple methods

The reliability/validity debate shows that there are fundamental differences in the way different research methods meet design criteria. These methodological differences are associated with the main epistemological positions of positivism and interpretivism which can broadly be divided into quantitative and qualitative approaches.

Methodological purists urge caution about combining research methods which derive from conflicting epistemological foundations and are therefore incompatible. (Mason, 2002; Pawson and Tilley, 1997: xiv) However, it is now generally accepted in the social sciences that the conflict between quantitative and qualitative methods (the so-called 'paradigm wars') has been overdrawn, and that there is value in combining techniques within a multiple-method strategy to give a more complete account of the subject in question (Bryman, 2001:20). *Triangulation* (using multiple methods to bear on the same research question) is argued to give researchers greater confidence in their findings if they are supported by the use of different methods which result in the same conclusion.

But is it necessary or even likely that different methods should produce similar results? Bryman for one (1998: 134) argues that discrepancies between the findings of different methods are normal and should be expected. The issue is not to judge which findings (or which methods) are 'right', but to probe further to explain the discrepancies. This might require developing a new theoretical explanation and then, if possible, collecting fresh information to test this out.

Triangulation also means that quantitative and qualitative methods do not need to be seen as uniquely distinct: questionnaires can include open-ended as well as closed questions, while interviews can yield data that are amenable to some counting and quantification. Evaluation in particular has adopted a pragmatic approach to the choice of research methods. For instance, with a number of groups of stakeholders to cover, it is quite normal in evaluations to find that research conducted with different stakeholder groups uses different methods, such as questionnaires and interviews, or interviews and focus groups, according to the size of the relevant groups, the depth of information sought and the problems of access to such group members.

The choice of methods is made according to their respective advantages and disadvantages. The strength of the questionnaire is in accessing, in a standardized format, high on reliability, a large number of respondents in a short period of time. The strength of the interview is in the richness and depth of information, high on validity, where the outcome is not predetermined by the researcher, and where the interviewee can provide a narrative on the process of interaction. Darlington and Scott (2002: 120) conclude that qualitative research is particularly useful for questions about meanings, while questions about quantity, about how much or how many, require quantitative analysis.

So questionnaires – for example, in the forms of street interviews using a pre-coded schedule – might be used to assess public opinion regarding a community centre and its services, while interviews would be more suited to finding out from volunteers or service-users at the centre what they thought about the program, what it meant for them, and how the services might be developed in the future.

Kvale identifies the characteristics of qualitative research as moving away from knowledge gained from scientific manipulation towards knowledge created with subjects through conversation:

> The subjects not only answer questions prepared by an expert, but themselves formulate in a dialogue their own conceptions of their lived world.
>
> (Kvale, 1996: 11)

Another common strategy is to use both a questionnaire survey and a series of semi-structured interviews to gain different types of information from the same group of stakeholders. This could be either

1. a short series of interviews to a few respondents, before a questionnaire to a larger number of people, or
2. an introductory questionnaire to the sample, followed by longer interviews with a selected number of respondents.

The first strategy uses the interviews as an initial stage to identify and clarify issues and to investigate the range of opinions and responses. This is then used to construct a questionnaire that can reach more respondents, with confidence that the questions have validity – they address the issues raised by participants, and follow their understanding rather than relying solely on the researcher's own interpretation of the situation. This strategy is particularly appropriate for exploratory research, where the details of the research questions are relatively less defined and it would be unwise to assume that the researcher has enough knowledge or information to devise a standard questionnaire at the outset.

The second strategy uses the questionnaire as an initial instrument to 'map the field', and to gain basic information on the research questions. While this information can provide a valuable summary of program provision and impact, it does not necessarily provide much detail on processes. Open-ended questions in questionnaires can be ignored, as respondents just 'tick the boxes'. But if the questionnaire includes a question asking if the respondent would be prepared to be interviewed further on the issue (and to give contact details), then semi-structured interviews can explore with respondents, who have now agreed to be interviewed, the detail of their answers and any further questions arising from the questionnaire findings.

Example 4.4   Interviews preceding a survey

A student was asked to evaluate a treatment for drug dependency using electric stimulation therapy (a form of acupuncture without needles). She interviewed a number of users of the therapy, and received detailed information on how the therapy was used, and how people thought about it. This information was later built into a questionnaire that was distributed to a larger sample of the therapy users, providing a means of contacting more people than could be interviewed in the time available, and of creating an overview summary of the experiences of therapy users.

Example 4.5   Survey followed by interviews

Two students were asked to investigate the responses of law firms to an independent organization's work in family mediation. An initial questionnaire was chosen as the means for contacting professional law firms. A listing of law firms in the city was available as an address list, and it was assumed that busy lawyers were more likely to respond to a fairly short questionnaire than to make time available for interviews. Though the response rate was not as good as hoped for – the address list contained inaccuracies, and some firms ignored the questionnaire – enough returns were received to provide the required information, and several agreed to be interviewed later, which gave important detail on how the family mediation service was developing.

Research plan checklist

A useful checklist for planning research is given in the resource pack for community research produced by Sue Gorbing and Jill Bedford for ARVAC, the Association for Research in the Voluntary and Community Sector (ARVAC, 2002). Although the checklist is designed for community groups negotiating with researchers, it works just as well for researchers negotiating with community groups. The checklist covers the following steps for any research project:

1. *Research proposal* – Establish the broad area of the research.
2. *Purpose of the research* – Specify the outcome expected from the research.
3. *Issues to be studied* – Involve as many different people's (stakeholders') perceptions as possible.

4. *Defining the research questions* – Specify closely to narrow down the scope of the research
5. *Determine what data will be collected* – Quantitative questions of 'how many' or qualitative questions of 'why' or 'how'.
6. *Decide where the Information will come from* – Specify the type and source of information.
7. *Decide who will collect the data* – Determine individual responsibilities.
8. *Decide how the information will be recorded* – Tape recording of interviews, or written notes.
9. *Decide how the information will be put together or analysed to answer the research questions* – Interviews to be transcribed in full or part, and analysed thematically
10. *How will the findings be presented, disseminated, used or passed on?* – Think creatively about using the information, and interesting others in it.

RESEARCH ACTIVITIES AND METHODS

Research can be conceived of as either *discovery* or *generation* of information. Data discovery or capture or excavation (the metaphors vary) implies finding out about an external reality, while data generation draws attention to the way in which knowledge is created from social encounters and interaction shared by the researcher and the subject.

Epistemology and the role of the researcher

For both of these approaches, the role adopted by the researcher with regard to the subjects is crucial.

In the *positivist* approach, the researcher is detached and disinterested, collecting data with the aim of objectivity. The researcher is the expert and the subject or interviewee is the source of the data. Observation is non-participant. *Data discovery* requires a standard approach revealing the minimum to the interviewee in terms of help or direction in answering the question – to avoid bias. Questions are likely to be carefully structured, so that there is little room for variation by different interviewers and the emphasis is on reliability – that anyone asking the questions would get the same results. Measurement scales are used to gauge opinion, and the results are quantifiable.

Phenomenological researchers are more interested in *data generation* – with the interview being regarded as where knowledge is constructed through interaction. The aim is to understand what meaning the interviewee gives to the areas they are being questioned about. Asking is therefore less structured and more open-ended, with in-depth data being sought as a valid way of exploring the research topic. The subject is seen as being the expert in their own situation, and the interviewer the learner. Good listening skills are required by the researcher, rather than the interviewer actively presenting information and ideas (Babbie, 2004: 300–02). Kvale notes that

> Qualitative interviews are not in themselves progressive or oppressive; the value of the knowledge produced depends on the context and the use of the knowledge.
>
> (Kvale, 1996: 72)

However, *critical research*, particularly under the influence of feminism (Oakley, 1981), has challenged the notion of the active questioner and the passive research object because the power relationship is balanced in favour of the researcher and is exploitative of the researched. Such research is seen as contributing to the alienation of powerless groups through a knowledge production process that benefits the academic research community at their expense. Instead, a new paradigm model is needed to

> [s]hift the research perspective to that of doing research with, not on, people; to accepting those researched in the role of co-researchers; to acknowledge the researcher as part of the process; and to welcoming the change brought about by the research experience.
>
> (Ledwith, 1994: 16)

Wolcott's (1999: 46) classification of fieldwork techniques in qualitative research in terms of the three dimensions of participant observation, interviewing and archival research, or more alliteratively, *experiencing, enquiring* and *examining,* is a useful starting-point, whether research is seen as discovery or generation. Each of these activities uses different sources of information, and can be quantitative or qualitative, more or less structured, according to the epistemological position of the researcher – that is, how they see knowledge as being created – and how they see the researcher's own role in the process.

Methods of experiencing

Observation

'Seven per cent of communication is verbal.' So ran a recent advertisement on television. The importance of using observation as a method for investigating how an organization carries out its activities, and the locations in which it works, cannot be over-estimated. Mason points out that

> Observation in a busy hospital ward might include the predominance of a smell of disinfectant or the sounds of people, bodies and equipment, as well as aspects of spatial and temporal organization such as where beds, patients and visitors are located, what kinds of movements occur, in what sequences and at what times.
>
> (Mason, 2002: 105–6)

Mason adds that the social sciences have tended to regard observations and interviews as *data* when they are transformed into text, but observational fieldnotes should be as subject to critical scrutiny as any other form of document. This point refers to qualitative research, where observation is a major and accepted method. However, observation is also practised in survey research, and many quantitative researchers fail to appreciate, unless it is pointed out to them, that while using the seemingly 'proper' research methods of questionnaires and interviews, they are also 'in the field' and engaging in observation almost by default.

The question, then, is not whether to do observation, but how to do it in a way which will contribute to the study. While non-participant observation is more likely, there are often advantages, particularly for the student evaluator, of taking on a participant observer role, although there are potential ethical dilemmas with this, as Chapter 3 discussed.

The same criteria that were advanced earlier regarding evaluation – of relevance, credibility and quality – can be applied to observation. A first visit to a community location can provide an almost overwhelming set of impressions – what should the researcher focus on? What are the things that are going to be relevant to the study? What should one note down, what omit?

McCall (1984: 200) concludes that observation can never be undertaken without some kind of focus, explicit or implicit, as 'observation is always selective and purposive'. So the evaluator needs to work out in the situation what to focus on and why. In Chapter 7 the use of the research diary as an aid to reflection is discussed. Here it can be noted that a good plan is to note down initial impressions in the research diary, to do with the area, the buildings, the people, observed program activities, and to make comments on any things which appear strange or unusual.

Later reflection can be used to tease out the reasons for strangeness, perhaps a contrast with implicit expectations, and an opportunity to explore the evaluator's own assumptions and taken-for-granted meanings. Further activity can then be given over to documenting and making sense of strange appearances and events. Initial observations may be replaced by a more systematic observational survey, for example by taking photographs to record aspects of what has been seen and found to be significant for understanding the context or the program under investigation.

If the initial notes are kept for further reflection, this may aid the researcher in reanalysing the sense of strangeness when they become more familiar with the setting. Testing personal observations against that of the participants can be useful. A researcher conducting an evaluation of support for families with hospitalized children pointed out to a consultant paediatrician a sign at the entrance to a hospital reading 'No entry except on official business', and said that it must be off-putting to patients' relatives. The consultant replied that though he drove through the entrance every day, he'd never noticed the sign.

Observation as introduction

The evaluator's observations can be an important part of initial familiarization with the setting and the organization, where field notes in the research diary flag up immediate impressions and questions that can be explored more systematically later on. Observation begins as the evaluator starts negotiation with an organization regarding a program. For this reason, it is advisable for the negotiation stage to take place on the premises of the organization rather than that of the researcher. 'Getting to know' about the program means seeing what goes on, and meeting the people involved.

The observation is of course two-way, as the intending researcher is observed by those within the organization. Participant observation of this kind can form a useful prelude to a later period of

Example 4.6   Observation as orientation

A study of a play scheme for young children concerned the recruitment and retention of volunteers. The student researchers observed the play activities, and found themselves actually called upon to help run some activities for the children. They did not particularly enjoy the experience, but it provided a starting-point for talking to the children about what they wanted, and it gave an insight into the experiences of volunteers – an experience they could use themselves later to draw up an information pack for volunteers as part of their research report.

interviewing, as the researcher becomes aware of the organizational dynamics, and the service users become familiar with the presence of the researcher.

Systematic sampling in observation

If observation is used for evaluation within an organizational setting, the research needs to ensure that the range of an organization's activities is covered, and that effort is made to observe what goes on in different days, even if the main focus of research activity will be concentrated on particular users at particular times. Systematic studies of the work of an organization require random sampling of time elements if the study is to be capable of providing quantitative data on interactions.

Just as a temporal grid is used for time sampling, so a geographical grid is needed if the observer is to cover an area like a neighbourhood systematically rather than through their own choice. The researcher samples randomly from the grid (Chaplin, 1994). Such techniques seek to apply the methods of quantitative research to what is largely a qualitative and subjective practice. As with other qualitative methods, the use of theoretical sampling, and the search for instances that break the rules can be applied to observation, but there is often a large element of *'serendipity'* in observation, of being in the right place at the right time.

Covert observation

If the arena for a program is a public place, the evaluator is but one of many people present, all of whom are observing (but not necessarily recording) what goes on. There is no obligation on the evaluator to explain their actions. But for arenas, which are not public, for example, a playgroup or a day centre for older people, it is essential to ensure that participants are aware of the reasons for the observations, and that they consent to notes being taken. Covert research is regarded as unethical by many researchers, and generally advised against in ethical guidelines, except in certain defined circumstances. The British Sociological Association Statement of Ethical Practice (BSA, 2002) cites two possible exceptions:

> For example, difficulties arise when research participants change their behaviour because they know they are being studied. Researchers may also face problems when access to spheres of social life is closed to social scientists by powerful or secretive interests.

Covert research certainly goes against the ethos of openness of small-scale evaluation, and examples were given in Chapter 3 where students ensured that consent to use information was obtained from participants who might have been unaware that they were being researched.

Visual images

Using a camera to record a scene moves observation to a different plane, as the record becomes more permanent, and individuals may be identifiable in photographs. The same distinction between public and non-public places needs to guide the photographer as to when permission of the person photographed is required:

> Because they potentially compromise the anonymity of research participants, the use of video or photographic data can present ethical problems.
>
> (Lee, 2000: 58)

Consent issues were discussed in Chapter 3, and in close encounters, and in closed-access situations, asking the permission of the subject is always necessary. It is also possible that photography in a public space may also have legal as well as ethical issues – it is increasingly being recognized that if people are identifiable and the material will be publicly viewed, then they have a right to their 'image' and consent for its use needs to be given.

There is considerable debate about whether photographs are 'truthful' or not (Rose, 2001: 167; Chaplin, 1994: 154). In everyday life, it can be noted that especially for identification purposes, photographs are normally taken to provide an accurate record, for example for passports, although they can be doctored for legal and illegal purposes. For research, these issues of authenticity need to be recognized if photographs are to be used for analysis and reporting.

For instance, the photo-elicitation technique can be applied to locality research. Photographs are used with groups of inhabitants to draw out their experiences and recollections of an area through discussion of a selection of photographs (Banks, 2001). This technique relies on the photographs being accepted as authentic 'slices' of the community. Banks himself distinguishes between 'found' photographs volunteered by community members (and perhaps better considered under the use of documents) and those taken specifically by the researcher for the purpose of the study.

Some evaluations may actually lend themselves to the active participation of the subjects in making the images themselves. For example, as an offshoot of a study of social exclusion, an arts training project for young people was enlisted to encourage the young people to take digital images of their streets and significant others to empower them to become recognized evaluators of their locality. (Hall *et al.*, 1999; Hall, 2003) The images not only provided a view of the area from the point of the youth, to set alongside their verbal descriptions, but also showed them in their everyday settings with their friends. Copies of the eventual publication were given to local libraries as a record of the young people's views of their neighbourhood.

Role of the observer

A distinction is usually drawn between participant and non-participant observation. For many small-scale evaluations, the evaluator occupies an ambiguous role, both outside and within the organization. This gets to the heart of the dilemma about collaboration and participation. Where the evaluator as observer keeps to an external role of non-participant, then the report is distanced from the organization and has independent credibility, which is useful both for the evaluator and the organization. But in the close confines of a small organization, it is difficult to maintain a strictly non-participative stance. The advantages of a (sometimes) participatory role within the organization are that it reduces participants' suspicion and increases personal awareness of what the organization is about. There are potential dangers of the researcher being 'enlisted' into the organization, and being 'captured' by one party or another within the organization, which might prejudice independence and reduce the value of the observation.

Non-reactive observation

Much of the observation described above, where the observer is close to the observed, either participant or non-participant, can be classed as 'reactive', in the sense that the presence of the observer affects changes in those being observed. While this does create problems in working out what 'usually' happens as opposed to what is happening at the precise moment of observation, it can be lessened by repeated observations and also by reflection on the activity by the observer.

There are, however, some classes of observation which are non-reactive. Collectively these go under the term 'unobtrusive measures' (Webb *et al.*, 1966; Lee, 2000) and rely on the evidence of signs visible in the situation under concern.

Unobtrusive measures are particularly appropriate for the settings, locations and neighbourhoods that program organizations work in. Areas of social exclusion can be observed and described in terms of the presence or absence of shops, public transport, and community facilities. The type, age and condition of local housing

---

Example 4.7 Unobtrusive observation in a women's shelter

A women's aid organization required an evaluation of the service provided for women who had suffered domestic violence. Two shelters were involved which were very different in size, location, security and standard of furnishings. The researcher felt these features were relevant to the recommendations she needed to make, but could not take photographs because of the need to maintain the secrecy about the external views of the shelter, and because internal photographs would have been an invasion of privacy. She therefore provided a 'word picture' of the shelters, a 'walking image' of what she saw as she approached the homes and walked inside – describing only the physical features and not the occupants. This was effective as well as non-intrusive and in keeping with the sensitive way in which the research had to be conducted.

Example 4.8   Describing a locality

A study sought to evaluate an innovative method of tackling young people's social exclusion from transport by a loan system of motorized scooters so they could travel to work or further education. Though the area could be categorized on the basis of available statistical indicators as one of social exclusion, the researcher also provided his own observations of the condition of the estate, its physical location in respect of transport routes into the centre of town, and the state of public transport. Although this was subjective and descriptive, it highlighted the environmental circumstances surrounding the scheme.

can be described or better photographed – and a selection of images included in the report.

Unobtrusive measures may focus on physical 'traces', particularly on the extent of changes visible in the area, the two main organizing categories being measures of *accretion* or *erosion*. Accretion looks at things added to the environment – the extent of litter and graffiti, for example, the availability of signposting, or ramps to aid disabled access. Erosion looks for evidence of wear and tear – broken windows, lack of repairs, holes in the road and so on. Such measures can give a concrete indication of the more abstract concept of social exclusion, and may be relevant to the organization's activities. However, understanding the reasons for what is seen will require asking questions of knowledgeable residents, and representatives of responsible public bodies.

In impressionistic surveys like this, having a guide from the area can help reveal issues and conditions which the researcher might miss, as well as providing the opportunity of bringing local people into the research. There are advantages in the researcher reflecting back their observations to the local inhabitants, and tapping their understanding of the situation. Observation of this sort is a valuable tool, but is best seen as part of a research strategy rather than an end in itself.

Methods of enquiring

The survey

Surveys use structured questionnaires to collect standardized information. At least five different methods of administering a questionnaire can be distinguished, each of which has its own strengths and weaknesses, as follows:

- **Postal (self-administered) questionnaire**: the questionnaire is mailed out and mailed back, so there is no direct contact between the researcher and the respondent. Large numbers of respondents can be surveyed in a short period of time. But the researcher has no control over how the questionnaire is filled in, or even who in the household actually completes the questionnaire. Non-response may be high, so the questionnaire needs to be designed to encourage response. The cost of postage, including returns and reminders, though small for each questionnaire, may be considerable for large samples.
- **Personal interview**: the researcher asks the questions of the respondent face-to-face and notes down the answers. The researcher controls the process, and response rates are typically higher than for self-administered questionnaires. As in market research, 'show cards' are often used to allow the respondent to see and choose from closed answers to questions. The main cost is in the interviewer's time, so structured questions on the interview schedule will speed up the delivery time. Interviewer bias can occur as responses may be affected by the interviewer's characteristics – interviewers local to the area may achieve better response rates.
- **Telephone interview**: similar to a personal interview, except that only verbal cues are present. Explaining the purpose of the interview, and asking complex questions, can be difficult. Telephone interviewing works best with a screening call or initial letter so that the time of the interview can be pre-arranged to suit the respondent, in order to increase the response rate. The time can then include the evenings when there might be issues of safety for personal interviews door-to-door or in the street.
- **Email or internet survey**: similar to a postal questionnaire, but with the possibility of a speedier response. This is a low-cost method, but, like the postal questionnaire, with low response rates. It will exclude those without the technology, and so those responding may not be representative of the population of interest. This method is particularly appropriate for evaluating services with an ICT component, and may increasingly be used in the future on the grounds of speed and low cost.

- **Third-party administration**: the questionnaire is handed out for self-completion and/or collected in by an intermediary. Where organizations are unwilling to provide addresses or telephone numbers for service users, on the grounds of confidentiality, this may be an unavoidable tradeoff for access to particular groups and situations. The third party could be someone in a gatekeeper role, connected with the program being evaluated. This may increase the likelihood of respondents completing the question- naire, but it can leave the administration with someone who may have little interest in the research, and experience has shown that this results in a poor response rate. The researcher needs to keep frequent checks on how the questionnaires are being handed out and returned and may need to remind the intermediary of research deadlines. This means keeping 'on their back' – which is not always easy when the researcher has no control of the situation and is trying to maintain relations of cooperation.

While there are also developments in computer-assisted perso- nal interviewing (CAPI) and computer-assisted telephone inter- viewing (CATI), which undoubtedly will affect large-scale surveys, these developments are unlikely to be relevant for small-scale, locally based research and evaluation (Miller and Brewer, 2003).

Designing the questionnaire

Experience shows that designing a questionnaire is rather more complex than simply coming up with questions. Building a ques- tionnaire requires a good deal of testing and revision to make sure that the intended audience understands the questions and is able to respond as the questioner intends. Questionnaires for evaluation are likely to need to cover both outcomes and processes of social pro- grams – how people have changed as a result of contact with the program, as well as how they understand the program to work, and what they think and feel about it. Social programs operate in specific local contexts, (Pawson and Tilley, 1997) so it will also be important to conceptualize and investigate aspects of context likely to have an effect on programs either for better or worse.

There are a number of steps to questionnaire completion, as follows:

Define the sections or building blocks for a questionnaire
Begin by breaking the task down into separate blocks or clusters, each dealing with a different aspect of the overall evaluation

question. Once the scope of the questionnaire has been defined by these clusters, each can be worked on in turn to develop actual questions. The questionnaire benefits from having a structure which groups similar questions together, as this makes it easier for respondents to understand what is being asked and may encourage them to reply. It also helps the question designer to avoid asking unnecessary questions. The headings for these clusters may become the headings for the sections in the evaluation report, where questions are grouped into themes (see Chapter 6). Thinking ahead in this way will also help to keep the questionnaire focused.

Operationalize the evaluation questions
Operationalization is the term given to the rules which govern turning abstract concepts into questions whose answers can be quantified as variables. For example, an evaluation, concerning user satisfaction with a program, might operationalize this into a series of specific questions about particular aspects of service, as closed questions measured on a five-point answer scale:

> very satisfied/quite satisfied/neither satisfied or unsatisfied/quite unsatisfied/very unsatisfied

Punch (2003) provides several examples of similar scaled responses to questions on quality, importance, effectiveness etc. For instance:

> *Quality*: Very poor/Poor/Average/Good/Very good
> *Importance*: Not at all/A little/Reasonably/Very/Extremely
>
> (Punch, 2003: 59)

Adapt the questions to the intended audience
Do the intended respondents have the *ability* and *willingness* to answer? Respondents must have knowledge of the topic to be able to answer the question; questions about the past involving memory should be within fairly recent recall; particular care needs to be taken with questions for people with hearing or visual disabilities, or questions directed at children. Questions must be readily understandable, with no presumptions about technical knowledge (that is, avoiding acronyms and special terms).

Willingness to answer can be affected by the perceived intrusiveness and relevance of the questions, as well as the length and presentation of the questionnaire. Willingness also relates to how included stakeholders feel in the way the evaluation has been negotiated.

Follow generally agreed question design 'rules'
Most textbooks on questionnaire design (see for example: Moser and Kalton, 1971; Hall and Hall, 1996; de Vaus, 1996; Bryman, 2001; Babbie, 2004) offer a number of useful 'rules' to avoid common errors in drafting questions:

- Avoid double questions, which sneak in the words *and* or *or*, making it unclear which part of the question a 'yes' or 'no' answer would apply to. Unpack these into two or more different questions.
- Avoid vague measures, such as 'a little', 'often', 'a lot' or 'recently' as people will differ on what they mean by these terms. Specify quantities or periods of time with as much precision as possible.
- Avoid leading questions, which presume a particular answer or offer alternatives slanted more towards one that the other. Ensure that people can respond without feeling that one answer is the right one.
- Avoid long questions, which increase the difficulty of understanding what is being asked. Sometimes it is desirable to present information and ask a person to choose; (an example would be, 'Some people say…, others say…, which do you prefer?'. The question should be kept short, and put at the end of the preamble.
- Avoid the use of negatives, and especially double negatives, in questions where 'no' answers become confusing both for the respondent and the researcher.
- Avoid hypothetical questions (for example, 'what would you do if…'), which will produce hypothetical answers that may be little guide to future actions.
- Use closed questions with precoded responses for the majority of questions. This speeds up the response time if the person has merely to circle a response number or tick a box. (Questions are often closed after the pilot stage of a survey – see below.)
- Choose measurement scales for attitudes, such as satisfaction, as these provide more information than simple yes/no answers. They show strength of feeling as well as the direction of that feeling.

- Use questions that will engage the respondents' interest, in order to increase their likelihood of response. For a community survey, collaborative design of questions with community members is a good way forward.
- Avoid intrusive questions which respondents may find objectionable. If questions are required on sensitive issues, consider carefully how these might be worded, perhaps with less specific response categories, or as attitudinal rather than behavioural questions, about *what people in general think* rather than how the respondent acts.

Questionnaire length

Avoid long questionnaires which fill the respondent with foreboding before the first page is completed. Printing the questionnaire in small type to reduce the number of pages is not the answer either, if readability suffers. Consider whether there are questions from other surveys which can be used to save time in design. The Question Bank website (www.qb.soc.surrey.ac.uk) is an excellent source for questions used in official surveys. The Office for National Statistics has an interesting section on Harmonized Questions and Concepts for Government Social Surveys (www.statistics.gov.uk/Harmony/default.asp) that discusses the standard questions used (inputs) for ethnicity, housing tenure, economic status etc. and how these are presented in tables (outputs).

Pilot test the questionnaire

Try out the questionnaire on a small sample of respondents. Even after following the design rules, it is still necessary to pilot the questionnaire. This will show if the questions are understood, and if the response categories provided cover the full range of responses. It should also show if the questionnaire is too long or complex to sustain the respondents' interest. At this stage more questions can be kept open, and the responses received will help devise the categories for the main survey.

Maximizing response rates

Response rates to surveys vary widely, and low response rates cast doubt on whether it is possible to generalize from the answers. Postal self-administered questionnaires can result in response rates of 30 per cent and lower. To have confidence in a questionnaire's ability to reflect the views of the sample more responses than non-responses are needed (Babbie, 2004: 261), while a 60 per cent response rate is preferable (Punch, 2003: 42) and 75 per cent is a good target to aim at (de Vaus, 1996: 107). This means increasing the *incentives* to reply and avoiding any disincentives.

A post-paid reply envelope is necessary for mail questionnaires (and should be costed into the project design), together with provision for a reminder questionnaire after a fixed period of time, usually two weeks. The questionnaire should be well presented, easy to read, not in small print, and not too long. Instructions for filling in the answers should be clearly marked.

A covering letter is essential. Salkind (2000: 140) gives the following tips on a good covering letter: it should

- be on an official letterhead;
- be dated recently;
- be personalized to the name of the intended respondent;
- clearly state the purpose and importance of the research;
- give a time estimate for response;
- assure anonymity;
- offer the respondent a copy of the results when the study is complete;
- make a clear statement of thanks for cooperation;
- be signed by 'the big boss' as well as the researcher.

For collaborative evaluations, it is also good practice to state that the research is being conducted with the program organization and that the results are intended to be used to improve services. In case of queries, the name of a contact person in the organization should also be supplied. Reassurances like these can be mentioned verbally at the start of an interview, when the questionnaire is administered in person face-to-face, but it is still good practice to leave the respondent with a written letter at the end with information on what the research is for, contact details and thanks for cooperation.

Incentives in the form of payment, or entering of names of respondents into prize draws, are becoming more common in commercial surveys, and voluntary and community organizations may be prepared to offer a small prize to encourage local response. But as their funds are often limited, so it is likely that incentives will be outside the scope of small-scale evaluation and student projects.

If personal interviewing is chosen, for example for a street survey where respondents are selected by quota sampling, there are some practical steps that can be taken to improve response rates:

- Begin by asking people 'Can you help me?' rather than 'Can you spare a few minutes?', as the first question is less easy to turn down than the second.
- Choose a place where many people pass, but recognize that some may not have the time to stop and answer questions. Shopping centres (malls) are private places, and permission will be required from the security office beforehand.
- Be within view of a colleague at all times for personal safety considerations. It is always a good idea to contact the local police station and make them aware of the survey. If the interviewer does not do this, it is quite likely someone from the public will.

Qualitative interviews

Qualitative interviewing uses semi-structured or unstructured questioning to create knowledge in the interaction between interviewer and interviewee. For Kvale, the characteristic of qualitative interviewing is its openness and flexibility:

> The absence of prescribed sets of rules creates an open-ended field of opportunity for the interviewer's skills, knowledge and intuition. Interviewing is a craft that is closer to art than to standardized social science methods.

(1996: 84)

Designing the interview guide or schedule

As with the structured questionnaire, evaluation questions drive the development of specific questions in the interview guide. The difference is that the semi-structured interview is more exploratory than the survey, and there is no clear delimitation as to what may be relevant or not relevant to the study. The researcher is interested in teasing out meanings and interpretations which may differ for different people. So probing questions may be used as follow-ups to earlier questions. The interviewer has to be much more flexible in practice to recognize if questions are being answered out of order and to sense when to follow up on new issues, and when to return to issues that might have been overlooked.

Because the personal involvement between interviewer and interviewee is greater with qualitative interviews, the interviewer has to be prepared to face direct questions back from the interviewee, and to decide how much information they are prepared to offer about themselves, their own experiences and their opinions. The interview becomes much more of an exchange of information. The more conversational style also allows the interviewer to 'repair' gaps in the conversation, offering clarification if the interviewee appears to have misunderstood the purpose of a question.

With semi-structured interviews, the interview guide may develop during the interviewing stage. It is the recommended practice to run analysis and interviewing concurrently, so there is the opportunity for introducing emergent topics into later interviews in a way which cannot be done with the survey questionnaire. This is part of the *progressive focusing* of phenomenological research.

The use of an interview guide is much more demanding on the interviewer (Mason, 2002; 68) than administering a questionnaire. It requires the interviewer to listen well to what the subject is saying, and to know when and how to probe for more information, while at the same time keeping a grasp on the process to ensure that all the topics are covered in the course of the interview, even if not in the order in the guide. If the interview is being recorded, then attention also has to be given so that the recording apparatus is functioning properly. If all that can be done while drinking the proffered cup of tea and stroking the interviewee's cat, which has got a sudden urge to sit on the interviewer's lap, then well done!

Qualitative interviewing can take on a number of forms such as face-to-face interview, group interview and focus group.

Face-to-face interviews

This is the most common form of qualitative interviewing. Interviews can cover situations and feelings in depth, but because of their length, only a limited number of interviews are likely to be possible within a given timescale.

Mason (2002) suggests that semi-structured interviewing shares the following core features:

- an interactional exchange of dialogue;
- a relatively informal style;

- a thematic, topic-centred, biographical or narrative approach;
- the perspective that knowledge is situated and contextual (so relevant contexts are brought into focus in the interview in order that situational knowledge is produced).

> In face-to-face interviewing, the 'relatively informal style' takes the appearance of 'a conversation or discussion rather than a formal question and answer format. Burgess's term "conversations with a purpose" captures this rather well (1984: 102)'.
>
> (Mason, 2002: 62)

For feminist researchers, and critical researchers in general, informal conversations do not go far enough. As already noted above (when considering the role of the researcher in epistemological terms), such researchers are committed to replacing the view from above – of academic researchers/non-participatory evaluators – with the view from below – dominated, exploited and oppressed groups, especially women (Mies, 1993). Interviewing is seen as a tool for consciousness-raising:

> The concept of consciousness-raising is incorporated into feminist methodology in a variety of ways. The feminist consciousness of the researcher (and the researched), the use of consciousness-raising techniques as a research method, and the consciousness-raising potential of the research act are the three most salient features of this aspect of epistemology (Richardson, Fonow and Cook, 1985).
>
> (Cook and Fonow, 1990: 74)

However Mies and others increasingly argue that there should be a shift from individual interviews towards group discussions to obtain more diverse data and also to help female subjects to 'overcome their structural isolation in their families and to understand that their individual sufferings have social causes' (Mies, 1983: 128).

Group interviews

Most interviewing assumes one interviewer asking questions of a single respondent. It's easy to see why – two interviewers could be confusing and feel more like interrogation, while having two respondents complicates the interview, as it runs the risk of one person taking over the interview and excluding the other.

But there can be situations where a group interview is more natural and productive. For people with language or communication

---

Example 4.9   Interviewing an older couple

At a day centre for older people, a student began interviewing an older man but became aware of the concern of his wife sitting some distance away in the same room. When the wife was invited to come closer and join in the interview, the rapport with the couple was much better and much relevant information was volunteered, particularly about coping mechanisms which the couple employed jointly.

---

difficulties, an interpreter may be necessary or for vulnerable people, or a companion may be needed.

In addition, when children are being interviewed, considerations of child protection apply and it is often a requirement that children must not be left alone with an adult. Group interviews are a better alternative.

As with all qualitative interviewing, the researcher has to be a good listener, able to pick up and follow points made by the group while at the same time ensuring that the research questions do get discussed at some stage in the proceedings. Group interaction allows commonly held views and disagreements to emerge, but reduces the interviewer's control over the situation. In this way it can be seen as more democratic than one-to-one interviewing.

Outlining a critical approach to public health research, Olsen argues that group interviewing can help to resolve the oppression which is part of individual interviews; for effective critical research:

> the gap in status between the researcher and the researched must be overcome, denied, overturned. Physical activities and jokes help to break traditional stereotypes that reflect entrenched authority. Groups can sit in a circle instead of lecture-style. Oakley has explained that interviewing often forces respondents to fit into the interviewer's verbal pigeonholes. However, less structured interviews, most focus groups, and democratically run group discussions can avoid this traditional power imbalance.
>
> (1994: 8)

Yet, even such democratic methods may present problems. For example, it has been noted that subjects may reveal things about themselves which present the researcher with ethical difficulties of knowing – and telling. And the opposite situation can arise when individuals may be reluctant to reveal their individual views in the group situation and there is the danger of one or two individuals monopolizing the discussion. Where this is likely, perhaps on questions which are of a sensitive nature, separate interviews may be preferable to group discussion.

Focus groups

Focus groups are a development of group interviews and were initially used in market research to focus on an experience shared by the participants which they could discuss in an open way. Focus groups have been intensively used in media and cultural studies research and are now being employed by social researchers to assess the views of *communities of interest*, such as residents in particular areas, and on topics where group meanings and norms are important (Bloor *et al.*, 2001).

The practical details of recruiting and running focus groups, including the researcher's role as moderator or facilitator, and the recording of discussion on tape, are all covered in a number of accessible texts on focus groups (Greenbaum, 1998; Bloor *et al.*, 2001; Krueger and Casey, 2001). For instance, it is generally agreed that the role of moderating or facilitating the discussion should be separate from that of recording the conversation, which implies at least two researchers present.

The size of the group is also important – it should be large enough to provide a variety of voices, but not too large that it allows some participants to remain silent. Six to eight participants is the size mostly recommended, though there are reports of successful groups with fewer participants. As focus groups may last up to 90 minutes or two hours at the most (Bloor *et al.*, 2001: 91), there is often hospitality provided (food and drink) and payment of expenses in return for participation. Small-scale evaluation research may not have access to a generous budget for the payment of expenses, but may be able to use a community centre as a location, for example, where refreshment facilities, even on the most modest scale (tea and biscuits), are available.

The advantage of the focus group is that individual opinions and attitudes are expressed in a non-threatening situation and tested against those of others in the group around a clear focus. Bryman notes that in conventional one-to-one interviewing, interviewees

Example 4.10   Focus groups for victim support

A local victim support scheme wanted to evaluate whether their services were being publicized sufficiently to meet the needs of specific groups – disabled people, students and older people. The student researcher held focus groups with people from all three groups to find out how they felt about their specific needs and whether there was awareness of what a victim support service could offer. While the disabled group had been supplied with information through their support organizations, the older people and the students were found to have little understanding of victim support, and the report concluded that these groups needed to be targeted with advertising.

are rarely challenged about inconsistencies, whereas

> [i]n the context of a focus group, individuals will often argue with each other and challenge each other's views. This process means that the researcher may stand a chance of ending up with more realistic accounts of what people think, because they are forced to think about and possibly revise their views.

> (2001: 338)

   To help reduce the likelihood of participants being unable to express their views, it is often suggested that the research strategy should make provision for a number of focus groups to be conducted, with separate constituencies, of women, older people, male youth, female youth, and so on.

Notifying subjects

Preparation and prior notification for an interview is important for gaining consent. When the interviewees are connected with a program being evaluated, an introductory letter should be sent beforehand from the organization to alert them to the research and to tell them that contact will be made with them shortly for an interview. The letter should also give each interviewee the chance to say if they are unwilling to participate.

Recording the information

For the structured interview, once specific questions have been finalized, and the answer categories decided, the interviewer records the respondent's answers, and can ensure that the correct boxes are ticked and that all questions are answered. The self-administered questionnaire relies on its design and layout to guide the respondents to making the correct marks to record their responses. This means a clear 'road map' for respondents on how to move through the sections and deal with applicable and non-applicable questions.

With qualitative interviews, and without predetermined categories, recording responses is more difficult. The choice comes down to the interviewer taking notes of the responses as she asks the questions from the interview guide, or of recording the conversation on audiotape. The advantages of tape recording are numerous: it allows all the verbal information to be captured, and to be reported verbatim, and, for the interviewer at least, it reduces the task of note-taking and allows more concentration on listening to and responding to the interviewee.

Consent has to be given before recording takes place; for many respondents, tape recording is a sign that their words are important and worth recording, and a guarantee that their views will be reported accurately. Where the interview is not face-to-face, as in a telephone interview, it is also vital for ethical reasons to obtain the interviewee's permission before recording an interview. However, it is important to note that in some countries (such as Austria) it is illegal to record a telephone interview, even with consent. Even when consent is given (and it is legal!) it needs to be recognized that recording can also create anxieties, and the researcher will need to explain exactly how the tape is to be used, and how long it will be kept, and to defer to the interviewee's conditions.

There are a few guidelines to the technicalities of recording: use good equipment, new tapes and batteries, test the recorder first, and check it is recording during the interview. Smaller tape recorders, with a built-in microphone, are likely to cause the interviewee less distraction, though an external microphone is preferable for focus groups (Darlington and Scott, 2002: 59). Mini-disks and digital recording may be about to replace tapes (Plummer, 2001: 139), but at the moment tapes are a cheap and reliable method of recording. Background noises, from passing traffic, aircraft flying overhead, grass mowing machines, televisions, and so on can seem not too noisy at the time, but prove a real distraction when the tape is replayed (Hall and Hall, 1996: 163). Sometimes it may be necessary to pause the conversation until the noise goes away.

Small-scale evaluation often involves working with programs which deal with specific groups, such as children and disabled people. For that reason, two short sections are provided below which indicate the issues and approaches which need to be considered when conducting evaluation with these groups.

Research with children

Children are increasingly being recognized as social actors able to comment on social situations, and research methods are being developed and adapted to increase the validity of the data from interviews and surveys. When the evaluation of a program serving children is called for, children's views have to be taken into account. *Listening* to children's responses in focus groups or interviews is as important as asking. Writing on research with children, Roberts (2000) comments:

> It cannot be taken for granted that more listening means more hearing, or that the cost benefits to children of participating in research on questions in which they may or may not have a stake is worth the candle.
>
> (Roberts, 2000: 229)

Roberts argues that children need to understand what a project is about, ask salient questions and become part of the process rather than simply become objects of study. As objects, they may be heard at the point of data collection, but their voices will be lost in the processing of the information so they will not be listened to. And that means that their experiences will not be listened to either.

Yet while poverty, for example, may be contested in academic and policy debates, the experience of a child living in poverty, vividly described, cannot be so easily dismissed by those who read reports:

> 'Research conversations' reveal that the context of generating such data is important – data gathered at school may be seen as 'fun schoolwork' whereas data from home interviews may be more detailed and personal.
>
> (Mayall, 2000)

Research methods need to be adapted for different age groups, with less structured interviewing and visual stimuli for younger

---

Example 4.11   Evaluating a service with children under ten years

Two students conducted an evaluation of a youth club which provided facilities for a variety of age groups, the youngest of which were aged seven to ten. Rather than isolate children in interviews, the context of the club made it possible to ask them questions in the context of a group game. The children and one evaluator (trained in youth work) sat in a circle and a large foam rubber 'dice' was thrown across the circle. The child (or evaluator) who caught the dice had to say two new things about the club (the other evaluator kept notes). This was found to be effective in generating ideas in a 'natural setting' as part of evaluating what the children liked or didn't like about the program and its setting. The children also enjoyed participating in 'The game'.

---

children and individual and group semi-structured interviewing for children over seven years. Interviewers may have to paraphrase questions more than they do with adults to make meaning clear, and for self-completion questionnaires with adolescents, it is important to pretest

> in order to identify problems with comprehension and ambiguities in question wording, to detect flippancy and boredom, and to discover discrepancies between the children's understanding and the researcher's intent...

(Scott, 2000: 102)

Research with and by disabled people

Emancipatory research shares its roots with the 'conscientization' process developed by Freire, the decisive characteristic being that 'the study of an oppressive reality is not carried out by experts but by the objects of the oppression' (Mies: 1993: 72). The social model of disability locates oppression not in the individual's impairments, but in the structures of a society which disables through the barriers it raises in terms of mobility, access, employment etc. So challenging oppression means challenging whatever contributes to disabled people being marginalized and passive, rather than being active and empowered.

Research should not therefore be conducted 'on' disabled people, but 'with' and 'by' them. Ledwith (1994) recommends 'respectful listening as a precursor of action' to rehumanize those objectified by society. For Barnes (1992) emancipatory research should systematically demystify the structures and processes which create disability. This has implications for the way the research is conducted, and

> researchers wishing to do interviews with disabled people should contact them well in advance of the main interview to arrange a preliminary meeting-to break down any social barriers between the interviewer and interviewee and to discuss the latter's possible involvement in the research.
>
> (Barnes, 1992: 122)

Barnes further suggests that details should be given about the interview, including the interview schedule where appropriate, and that such an approach would help redress the balance of power between the researcher and researched.

Methods of examining

Local area statistics

Many organizations are interested in how well they address the needs of the local community, and to gauge this they often require information on the local population, in terms of age and sex structures, numbers of young and elderly, as well as numbers in particular categories of interest, such as people with disabilities or lone parents. The baseline for much of this information in the UK is the national Census of population, conducted at 10-year intervals, and published in detail down to the local electoral ward. Because this information is so important to national and local government for establishing their policies and practices in relation to local need, the local authorities are likely to have available ward level (or neighbourhood) statistics, updated with estimates for the years between censuses. Education authorities and health authorities are also likely to publish, or to make available on request, information relating to social need on an area basis, for example, the numbers of school exclusions and free school meals.

Apart from statistics on local areas published by governmental authorities, local area profiles are often required as a basis for funding regeneration programs. It may be the case that consultants have already reported on the area's socio-economic profile and needs. These too can be useful background information, though the information has to be assessed (or evaluated) in terms of the quality and provenance of the information (Black, 1999). While the census information is trustworthy (though some inner city areas may have lower returns than other areas), consultants' reports based upon original survey materials should be assessed in terms of the sampling procedures and not just the size of the sample. It pays to read the small print on the methods used, as some are more reliable than others.

Organizational records

Organizational data are also a potential source of information. Provided access can be obtained, minutes of committee meetings can provide information (of variable quality) regarding the issues of priority for the organization, and decisions taken. Corporate statements such as mission statements, or self-evaluation reports or applications for funding provide an insight into how an organization chooses to present itself. As Hakim (1983) notes, relatively little concern is usually given in social research to using the records produced by the organization's own administrative purposes. Of course, some caution is necessary: such records are the outcome of social processes (Scott, 1990; Bryman, 2001: 376), and may conceal more than they reveal.

For small-scale evaluation, with students on placement in an initially unfamiliar area of practice, one additional advantage of accessing the organization's repository of written and stored information is that the organization is more likely to have up-to-date information on the issue and on policy recommendations than the university library, and so be a valuable resource for the researcher. The organization may even have conducted or commissioned research previously on its locality and its services. Again, the data collection methods have to be carefully scrutinized to see how much trust can be placed on the figures, and to what extent (if any) one may generalize from the findings. Many reports may not be too forthcoming as to how the data were actually collected, and where only percentage responses have been reported, sometimes the figures need to be reworked to find out the actual numbers of people questioned.

Personal records

A final source of documentary evidence may be provided by respondents themselves in the form of personal records, photographs, diaries, etc. Such 'documents of life' (Plummer, 2001) may be particularly relevant to studies which have a historical dimension, or are looking at changes in social situations over time.

It is not just other people who have personal records relevant to the evaluation. Whether observing, or asking questions, or dealing with information collected by others, the evaluator as researcher will be trying to make sense of what they see, or hear or find, to develop further questions and to understand better the subject of their study. These reflections are likely to be given a physical form in the shape of a research diary or journal, and it is useful to regard such diary records, comments and reflections on research in progress as data for analysis in much the same way as information gathered from others. As reflection is such an important topic for experiential learning, it is dealt with in more detail in chapter 7.

SAMPLING

Selection of participants in the research

The final issue in research design to be discussed in this chapter (although it may be one of the first considerations in practice) is the issue of who exactly will provide the information. In some circumstances, when the number of people in a stakeholder group is small, for example a dozen volunteers with a small organization, it may be perfectly feasible to interview all the volunteers. No sampling is required – though there may be issues to do with gaining access to all the volunteers, and in obtaining their consent. Where the number of people is larger, for example the number of service users of a small to medium organization, or the number is indefinite, as in the number of residents in a local area, then some form of selection or sampling will be needed.

It is difficult to answer the question 'How many interviews are needed for a sample?' Kvale's realistic but not very helpful answer is, 'Interview as many subjects as necessary to find out what you need to know' (Kvale, 1996: 101). Where the selection of the sample is likely to be biased, increasing the sample size does not remove or reduce the bias. Even when there is a form of control in restricting the sample to a particular category of interest, for example, women or young people, there is absolutely no guarantee that those questioned are representative of the wider population of women or young people.

In quantitative research, the aim is to make valid *generalizations* from the sample to the *population of interest* from which the sample is selected. For instance, the population of interest for one project was profoundly deaf people living in a locality and a sample had to be selected from these (to evaluate their views about a possible new support service). *Probability samples* are preferred in quantitative research – that is samples selected by chance methods rather than through the researcher's own subjective choice. In this way selection bias is reduced. If time and resources are limited, *non-probability* methods may have to be used, as discussed below, with consequent effects on the generalizability of the data.

In qualitative research the aim is often not to generalize from a sample, but to ensure that the sample is *representative* and encompasses the range of views held. Here *judgemental* and *theoretical* sampling are likely to be used as acceptable forms of *non-probability* sampling.

Probability samples

Probability samples offer the best way of making estimates of the *population of interest*, as they are derived from random methods of selection which reduce bias. In the case of a survey, using house-to-house doorstep interviewing with a structured interview schedule, the following steps are required:

1. the establishment of a '*sampling frame*', or list of all the houses in each of the streets of the area;
2. the selection of a sufficient number of addresses by the use of *random numbers* to provide the sample;
3. calling on just these houses and no others to obtain a response.

A *sampling frame* is a list of the population from which the sample is drawn. To evaluate the effectiveness of a program, a list of users is needed – and the list needs to be accurate, up to date, and with full contact details.

Essentially, *probability sampling* must ensure that every case (person/family/school and so on) in the population is available for selection into the sample and that each case has a known and equal chance of being selected. From properly conducted probability sampling, estimates of the population of interest can be made, with precision in the estimate depending on the number of people in the sample, and the range of responses on each particular variable.

So, for example, a survey of 100 people randomly sampled would permit a 95 per cent confidence interval of ±10 per cent around the sample average, with the inference that the unknown population value is most likely within 10 per cent either way of the known sample value. To reduce the confidence interval by half, to ±5 per cent, would require a fourfold increase in the sample size to 400 (see the table in de Vaus, 1996: 72):

> Sample size decisions are always a compromise between the ideal and the practical, between the size needed to meet technical requirements and the size that can be achieved with the available resources.
>
> (Blaikie, 2000: 200)

Alternatively, and more quickly, *systematic sampling* can be used, where every tenth address (or fifteenth, or twentieth, the sampling fraction being chosen to give a desired sample size) is contacted, with the initial starting-point on the list being chosen by random means (Blaikie, 2000).

In large-scale survey research, simple random sampling is not employed but complex designs are used such as *stratified* sampling (that is strata such as age groups, gender groups or employment types are identified, and individuals are randomly selected from the strata). These strata can be *proportionate* to the population (reflecting, say, a 40 : 60 ratio of men to women) or *disproportionate* (to allow minority groups to be represented). *Clusters* can also be used – that is, naturally occurring groups such as regions, cities, school districts and schools can all provide the basis for multi-layered sampling, in order for the researcher to be able to access samples of students whose views and experiences are representative. Such sophisticated designs are likely to be beyond the scope of the evaluator working at a local level.

In a local survey of small-scale evaluation, obtaining a hundred or more responses by probability sampling is a major undertaking, though not impossible if resources are available (such as a sampling frame). However, other methods of sampling may have to be adopted because of limited resources, and these will mean *non-probability methods*. These are easier to apply, but difficult to generalize from.

Non-probability samples

Quota sampling

This method of market research, is one that most readers of this book will have encountered at some time or another and involves stopping people in the street in busy areas. It depends on the availability of people to be questioned and the selection of people by the researcher – both sources of bias. This way of achieving a predetermined quota sample, representative of the major social characteristics of inhabitants of an area, is generally frowned on in academic research. But it has some utility in ensuring that the people stopped for questioning do match the local population in terms of such variables as age, sex, socio-economic status or ethnicity. The quota sample is also 'economical, easy to administer and quick to do in the field' (Blaikie, 2000: 205). Information from a quota sample may be enough to answer the questions the organization wants to be asked. There may not be the same need as in academic research for precise generalization – the results from a sample which includes a cross-section of age and sex may be sufficient guides for action.

Example 4.12   Survey using quota sample

Two students were asked by a neighbourhood support scheme to evaluate the public's awareness of the service they provided. After consulting the national Census data for the area, they devised a quota sample proportionate to the population parameters, in terms of gender and age, and conducted a survey in a variety of local shopping and market areas.

The results showed a common pattern. Most people said they had heard of the program, but few could say what it did. Fewer still could say where the neighbourhood office was located. Those with least awareness were young men, older people over 70 and members of ethnic minority groups.

The outcome enabled the program manager to re-evaluate whether the service was reaching potential users effectively and whether more targeted advertising was needed to reach the groups least aware of what was on offer.

Theoretical sampling

Quota sampling, where the quotas are chosen to represent the socio-economic features of the local population, could be viewed as a version of theoretical sampling. This has been defined by Strauss and Corbin as, 'Sampling on the basis of concepts that have proven theoretical relevance to the evolving theory' (1990: 176).

However, where quota sampling seeks to replicate the proportions of the population in the sample, theoretical sampling is a qualitative technique in which representativeness in terms of numbers is not the aim. Rather, theoretical sampling aims to explore

> concepts that are deemed to be significant because they are repeatedly present or notably absent when comparing incident after incident, and are of sufficient importance to be given the status of categories.
>
> (Strauss and Corbin, 1990:176)

With *theoretical sampling* the choice of subject is made initially according to the theoretical purpose of the research, and more interviews are added in the light of the information generated and the research questions remaining. This inductive process become complete at the point of 'theoretical saturation' when nothing new is discovered by increasing the number of interviews.

Strauss and Corbin (2000: 183–4) point out that the procedure for creating such a sample can be carried out in a variety of ways:

- purposefully, deliberately chosen by the researcher
- systematically, including all examples of a category
- fortuitously, finding things unexpectedly during research

'Judgemental' or *purposive* sampling is the name sometimes applied to theoretical and non-probability sampling where people are selected according to criteria set by the researcher or the relevant agency. So an evaluator of a service program might wish to obtain interviews from a sample of program users with different backgrounds, varying by age or social class, for instance. On theoretical grounds these variables might be expected to have an influence on how people use the program and on whether they benefit from it. But the evaluator might also be advised to look out for other categories to explain service user's responses to a program. It could be that whether a person lives on their own emerges as a new factor in interpreting their responses, and that more interviews need to be done with people in this situation.

Blaikie (2000: 206) argues, 'An important point about this method of sampling is that any notion of representativeness is irrelevant.' This does not mean that theoretical sampling should be *ad hoc* or unsystematic. As Mason points out (2002: 136), 'The key issue for qualitative sampling is...how to focus, strategically and meaningfully, rather than how to represent.' She adds that it is vital that the researcher keeps a record of the sampling decisions taken to justify the rigour of the procedures which have been used. This record can be kept in the research diary and form part of the reflective account of the research (see Chapter 7).

Snowball sampling

Particularly when dealing with 'hard to contact' groups for which no list exists, such as asylum seekers, the method of 'snowball' sampling may be the only practical approach (Atkinson and Flint, 2003). This involves beginning with a few members from the group of interest who are accessible to the researcher, and then relying on referral onwards to other members of the group from the initial contacts. Bias occurs from using such a social network – while relevant people will be included, others will inevitably be excluded – and it is impossible to work out how 'representative' the snowball sample is of the wider population of interest.

Atkinson and Flint suggest that one of the strongest recommendations for snowball sampling to access hidden populations is that, in contrast to the top-down or descending methodology of quantitative surveys, which often suffer from low response from particular groups, it uses an ascending or bottom-up methodology, starting from known individuals on the ground:

> In this sense snowball sampling can be considered as an alternative or complementary strategy for attaining more comprehensive data on a particular research question.
>
> (2003: 276)

Samples of convenience

Apart from the methods referred to above, a frequently encountered sample is just those people whom the evaluation researcher happens to meet – with all the potential biases that that implies. Known as an 'accidental sample' or a 'sample of convenience' or an 'opportunistic sample', this should not obscure the fact that this type of sample has nothing whatever to do with what statisticians would call a random sample, and that there are very serious drawbacks to making any generalizations from the sample – even if the sample is quite large.

Nevertheless, provided this important restriction on generalization is made clear to the organization, there may still be some usefulness in collecting information from such a sample. Pragmatically, it is quick, and it may be the best that can be achieved in the circumstances where access is difficult. Provided the results are treated with caution, they still represent the views of those questioned, if not the wider population. It is a judgement call on whether potentially biased information is better than no information at all – and organizations may well choose to have something over nothing.

Bryman (2001: 97) suggests two contexts where convenience samples may be valuable, despite their limitations, and these are

- to initiate preliminary analysis (as in a pilot for a larger survey), and
- where the opportunity of conducting research is too good to miss (where access otherwize may proved difficult or impossible).

Interpreting the information may depend on what other sources of information and knowledge the organization has gathered, whether it confirms prior knowledge or expectations, or introduces new responses which had not been considered before.

Suggestions for further reading

On evaluation

There are some excellent websites with many references to evaluation guides and 'cookbooks,' such as:

The World Wide Evaluation Information Gateway
http://www.policy-evaluation.org/

Resources for Methods in Evaluation and Social Research
http://gsociology.icaap.org/methods/

The CAQDAS Networking Project
http://caqdas.soc.surrey.ac.uk/

Herman, J.L. (ed) (1998) *The Program Evaluation Kit*, 2nd edn. Sage, Newbury Park, CA. An extensive collection of resources for all aspects of evaluation from start to finish.

In addition to those sources cited in the chapter, the following may also be found helpful:

On questionnaires and quantitative methods

Balnaves, M. and Caputi, P. (2001) *Introduction to Quantitative Research Methods*. Sage, London.
Converse, J. M. and Presser, S. (1986) *Survey Questions: Handcrafting the Standardized Questionnaire*. Sage, Newbury Park, CA.
Dillman, D. A. (1999) *Mail and Internet Surveys: The Tailored Design Method*, 2nd edn. Wiley, New York.
Oppenheim, A. N. (2000) *Questionnaire Design, Interviewing and Attitude Measurement*. Continuum, London.
Punch, K. F. (2003) *Survey Research: The Basics*, Sage, London.

On qualitative methods

Arksey, H. and Knight, P. (1999) *Interviewing for Social Scientists*. Sage, London.
Flick, U. (1998) *An Introduction to Qualitative Research*. Sage, London.
Wengraf, T. (2001) *Qualitative Research Interviewing*. Sage, London.

On social research methods in general

Gilbert, N. (ed.) (1993) *Researching Social Life*. Sage, London.
Sapsford, R. and Jupp, V. (eds) (1996) *Data Collection and Analysis*. Sage, London.
Robson, C. (1993) *Real World Research*. Blackwell, Oxford.

CHAPTER 5

Analysing the Data

Summary

The result of research questioning is a collection of information, in the form of audiotapes and interview notes of in-depth interviews and focus groups, or a set of completed questionnaires. There can also be the researcher's field notes of observations, a selection of photographs and videotape and a collection of documents relating to the program and the area, as well as the reflective diary. This chapter is about analysing such information. Analysis covers the stages of organizing, reducing and making sense of data. Data collection and analysis, although conceptually distinct activities, often proceed together in practice, as the researcher formulates ideas on the basis of initial responses, and decides if more information needs to be collected.

In addition, the end result of analysis is the presentation of findings in the evaluation report, as evidence for forming a judgement on the program being evaluated. Again, although report writing is a distinct activity, it does not fall into a neat chronological sequence of events. It will have been planned early in the process and this planning will influence both subsequent data collection and analysis:

> The final report should be envisaged from the start, and much of the analysing and verifying tasks should be pushed forward to earlier stages.
>
> (Kvale, 1996: 99)

For moderate amounts of data, the traditional methods of coding, sorting and analysing data by hand are still appropriate. However, computer programs for quantitative data analysis and, increasingly, qualitative data analysis, offer opportunities for greater speed and accuracy in analysis. But while such programs offer assistance, they do not remove the need for the researcher to understand the underlying rationale of analysis in order to control the process and choose the most appropriate ways of sorting, collating and presenting their information. Interpreting the findings still relies on the researcher's skill and judgement.

As with Chapter 4, there is much that has been written on the analysis of data, both from survey questionnaires and from qualitative interviews. Within this chapter, it is only possible to present an outline of the most common approaches to quantitative and qualitative data; a short list of suggested reading is included at the end.

QUANTITATIVE OR STRUCTURED DATA

Data and the rules of measurement

As Chapter 4 noted, quantitative research involves turning abstract concepts into concrete indicators which can be measured through the process known as *operationalization*. Indicators are what can be researched and the researcher needs to identify specific factors which are variables. In planning the research, links between *variables* were hypothesized. The analytical stage is the opportunity to test whether links exist and, if they do, how strong the connections are – for instance between the age of respondents (variable one) and their level of satisfaction with a program (variable two).

A variable has a set of categories and there are rules about how the different categories may be analysed, depending on the scale or level of measurement being used.

> Variables may be measured at different 'levels of measurement' (depending on the type of variable), and the level of measurement will determine what kinds of analyses may be performed.
>
> (Rose and Sullivan, 1996: 17)

Three different *scales or levels of measurement* for variables are usually distinguished as

- nominal;
- ordinal;
- interval/ratio.

In *nominal* scales, the different categories of a variable have no implied ordering; they are just different. So for gender, there are two discrete categories, male and female. Religious affiliation and political party preference could also be specified through a number of discrete non-ordered categories.

Ordinal scales exist where the various categories can be ranked in order from highest to lowest, though exact differences between each category remain unspecified. Educational level, in terms of the types of qualifications achieved, would be one example, and a scale of satisfaction, from very satisfied through to very unsatisfied, is another.

Interval scales use measurement in numbers on a scale with equal intervals. When interval scales have a true zero-point, these can also be called ratio scales. Examples would be age in years, height in centimetres, or income in the unit of currency. There is a correspondence between the values, so that a person aged 40 is twice as old as one aged 20, and an income of £25 000 per year is a quarter of £100 000 per year.

Interval scales can be reduced to ordinal scales through recoding, with a loss of accuracy of the information, and ordinal scales can be reduced to nominal scales as dichotomies, with just two categories. So a question on age, for example, could be asked expecting an answer in years (interval), or in a pre-coded age group category (ordinal), or as a dichotomy ('Are you aged 60 years or over?'). The scale of measurement to be used in the question should reflect the amount of detail to be used in the report. Where most accuracy is required, it is better to ask for a person's date of birth, and then to recode this in terms of current age in years and months. But if only broad comparisons will be drawn in the report between younger and older participants, then a small number of age groups may be enough – and less intrusive for the respondent to answer.

With questions about satisfaction and opinions, it is generally better to avoid the simple dichotomy of 'yes/no' answers, and to phrase the answer in terms of a rating scale. The answer then shows not simply the direction of the attitude, but also the strength with which it is held.

The categories of a closed-question answer must be mutually exclusive, except in compound questions where the respondent can tick all the options that apply. Where the categories are not exhaustive (there may be other possible answers not listed), it is necessary to include an 'Other' category for the respondent to specify whatever this may be.

The pilot phase of the questionnaire should reveal if respondents are replying outside the categories listed, but if new categories arise during the main research phase then the researcher has a dilemma. Kvale writes of the implications of the researcher becoming 'wiser' during interviewing as the research progresses:

> In hypothesis-testing studies, realizing significant new insights during the study may well create problems for the interviewer ... The dilemma will then be whether to improve the interview guide to include in the new dimensions, and not have comparable groups, or to refrain from learning more about the new dimensions uncovered during the study.
>
> (Kvale, 1996: 100)

Once data are collected, the researcher is faced with a number of tasks:

- *organizing* the collected information into a form suitable for analysis;
- *checking* the information for consistency and errors;
- *reducing* and summarizing the information;
- *looking for patterns* in the data;
- *testing* hypotheses to construct explanations.

Organizing quantitative data for analysis

de Vaus (1996: 3) emphasizes the importance of the data matrix in this process. Following Marsh (1982), he sees this way of systematizing data as the key feature of the survey. So the survey is not defined by its use of questionnaires but by 'a structured or systematic set of data which I will call a variable by case data matrix'. de Vaus points out that other research techniques, such as structured interviews, observations and content analysis, are all capable of producing information in a form that can be placed within a data matrix, that is, a 'grid in which we have the same information for each case' (de Vaus, 2001: 185). The data matrix holds information in separate rows for each information provider (or case), and in separate columns for each variable. In questionnaires, cases are individual respondents, but the case unit of analysis could equally be organizations or neighbourhoods, for example, were that the focus of interest.

Table 5.1   Case by variable data matrix

	Variable 1 Gender	Variable 2 Age group	Variable 3 Employment	etc.
Case 1	Female	21–45	Full-time	
2	Female	21–45	Part-time	
3	Male	60+	Not in employment	
etc.				

Each cell in the data matrix, formed by the intersection of row and column, represents the response of one case on a particular variable. This is the basis for statistical analysis. Because the same information is collected for each case, each cell contains an entry. In those instances where information has not in fact been collected from the case (perhaps because the respondent omitted to answer a particular question, or the question did not apply to that individual's circumstances), an entry signifying non-response, or refusal, or 'does not apply' must be placed in the data matrix so that every variable is accounted for (Table 5.1).

Putting information into the data matrix is the first stage. Statistical methods use numerical information, so responses in the form of words or phrases need to be turned into numbers. This requires explicit rules on coding responses, which are provided by the *codebook* (de Vaus, 1996: 245) or coding manual (Bryman, 2001: 186). The codebook identifies a different value for each possible response to a question, and includes values for non-response or 'missing data', which must also to be recorded to complete the data matrix.

In nominal scales, code values have no intrinsic meaning, and are applied merely to represent the different categories, as for example in coding voting preferences in UK elections:

1 = Conservative
2 = Labour
3 = Liberal Democrat
4 = Green
5 = Other
6 = None
−9 = No response

To avoid transcription errors, it is good practice to use a clearly distinguishable number for missing data, as here (−9). Yes/no questions are easily coded into a dichotomy, treated as a nominal level variable:

1 = Yes
2 = No
−9 = No response

Scales of satisfaction are ordinal scales, and again the code values are arbitrary (though there are arguments for treating these 'quasi-interval variables' as interval scales; see Corbetta, 2003: 168):

1 = very unsatisfied
2 = quite unsatisfied
3 = neither unsatisfied or satisfied
4 = quite satisfied
5 = very satisfied
−9 = No response

In interval scales, the answer is on a number scale already and requires no further coding.

Difficulties of coding sometimes arise when questions are asked for which it is possible to give more than one answer. A compound question, with a list of alternative responses and the instruction, 'tick all that apply', can produce none, one, two, or more positive replies. These 'multiple-response' questions are often used in evaluations, for example, where service users are asked to say how satisfied they are with a variety of services that they may have received.

But in the data matrix, only one entry can be made in each cell. The simplest way of dealing with such questions is to treat each possible response as a separate variable. So, for example, the question asking service users about satisfaction would be broken down into separate variables for each of the different services. Each variable is then coded 1 if ticked, or 0 if not ticked (or given a 'missing value' if the whole question has been ignored). de Vaus (1996: 237) calls this the 'multiple-dichotomy' method.

Open questions, on the other hand, require 'post-coding' (de Vaus, 1996: 233), once the questionnaires have been completed. This involves sifting through the responses, noting all the different answers to the open questions, then grouping these into a set of mutually exclusive categories which cover all the responses. The result is a nominal scale, to which code values can then be assigned.

The researcher's judgement is used in determining which responses are sufficiently close in meaning to be placed under the same category. The reasoning should be explained and consistently applied to ensure reliability. The aim is to have a balance between too many categories, with few cases in each, and too few categories, with little discrimination among the sample.

Using computers with quantitative data

While it is feasible to produce by hand on a few sheets of paper a data matrix for a small number of questionnaires, and to perform the analysis by counting up the entries in the columns, the possibilities of making mistakes, and the difficulty of producing cross-tabulations in the next stage of analysis, mean that for most circumstances, using a computer program for data analysis will repay the time spent learning the program and inputting the data. The availability of data analysis programs such as SPSS For Windows has shifted the balance in favour of using computer programs for the analysis of all but the simplest of questionnaires.

There is no shortage of books on how to use SPSS For Windows, and the Windows format also means that tables and graphs are readily exported to other writing packages for producing the final report.

Checking the information for consistency and errors

If the researcher is personally inputting the data into SPSS, each questionnaire can be screened as it is processed to see if the responses are complete and make sense. Each questionnaire should be identified by an index number that is input as the first variable of the data matrix. Any obvious inconsistencies in answers may be flagged up for attention, perhaps to be treated as suspect or missing data.

Once the data file is complete, the first run through the information should be to produce a frequency count for each variable, to check that the values recorded fit into the expected range of numbers. Any unexpected values can be tracked back by the index number to the originating questionnaire. This allows the researcher to check if there have been any transcription errors in entering the data.

Reducing and summarizing the information

Even a modest-sized questionnaire, running to two or three A4 pages, with 30 or more respondents, will result in quite a sizeable data matrix containing a mass of information. One of the first tasks of analysis will be to get an overview of the information by describing the information on each variable in condensed form.

Descriptive analysis reduces the information to show the main features of each variable, such as the average and the extent of variation around the average. As de Vaus comments, cross-sectional designs such as the survey are well suited for 'descriptions of things as they are at a given point in time.' They provide answers to 'questions of "how many" and "which types" of people do or think in particular ways' (de Vaus, 2001: 194).

Choosing the appropriate descriptive statistic (Table 5.2) depends on the scale or level of measurement for each variable. With a *nominal scale* variable, such as political party preference, SPSS will happily calculate a value for the mean average for this variable. However, the resulting number has no meaning as it depends on the code values assigned to the different categories and these values have no intrinsic meaning. All that can be done in the case of nominal variables is to report the numbers and percentages of respondents favouring each party, and the party with the largest number of adherents (modal value). This is done in a *frequency table*, which shows the numbers in each category of the variable, the number of 'missing' replies, and the percentages of each category (leaving out the missing replies) (Table 5.3).

A *bar chart* (Figure 5.1) or *pie chart* can also be used to display the number of cases in each category. In fact, diagrams such as these are good ways of displaying information in reports, and can often make the point better than tables of numbers alone. Bryman comments that

> [d]iagrams are among the most frequently used methods of displaying quantitative data. Their chief advantage is that they are relatively easy to interpret and understand.
>
> (2001: 223)

In the case of *ordinal scales*, the median is the appropriate 'average' to use as an indicator of the central point of the distribution.

With *interval/ratio scales*, it not necessary to list each value reported (for example, income level) and the number of people

Table 5.2 Descriptive statistics for scales of measurement

Scale of measurement	Measure of central tendency	Measure of dispersion
Nominal	Mode	Range
Ordinal	Median	Inter-quartile range
Interval/ratio	Mean	Standard deviation

Table 5.3 Example of a frequency table for political preference (mode added)

Party supported	Number	%	
Conservative	12	17	
Labour	24	33	←mode
Liberal Democrat	13	18	
Green	3	4	
Other	2	3	
None	18	25	
No response	1	–	
Total	73	100	

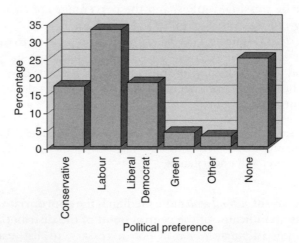

Figure 5.1 Example of a bar chart for political preference

on that value. Instead, the whole of the range of responses on that variable can be summarized using the appropriate descriptive statistic for the average – the arithmetic mean.

While averages can indicate the 'typical' value of a variable, their use as the sole descriptive measure of a variable is questionable, particularly where there is a great deal of 'spread' around the average. If a sample survey sample reported an average age of respondents of 45 years, there is nothing here to indicate whether the respondents were all between 40 and 50 years of age, or from a wider range of, say, 16 to 96 years.

So the spread or *dispersion* around the average also needs to be considered. For interval variables such as age, the *standard deviation* is appropriate, while for nominal and ordinal variables there is the *range* or *inter-quartile range* respectively. When interval scale variables are normally distributed, that is to say, have a symmetric pattern, with most data points close to the mean, and fewer and fewer data points the further away from the mean one goes, then the standard deviation allows fairly precise estimation of the percentage of data values between the mean and the standard deviation, and by extension, between any two values in the normal distribution (see, for example, Salkind, 2000: 151–5; Fielding and Gilbert, 2000: 144–51).

Looking for patterns in the data

Reports that do no more than go through a questionnaire answer by answer, reporting separately on each item, make for very boring reading. By giving equal attention to each answer, they lose any capacity to interest and intrigue the reader. Additionally, they fail to show connections or patterns in the data where one variable may be related to others.

The descriptive stage, with frequency tables, should be the first rather than the last stage of analysis. It has to be done, and done proficiently, but then the researcher needs to impose an order on the findings. This moves on from description to explanatory analysis. de Vaus comments:

> When trying to make statements about causal relationships, cross-sectional designs must rely on static comparisons between groups or on correlations between variables where measurements are made at the same point in time.
>
> (2001: 201)

Unlike experimental research, where different experimental and control groups can be directly compared, and differences explained in terms of the experimental treatment applied to the experimental group and not the control group, the logic of causal inference is more difficult to apply to questionnaire data. Here there is only 'statistical control', that is, comparison of groups formed on the basis of existing differences (independent variable) in terms of their outcomes on a second variable (dependent variable).

Represented graphically, the situation is as in Figure 5.2, where prior variables influence dependent variables, either directly or through the influence of one or more intervening variables. Depending on the particular link examined, the main research question may be treated as a dependent variable, whose outcome is influenced by the different characteristics of the sample, or as an independent variable, which influences further dependent variables in consequence.

The task of quantitative data analysis, in hypothesis testing designs, is to relate the main research findings to the characteristics of the sample, or to other intervening or consequential variables. This may mean prioritizing some findings in terms of greater importance for explaining responses, and relegating other variables to the background.

In evaluation research, people's experiences of and attitudes towards the program under evaluation may be interpreted or explained by background factors such as gender and education level, or by intervening variables such as levels of income or

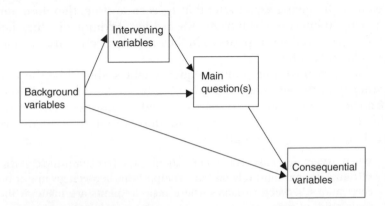

Figure 5.2   Schematic of explanatory causal model

participation. The report needs to tell a story that will interest the reader, and have sufficient accurate and well-presented information, whether in tables or graphs, to be persuasive.

Crucial to this is that the report of the findings be made in sufficient detail – of the numbers involved (and numbers of non-responses), how the questions were worded, and the representativeness of the sample – in order to allow the reader to make up their own mind about what the data mean.

Comparison of responses from different groups within a sample is central to the task of analysis. For example, what are the residents' views of the role of a community centre? And are these views the same or different for women and men, for old and young? Comparison between samples is important too. What do paid staff, volunteers and service users feel are the best services provided – and the worst? Do these views coincide or differ?

Testing hypotheses or constructing explanations

Making comparisons, and tracking differences and similarities means moving on in a report from simply describing each answer or variable one at a time (univariate analysis) to looking at how two or more variables are related (bivariate and multivariate analysis). For two variables, cross-tabulations (also called contingency tables) provide a readily understandable way of showing any association or relationship between the variables (de Vaus, 1996: 155; Bryman, 2001: 227).

Cross-tabulations are best applied to nominal and ordinal level variables; more powerful techniques of correlation are available for interval variables, though these are likely to be in the minority in most questionnaires used in social research.

A cross-tabulation shows how the distribution of responses on one variable lines up with the distribution of responses on a second variable. It is then possible to see if the two variables are associated. The logic of association is as follows:

- A *positive association* is where high (or positive) values on one variable are associated with high values on the other variable.
- A *negative association* is where high values on one variable are associated with low (or negative) values on the other variable.
- Where the values on one variable bear no relation to the values of the other variable, there would be *no association*.

Example 5.1 Preferences for a coffee shop

A study of young people's attitudes towards a proposed coffee shop with
advice centre and homework club found that about half the young people
said that in the evenings they just hung out on the streets. Would those who
'hung out' feel the proposed coffee shop to be a safer place than the streets
than those who did not 'hang out'?

The cross-tabulation was shown in Table 5.4 (adapted from Richmond,
2001). The numbers show how the total of 154 responses were cross-tabu-
lated, and the addition of column percentages allows easy comparison
between the two columns of those who did and did not stand around on the
streets, despite the (in this case, slightly) different totals.

As might be expected, those who habitually stood around on the streets
were less likely to view the proposed coffee shop as a safer option, but
nevertheless a large majority in each case thought the coffee shop offered
safety. There is some evidence of a small negative association here.

The report also discussed whether there was a difference between those
who did and did not hang out on the streets in liking the idea of a coffee
shop.

This cross-tabulation was as shown in Table 5.5 (adapted from Richmond,
2001). Here the cross-tabulation shows virtually no difference in the percentages liking the idea of the coffee shop. The conclusion is that the young
people's activity of hanging around on the streets has no relationship to their
approval of the idea – in each case well over two-thirds were in favour, and
the coffee shop was likely to appeal equally to both groups. Notice that in the

Table 5.4 Views on safety by evening activity

Is the coffee shop safer?	Stand on the street in the evenings		
	Yes	No	Total
Yes	61 (77%)	67 (89%)	128 (83%)
No	18 (23%)	8 (11%)	26 (17%)
Total	79 (100%)	75 (100%)	154 (100%)

Table 5.5 Preference for coffee shop by evening activity

Like the idea of the coffee shop?	Stand on the street in the evenings		
	Yes	No	Total
Yes	54 (72%)	52 (71%)	106 (72%)
No	21 (28%)	21 (29%)	42 (28%)
Total	75 (100%)	73 (100%)	148 (100%)

two tables the totals are slightly different, because of missing data – some people had not answered both questions, and were therefore excluded from the relevant table.

An accepted standard rule for setting out tables is that if a causal link is proposed between the two variables such that one variable is dependent on the other then the dependent variable is presented as the row variable, reading across the page, and the independent variable as the column variable, reading down the page. Calculation of column percentages *down* the table allows comparison between the groups for similar responses *across* the rows (de Vaus, 1996: 159).

In these examples, the supposition is that young people's habits of standing on the street in the evening (independent variable) would influence their attitudes towards the coffee shop (dependent variable). Table 5.2 gives a percentage difference across the rows of −12 (77 per cent − 89 per cent), while Table 5.3 gives a percentage difference of 1 (72 per cent − 71 per cent). So the conclusion is that there is a small and negative association between the variables in the first example, and no evidence of an association in the second example.

Of course, finding an association is not proof that a causal link exists. All that cross-tabulations will show is whether there is an association between two variables. Attributing causality is part of the explanatory process generated by the researcher, and there may be other, as yet unexplored variables, which are really responsible for the findings.

Recognizing associations

How big does a percentage difference in a table have to be in order to be confident that the association is not just down to chance? Some precision to that answer can be given through the use of statistical tests, and the *chi-square* test is an appropriate one for cross-tabulations. SPSS will calculate the probability of the values in a cross-tabulation occurring by chance. Where that probability value is small ($p < .05$) the researcher has confidence that there is a statistically significant relationship between the variables.

However, as both Blaikie (2000: 207) and Hakim (1987: 7) warn, establishing a statistically significant relationship is not the same as establishing the strength of the association between the variables. The size of the sample must also be considered. With large samples, even a small association may be statistically significant, though unimportant. And with small samples, even an important relationship of moderate strength may fail to be detected. To test the strength of an association, a measure independent of the size of the sample is preferred, such as the *phi correlation* statistic (or for tables with more than three rows and columns, Cramer's V; see Rose and Sullivan, 1996: 136).

The chi-square test does have to be used with caution. It is unreliable when the expected frequencies are low (<5), so for large tables with many cells, it may be necessary to recode the variables into a smaller number of categories to avoid having cells in the table with low expected frequencies. The test also assumes a random sample, and if the sample is not random, as may be the case in small-scale evaluation, then the results may be invalid.

Where small-scale evaluation is concerned, there is a tradeoff between the power and complexity of statistical tests, and the ease of analysis and understandability of the report. Keeping it simple means there is greater chance of the evaluator producing a report which is clear and comprehensible to the intended audience.

QUALITATIVE OR NATURALISTIC DATA

Qualitative research is about understanding the world of the subjects, listening to their voices, and allowing those voices to be heard in the analysis and the report. This means the researcher will want to analyse the information in terms of the ideas, concepts, and words used by their subjects, rather than, or as well as, those the researcher thinks are important. The researcher needs to illustrate the analysis with direct quotations from interviewees. Qualitative research emphasizes understanding social processes rather than collecting a 'snapshot' through a structured questionnaire, and aims to provide the 'rich' and 'deep' data of qualitative research in contrast to the reputedly 'hard' information from quantitative research.

As Plummer suggests, there is humanistic interest in people's lives, and in how these lives are told in 'stories' and 'narratives'. The influence of postmodernism has been to view the world as 'less dominated by generalities and "master narratives"' Plummer (2001: 12), and more open to a multiplicity of perspectives and a multiplicity of local stories. For the purposes of evaluation, it can

Example 5.2   Using stories in evaluation

Two students worked with an organization providing assistance to people with physical and learning difficulties to live in ordinary housing in family situations. The organization was concerned that when its service users went into hospital from time to time they did not always receive the best standards of care, and wanted to document their experiences more systematically.

As the people with special needs were unable to speak or communicate clearly, the decision was taken to interview their carers about the hospital experiences. The report indicated that 'the treatment patients received was usually of a high standard ... Nevertheless some problems were experienced.'

An example of a serious problem was the following report from the carer Eleanor about the treatment of Jillian: 'I asked the nurse to keep an eye on Jillian while I went home. When I got back, the Sister and nurses were chatting three yards from Jillian's door. I went into Jillian's room to find the blinds were closed, the door closed, and it was pitch black. She had fallen forward, the elastic from the mask had twisted around her neck, and the mask was under her chin.' When Eleanor asked the nurses why Jillian had been left in the dark, the nurse said that when she had gone to turn the light on, Jillian had shaken her head, and the nurse assumed this meant she wanted the light off. But the carer knew that 'Jillian cannot communicate like this and she hates the dark.'

(McCulloch and Quarrie, 1998)

be revealing to listen to stories of people's encounters with others, their feelings, and the sense they make of their own lives in order to understand how services affect them, in ways that the standard questionnaire would be unable to detect.

Analysing recorded interviews

The researcher has a number of tasks to perform:

- organizing the information into a form suitable for analysis through full or partial transcription of audiotapes;
- checking the information for consistency and accuracy in transcription;

and, as with all qualitative data:

- coding the information;
- categorizing the codes, reducing the information and developing hypotheses or constructing explanations.

Transcription

The decision has to be made whether a detailed transcription of the whole tape is necessary. For an academic research study, without a doubt a full transcription is required, but for small-scale evaluation it may be sufficient to transcribe only selected parts of a tape which bear directly on the program and relevant groups, focusing on the evaluation questions agreed with the organization.

Full transcription is a major commitment, and estimates of the amount of time required vary from around 3 hours per hour of tape (Darlington and Scott, 2002: 143) to up to 10 hours (Plummer, 2001: 149). It is wise for planning purposes to allow for somewhere in between, say around 6 hours per hour of tape (Hall and Hall, 1996: 162). Good advice is always to do the transcription as close in time to the recording as possible, as this allows checks on unclear passages while the interview is still relatively fresh in the researcher's memory, and to begin analysis by looking for key themes and emergent concepts while the interview process is continuing.

In small-scale evaluations, where there may be no budget to employ a separate paid transcriber, the researcher will be able to begin identifying themes as she or he works through the task of transcribing. Where a transcriber can be paid, it is important to give clear instructions about the level of detail to be included, and to have consistent conventions for what to do when the tape is inaudible. In addition, Darlington and Scott (2002: 144) warn that transcribing 'can also be hard work emotionally', when the interview has been about a sensitive issue and the interviewee has been speaking frankly, so that the concerns of the transcriber also need to be considered. But in contrast, transcribers can be enthused and involved in their role by interviews that give evidence of successful programs and the subject's personal development.

Accuracy in transcription

The level of detail in a transcription for evaluation research is much less than would be normal for a conversation analytic study where silences and hesitations would also be recorded (for this, see Silverman, 2001: 163). Plummer (2001: 150) indicates that some slight editing may be advisable, and offers the advice given by

Finnegan:

1. Leave out 'uh's' and other hesitation phenomena including false starts and fil-ins like 'you know', or 'I mean'.
2. Repair false starts and corrections (unless these, or an unusual pause, seem significant for content).
3. Omit interviewer responses like 'I see', 'yeah'.
4. Use standard spellings, not dialect or pretend dialect.
5. Do not use 'eye' spellings ('enuff' for 'enough', 'wuz' for 'was').
6. Use punctuation as for normal written prose, without over-reliance on under-lining or exclamation marks.
7. Subject to the provisos above, do not correct or interpret: put down what the speaker actually said, not what you thought he meant.

(1992: 196–7)

Finnegan herself argues that the urge to 'correct' or 'improve' must be resisted, but that there are different ways of being 'accurate'. In transcriptions, non-standard dialect speech (for example, 'I done/dun this') is a recurring issue – should local speech patterns be preserved in the transcript for 'accuracy', or is it allowable to transcribe as standard English 'I did this', so that the reader of the report does not focus on the pattern of speech to make negative inferences about the speaker? For evaluation purposes, accuracy is needed, but not at the expense of the subject, whose spoken English may contrast poorly with the written English of the report. This could lead to such subjects being regarded as of less importance than those who use standard English.

The outcome of transcription is a computer-readable file of the interview, plus one or more printouts on paper. It is sensible to set wide margins and line spacing so that the researcher's comments can be written alongside. Where a full transcript has not been completed, there should be notes at least on themes and topics in the non-transcribed parts of the interview, in case it is decided to return to these issues at a later date.

Thematic analysis

Where the information comes from semi-structured interviews, following a set of themes in an interview guide, the themes can be treated as separate items for analysis. In a similar way as with the variable/case data matrix of quantitative data, a qualitative data matrix can be drawn up to show the responses to each theme by the different interviewees. This can be done either on a large sheet of paper ruled into boxes or, perhaps more flexibly, in a computer spreadsheet program, where the individual cells can hold either the full text or just the main phrases used by interviewees in response to each theme. This then permits an overview of the total number of interviews, though the amount of detail given by different interviewees on the same themes will vary from subject to subject. A simple qualitative data matrix like this makes possible some quantification – counting – of the responses, such as whether people are generally positive, negative or neutral about certain items. Measurement of this kind is not antithetical to qualitative analysis, and indeed can help to answer initial hypotheses, and provide the reader with some assurance of the validity of the conclusions as not being based solely upon 'anecdotal' evidence (Silverman, 2001: 68).

The qualitative variable case data matrix also facilitates comparisons across different cases. Comparison has been suggested as a way of hypothesis testing, and bringing rigour to qualitative analysis (Silverman, 2001: 69; Gibbs, 2002: 189), rather than relying on untested hunches. The method can be extended to cross-tabulate responses to different questions by various background variables such as age and gender, in much the same way as in a quantitative table. The difference now is that the cells defined by the intersection of rows and columns hold not the number of cases on that combination of variables, but phrases and responses from the whole sample of interviews, documents and so on for the corresponding combination of questions and background variables. In this way, for example, all the responses from men on a particular theme could be compared with the responses from women.

There are however dangers with treating themes, which may arise at different points within unstructured interviews, as if they were variables coded under the same heading. Mason rejects this approach of using the logic of variable analysis and its search for cause-and-effect relationships for qualitative data. Instead she prefers to consider such collections of information under the same theme as 'unfinished resources for a variety of further uses rather than end products (such as variables) in themselves' (Mason, 2002: 157).

Coding data

Applying codes

As with quantitative data, question-by-question analysis is unlikely to provide an either very insightful or very interesting way of developing understanding of the information, even with selected illustrative quotations. What is required, especially for loosely structured interviews, where people's responses do not fit neatly into boxes for answers to particular questions, is a way of coding the data into a variety of themes, of grouping similar thematic materials together, and of developing and extending broader explanatory categories.

Gibbs points out that whereas in quantitative analysis coding is used to simplify the data, reducing it to a few categories so that it can be counted,

> [i]n contrast, coding in qualitative analysis is a way of organising or managing the data. All the original data are preserved. Codes are *added* to the data... Whereas quantitative analysis can be seen as a consistent move away from the original data towards a summary, qualitative analysis constantly cycles around between the original data and the codes, memos, annotations etc. that the analyst constructs.
>
> (Gibbs, 2002: 4)

Coding, as Bryman (2001: 398) indicates, 'is the starting point for most forms of qualitative data analysis'. At its simplest it means the researcher identifying a word, phrase, or sentence as an example of X, where X is a concept or area of interest. In program evaluation, for example, the evaluator is likely to be guided by the aims of the project and the evaluation questions to look for and code instances where aspects of service are mentioned, and to code statements as to whether respondents are favourable, unfavourable or neutral towards those aspects. Codes would also be used to identify themes mentioned by the interviewee that seem to the researcher to be interesting, significant and indicative of the meanings of the situation held by the subject.

Coding can be done manually, with coloured pens and highlighters for example, and grouping can be done physically as well through a cut-and-paste of copies of transcripts or field notes, though Plummer (2001: 151) recommends that the resulting 'analytic' files – distinct from the transcripts or 'core' files – should also be created by computer. Plummer also recommends keeping a third set of files, that of the 'personal log', where the researcher can record impressions, comments and new ideas as the analysis progresses. The log then becomes a summary of 'ideas in progress' as it records original guiding assumptions or hypotheses for the analysis, together with any emergent ideas or insights as the work progresses. This is in line with a reflective approach to evaluation.

Categorizing codes, reducing information and developing explanations

After coding has identified different sections of the data, comparing within and across documents allows the researcher to view passages where similar codes or combinations of codes occur. This is an occasion for reviewing the first coding, and looking for finer detail within the texts that might be dealt with under new codes. Essentially this is a repetitive task of working with the data, reading and rereading, and noting any new ideas for further exploration in the personal log or memo.

According to the precepts of 'grounded theory' (Glaser and Strauss, 1967; Strauss and Corbin, 1990), initial open coding is followed by organization and reordering of codes into categories to make connections between different codes. The research and data-collection/data-analysis process is continued until no new information on the category is being generated ('theoretical saturation'). Out of these categories may emerge core categories that are then used to explain the phenomena in the texts. Such explanation becomes a theory grounded in the data rather than in the researcher's own models and assumptions.

Because of its iterative and open-ended character, full application of the ideas of grounded theory is unlikely to be used in a small-scale evaluation – or indeed in many research studies which claim to do so (Bryman, 2001: 391). But the basic process of ordering codes into categories which are empirically related in the data, as well as being theoretically justified, can be applied, and is what computer programs such as NVivo are designed for.

Some forms of computer-assisted qualitative data analysis software (CAQDAS) are now gaining popularity (Fielding and Lee, 1991; see also the CAQDAS networking project website at www.caqdas.soc.surrey.ac.uk). With qualitative data, the amount of information in even a moderate number of interview transcripts can be overwhelming, and a method of handling such data by computer has advantages. But as with quantitative data, the evaluator will need to consider whether the advantages outweigh the costs of time and effort in learning to use the program effectively. Moreover, time is not usually on the side of the small-scale evaluator. Effective use of qualitative data analysis programs is iterative, going through the data repeatedly a number of times to interpret text and develop explanatory categories. As Silverman (2001: 67) notes, (perhaps in a warning!) 'tapes and transcripts... offer endless opportunities to redefine our categories'.

If the decision is to use computer programs for qualitative data analysis, there are a variety of choices available. One currently finding considerable support from researchers is NVivo, for its flexibility in storing and editing documents and codes, memos and annotations, and organizing and displaying codes in broader interpretive categories. There is a growing number of books on how to use NVivo (and its earlier version Nud*ist). As with SPSS For Windows, the Windows format means that interview transcript files are easily imported, while reports and tables can be readily exported to other writing packages for producing the final report.

Computer programs will not do the analysis for the researcher; they are just tools to manage the information. Analysis still depends on the skill of the researcher in developing codes to apply to text, in generating categories to link codes together for explanation, and in interpreting the information.

Narrative

One objection to the coding approach to qualitative data is that is breaks down the text into small fragments, coded in one or more different ways, so that the larger structure of how people say what they say is lost (Bryman, 2001: 401). Riessman (1993) points out that in interviews, people often include 'stories' in what they say. Plummer (2001: 186) agrees that people use narrative to organize and give meaning to their interactions with the world, and that in representing this to others they are likely to use stories.

Stories are often a way of linking a sequence of events with a moral message. Stories have actors, and plots. Often there is a conflict or complicating action, an evaluation of the significance and meaning of the action, followed by its consequences which may include a resolution (Riessman, 1993: 18, following Labov, 1972). By recognizing these elements of story-telling one may have a better understanding of the structure of what people say, and how they see the world. Plummer (2001: 174) comments that

> The analysis of narratives, stories and biographies allows us to examine the rhetorical devices that social actors use and the way they represent and contextualise their experience and personal knowledge.

Example 5.3   Narrative in understanding need

A student was conducting a needs evaluation of support for hard-of-hearing people on behalf of a local charity which offered social and practical help and advice. In an interview with a hard-of-hearing man and his normal-hearing wife about their experiences, the wife recounted the following 'incident':

> We had one particular incident when we were out.
> I was waiting for Jim,
> No, I'd gone off, Jim was waiting for me in a shopping centre,
> and somebody came up, a young man.
>
> As I was approaching,
> a young man came up to him,
> young, purple hair, studs everywhere, tattoos, everything,
> and he stood behind Jim and said 'Have you got the time mate?'
> and Jim saw him and just turned away.
>
> I could see this young man bristle
> as if to say, 'I see you don't like the look of me',
> and I had to step in and say,
> something I shouldn't really say,
> but I said 'I'm sorry he can't hear you, he's deaf.'
>
> At which point the young man then went, 'I'm sorry,'
> and turned round and they both communicated,
> and Jim told him the time
> and he went away happy.

(Hall and Hall, 2000b)

The story was one complete and unbroken response to the question, 'Do you believe isolation is a big problem if you are deaf or have hearing difficulties?' It has been transcribed word for word from the video-taped interview. But presenting here as a four stanza 'poem' highlights the narrative elements, which were not immediately recognizable in the original transcription.

Riessman (1993: 45) also gives examples of transcription as stanzas to bring out the poetic structure which lends coherence to narratives. Although this example is about one incident of fairly short duration, it contains a strong narrative element, 'recapitulating past experience by matching a verbal sequence of clauses to the sequence of events which (it is inferred) actually occurred' (Labov, 1972: 359). The sequential structure is flagged by the repeated use of the word 'and'.

There is a conflict or complication in the story, which is given as an example of the social problems facing hard-of-hearing people. This complication is given dramatic emphasis by the description of the antagonist as extraordinary in appearance – the hard-of-hearing person has normal eyesight and can be expected to react normally to the 'threat'. The husband's response is taken as rejection. His wife acts to break the conflict by introducing the reason to explain her husband's behaviour, though she feels uneasy about doing this. The explanation is accepted, and the protagonist and the antagonist resolve their differences.

It can be understood as an interesting example of how the social problems of hard-of-hearing people extend to close members of the family, and of the ambivalence of the family member in knowing how to be protective, how to intervene and whether to disclose the partner's disability. Recognizing it as a narrative, with the elements of a story, helps to understand how it is constructed and why it is effective in conveying the meaning of hearing loss to others.

Contrast this with a very different type of response to another open-ended question in the same interview, which generated just a short reply:

INTERVIEWER: Is awareness in the general public getting better?
INTERVIEWEE: Yes, it's much better than it was twenty years ago.

(Hall and Hall, 2000b)

Oral history

A longer form of narrative is provided by auto/biography and oral or life history (Yow, 1994). These can provide interesting and illuminating counterpoints to other methods of data collection, and open up people's understandings of the social worlds in which they live, and the meanings they give to their lives and interactions with others.

Within evaluation research, oral histories can provide useful information about the development of neighbourhoods and communities in which the program is set, acting as a counterpoint to quantitative cross-sectional information from a survey of residents.

Example 5.4   Oral history in a housing survey

In a study for a housing tenants' association investigating residents' views on a possible future move from local council ownership and control to that of a housing association, a student undertook a representative sample survey of residents' opinions. She also conducted an extended unstructured interview with a resident who had lived in the same house on the estate for 70 years.

The interview covered aspects of his life on the estate since he arrived (at the age of four) and comparisons between earlier times and the present. The interview was reported in full in the appendix to the final report, and sections were used to illustrate the changing conditions of housing repair, to show in detail the process of deterioration and decay which the interview sample documented for the present day.

The housing estate was of particular interest through its method of construction, an experimental method using pre-cast concrete developed in the mid-1920s to speed house building after the First World War. At first, the houses were desirable and not that cheap. The interview records:

> I can just remember coming here ... it was only later in conversation with my parents many years later that I realized why we left [former location], simply because there was a garden for me to romp in as a kiddie, instead of dashing out onto the street ... but in those days there was hardly any traffic down the road [here].
>
> So if we came in 1932, those houses were only six years old, and I suppose we were quite happy, but when you think about it, 1926, the wages that were going, these houses were 16 shillings and 6 pence a week which was a lot of money even for a council house.

Problems arising from the form of housing construction only became apparent after the end of the second world war, where rainwater penetration deteriorated the concrete.

> You noticed with these houses that the corners fell off quicker than anything. And they [Council workmen] came along and patched them up, and then they'd come along and patch that bit up so it was a different colour. So I would say it was just after the war where you started to notice – somewhere around the back end of the 1940s – that you started to notice the corners falling off.

The houses are currently declared defective, and the sample survey showed that over 70 per cent of those interviewed thought their houses were in a state of disrepair.

The oral history interview had a number of other things to say about community, neighbourliness, wartime conditions, and contrasts between the present and the past, though these were not so relevant to the main purposes of the study, and so were left for the appendix to the report.

The student also discovered another resident on the housing estate with a similar length of residence, but was unsuccessful in gaining her permission to participate in the oral history. This does show the researcher's dependence upon circumstances and chance encounters for oral and life histories (Plummer, 2001: 133).

Representation in qualitative analysis

The reason for attending to the actual words of the subjects of qualitative research, as in the example above, and for considering the nuances of the ways in which they speak, is to give back to the subjects the initiative which in the past was appropriated by the researcher who alone sought to depict the experiences of others. The dilemma of doing this – that such voices may be discounted in a written text as uneducated or of low status – has already been discussed in this chapter.

However, there is a further issue in whether the researcher can 'let the data speak for themselves'. The 'representational crisis' draws attention to the fact that researchers do not have direct access to the experience of others, that such experience is always mediated by representations in terms of interview talk and written text. When the researcher attempts to present that experience to others, there is a further selection (which may be acknowledged through reflexivity by the author). All information presented in a report has been selected in some way by the researcher, and she or he cannot escape the responsibility for the 'authorial voice' which makes the selection.

Riessman argues that 'the idea of representation brings into view the constructed nature of social scientific work' (Riessman, 1993: 16). She concludes that awareness of the crisis of representation should make researchers 'more conscious, reflective and cautious' about the claims made in research reports. Lincoln and Denzin (1998) reflect that such concerns about how the experiences of others can be authentically presented leads some researchers towards more participatory and collaborative research and evaluation methods, others to liberating and emancipatory investigations by subjects themselves, and others researchers still to becoming 'coauthors in narrative adventures' (Lincoln and Denzin, 1998: 411).

The crisis of representation is further considered in the following chapter on report writing, while reflexivity is the subject for Chapter 7.

Suggestions for further reading

On using SPSS for Windows

Bryman, A. (2001) *Social Research Methods*. Oxford University Press. (Chapter 12).

Bryman, A. & Cramer, D. (2001) *Qualitative Data Analysis with SPSS Release 10 for Windows*. Routledge, London.

Colman, A. & Corston, R. (2002) *A Crash Course in SPSS for Windows*. Blackwell, Oxford.

Field, A. (2000) *Discovering Statistics Using SPSS for Windows*. Sage, London.

Kinnear, P. & Gray, C. (2000) *SPSS for Windows Made Simple*. Psychology Press, Brighton.

Miller, R. et al (2002) *SPSS for Social Scientists*. Palgrave, Basingstoke.

Pallant, J. (2001) *SPSS Survival Manual*. Open University Press, Buckingham.

On using NVivo and Nud*ist

Bazeley, P. & Richards, L. (2000) *The NVivo Qualitative Project Book*. Sage, London.

Bryman, A. (2001) *Social Research Methods*. Oxford University Press. (Chapter 20).

Gahan, C. (1998) *Doing Qualitative Research using QSR Nud.ist*. Sage, London.

Gibbs, G. (2002) *Qualitative Data Analysis: Explorations with NVivo*. Open University Press.

Richards, L. (1999) *Using NVivo in Qualitative Research*. Sage, London.

On statistics for social research

Clegg, F. (1983) *Simple Statistics*. Cambridge University Press.

Fielding, J. and Gilbert, N. (2000) *Understanding Social Statistics*. Sage, London.

Salkind, N. J. (2000) *Statistics for People Who (Think They) Hate Statistics*. Sage, Thousand Oaks, CA.

Walsh, A. (1990) *Statistics for the Social Sciences*. Harper & Row, New York.

CHAPTER 6

Reporting on Evaluation: Communicating to Audiences

Summary

Because evaluation aims both to understand a program and to provide a judgement on it, the findings need to communicate clearly to the audience or audiences who will receive the report and, it is hoped, act on it. This communication can be done orally or in written form. Oral communication is less formal than a written report; it can be used at a formative stage, to provide two-way feedback throughout the evaluation, or to supplement a final report. When negative findings need to be communicated, this feedback is best done orally before being committed to writing.

There are many other forms of expression that can be used in addition to or in preference to the written report, including posters, poetry and drama, which may be particularly appropriate where the aim is empowerment and emancipatory evaluation through stakeholder action.

The main form of communication, however, is the written report. This chapter is designed to help make written communication effective by explaining how a well-written and clearly presented report can be produced. Many of the ideas on content, style and presentation can be applied to any social research report. However, evaluation reporting differs in a crucial way. The evaluation report is envisaged not simply as an end product, but also as an input to a further stage of decision-making or policy formulation, so issues of dissemination must be considered.

Evaluation is designed to be used, and the evaluator has to have in mind how to produce a usable report for the various audiences. The quality of the report is not the sole determinant of whether a study has impact or not, so a deliberate dissemination strategy may encourage wider reception of the findings.

The final report – structure and audiences

There is considerable agreement as to what an evaluation report should look like and what it should contain. Guides and toolkits such as those by Gosling with Edwards (1995) and Rubin (1995) suggest a basic structure as follows, which is similar to the authors' own practice with their students in applied research (Hall and Hall, 1996: 238):

- title page;
- contents list;
- acknowledgements;
- executive summary;
- introduction and background information;
- purpose of evaluation and methods chosen;
- results and findings;
- conclusions;
- recommendations;
- appendices.

The content of these sections will be reviewed in detail later in the chapter. But first the question of the audiences for the report needs to be considered.

In collaborative evaluation, the primary audience is that of program practitioners, where the organization manager in conjunction with staff, volunteers and service users has the responsibility for taking forward action from the findings and recommendations of the report. A secondary audience may be other stakeholders such as funders of the program and residents of the area where the program operates.

Robson (2000) agrees that it is difficult to provide universal rules for the way in which the findings of small-scale evaluations are communicated as consideration of the audience takes precedence:

> The ideas of *audience* and *purpose* are important; who are you seeking to communicate with, and why? There can be multiple audiences and multiple purposes. It is highly likely that one audience will be the sponsor of the evaluation, but key stakeholders including program personnel and, possibly, clients may be others. One purpose will probably be to fulfil the terms of any contract or formal agreement (which may have specified the kind of reporting required). Similarly, undertakings about feedback made to anyone involved should be honoured. Another purpose might be to facilitate implementation of the findings.
>
> (Robson, 2000: 121)

Evaluation with a student input may also have an academic requirement in the report, yet the majority of the intended audience remains non-academic, and this must influence the style and language of the report.

Style and language

Locke *et al.* (1998) identify language used as the major problem facing the non-specialist reader of academic research reports:

> People simply do not understand why reports cannot be written in plain English. For the outsider, reading becomes a problem of translation as well as one of comprehension. The problem is more than mechanical, however, because the impenetrability of specialized language leads to scepticism about the motives of researchers, and, thereby, to a devaluing of results.
>
> (Locke *et al.*, 1998: 3)

Texts which are full of jargon and difficult to read, failing to convince readers that the results are worthwhile, would be fatal for the presentation of an evaluation. Locke *et al.* aim their main criticisms at reports which come from 'investigations motivated by the need to know (basic research)' rather than investigations motivated by 'the need to improve (applied research)'. The latter, including evaluation reports, are likely to be exempt from such criticism because with their focus on the user audience 'they make less use of cryptic shorthand and more use of carefully selected common language' (Locke *et al.*, 1998: 59).

Using language sensitively

It is important for the evaluator to be aware that in the area of
social welfare, groups use language about themselves or their service
users in very specific ways – to avoid stereotyping and disadvan-
tage. It is a good idea to clarify at an early stage what terminology
is acceptable – and this can sometimes differ between groups and
organizations as well as over time. Thus, two evaluation projects
running concurrently with different organizations required the use
of the term 'people with difficulties' in one instance and 'people
with disabilities' in the other. Users of the programs may have
preferred a third term, 'disabled people' (see below).

The main advice on the avoidance of pejorative and prejudicial
language is 'Don't make assumptions' and 'Don't generalize'.
Freeborn explains:

> Of course, groups by definition have a common identity, but too often
> this is presented and described in an oversimplified way. For example,
> referring to people with disabilities as 'the disabled' or 'the handicapped'
> implies that there only exists one homogenous group 'without parti-
> culars or exceptions'. The same happens when someone is called ... 'an
> epileptic' etc. which reduces the person to a medical condition.
> Generalisations are also made when particular life experiences are
> attributed to all disabled people. A common example is when people
> with disabilities are depicted as 'victims' or as 'suffering' from their
> disability. Many disabled people do not suffer from their disability, and
> object to being portrayed as victims.
>
> (Freeborn, 1986: 235)

Categorization as 'the disabled' or 'the elderly' is dehumanizing
and to be avoided. Always use 'people', as in 'disabled people' and
'older people'. Currently, disabled groups in Great Britain prefer
'disabled people' to 'people with disabilities' because this term
better expresses the social model of disability – that people themselves do not inherently have the problems, rather that society is
disabling them through lack of access to public transport, buildings, decent housing and so on. Using the language which disabled
people themselves choose to use, is in turn preferable to accepting
the language of the service providers, where this differs. Choice
of terminology can be part of ensuring that the evaluation has
sensitivity and some recognition of the emancipatory issues
in evaluation, which were discussed in Chapter 4. The British

Sociological Association provides guidance on 'ablist' and 'disablist' language on its website, www.britsoc.org.uk.

Constructing the text

The aim of the evaluation report is to describe the program, to present the findings, and to make recommendations. Under the positivist model of research, the researcher is typically absent from the report as the passive voice is used ('A survey was conducted ...'). Findings are presented as objective facts, and the creation of the text of the report is a technical issue.

However, ethnographers, in particular, now emphasize how the construction of a text is an important part of the research process. Rather than text construction being a 'taken-for-granted', part-of-the-research endeavour, in which findings are reproduced in a fairly straightforward way, it is seen as problematic. Issues of concern include the writer's own part and place in the text, the style of discourse which is used and how evidence is treated. Why do some items get included and some excluded? How much detail is given? How authentic are the 'voices' reproduced, and have they been incorporated into a world view which is not theirs but the writer's own?

Richardson notes:

> I consider writing as a *method of inquiry*, a way of finding out about yourself and your topic. Although we usually think about writing as a mode of 'telling' about the social world, writing is not just a mopping-up activity at the end of a research project. Writing is also a way of 'knowing' – a method of discovery and analysis ... Form and content are inseparable.
>
> (Richardson, 1998: 345)

Richardson argues that it is important to tackle the mechanistic view whereby students are trained to conceptualize writing as 'writing up' rather than as a method of discovery. Such texts are likely to be formulaic and boring, where the 'self' of the researcher is suppressed and where language is homogenized.

This is a particularly important issue for postmodernism and particularly poststructuralism, which emphasize how reality cannot be separated from the discourse which expresses it. Language is central to discourse and Richardson quotes Weedon (1987):

> The centrepiece is language. Language does not 'reflect' social reality, but produces meaning, creates social reality.
>
> (Richardson, 1998: 348–9)

Reason (1998) summarizes the postmodern and poststructuralist perspectives as arguing

> ...that we cannot sensibly speak of raw, lived experience because experience can be accessed only through the discourse or text through which it is expressed, and that there are multiple shifting discourses, all determined through the social context.
>
> (Reason, 1998: 281)

However, Reason is dismissive of the postmodern/poststructuralist view that experience cannot be directly known. Instead he argues that our discourse deeply influences our experience, but that we can approach experience more directly through 'cycles of action and reflection' – for instance through the types of experiential and reflective learning models developed in Chapter 7.

Reason concludes that

> Participative, action-oriented approaches to inquiry work to move beyond this overintellectualized approach and to ground knowing and action literally in the body of experience.
>
> (Reason, 1998: 282)

This argument makes the construction of an evaluation report text an achievable ideal for an evaluator writing from the 'body of experience'. However, it is worth noting that as a participatory researcher, Reason is keen to move beyond such formal reporting to include such 'data' as storytelling and metaphor, and even song, dance and theatre as 'expressive forms of knowing'.

This discussion on text construction relates back to the representational crisis mentioned at the end of Chapter 5 and looks ahead to the issues of reflection and reflexivity in Chapter 7. At this stage, the key point is to raise awareness that report writing is far from a 'natural' or unproblematic process, but one which requires thought about how language is to be used, and about how evidence is to be treated.

A second issue to be noted at this stage is that awareness of text construction issues means the nature of the evidence in the evaluation report is problematic – should it consist of different accounts which have been combined to produce quantitative data, perhaps enhanced by 'typical' or 'illustrative' quotations, or should there be a way of adequately representing the individual experience of participants? Third, there is the interesting question about whether the 'personal' (the evaluator's views and feelings), is to be expressly and openly treated, or whether it is to vanish within the text as a 'given'.

The way these questions are answered depends on the evaluation paradigm within which the evaluator is working. So for Guba and Lincoln (1989: 8), for instance, report writing is part of the social construction process which characterizes research and evaluation. Findings, as outcomes of evaluation, are not descriptions of some objective reality 'out there' but represent meaningful constructions formed by individual actors and groups to make sense of the situations in which they find themselves, and the evaluator is included in this interactive process. It follows, therefore, that the 'report cannot simply be *about* the evaluand and its context, but must enable readers to see *how the constructors make sense of it, and why*' (Guba and Lincoln, 1989: 223).

Guba and Lincoln recommend a report of a case-study should in turn enable the reader to further reconstruct the joint construction. To do this, the writers argue that the report must exhibit certain qualities which derive from their Fourth Generation (constructivist) model of evaluation, but are not unique to such a model. These qualities are categorized into a fourfold classification which comprise the following:

- *Axiomatic criteria*, by which we mean that the study must resonate with the axiomatic assumptions (the basic belief system) that underlie its guiding paradigm. It must, for example, reflect multiple rather than single realities.
- *Rhetorical criteria*, by which we mean those relating to form and structure, including (following Zeller, 1987) unity, overall organization, simplicity or clarity, and craftsmanship. The latter is characterized in a case study that displays power and elegance, creativity, openness, independence, commitment, courage, and egalitarianism.
- *Action criteria*, by which we mean the ability of the case study to evoke and facilitate action on the part of readers. These criteria include fairness, educativeness, and actionability or empowerment.

- *Application or transferability criteria*, by which we mean the extent to which the case study facilitates the drawing of inferences by the reader which may apply in his or her own context or situation. These criteria include the presence of thick description, provision of vicarious experience, metaphoric power, and personal reconstructability.

(Guba and Lincoln, 1989: 224)

This sets a heavy agenda, particularly for small-scale local evaluation, in its requirements for 'power and elegance', for example, or for 'commitment, courage and egalitarianism', although these may be worthwhile aims to aspire to. More contentious is the constructivist paradigm itself, with its requirement for 'personal reconstructability' and the eschewing of all forms of 'facts'. Yet however evaluators position themselves in relation to these debates, they can still find in such criteria some thoughtful pointers to the way their own position will influence their report. Will it include 'thick description' (Geertz, 1973) as well-summarized feedback and will it reflect multiple rather than single realities in the way voices of subjects are heard?

Several of these themes are developed by Kushner (2000) in his plea to 'personalize' evaluation. He argues the voice of participants is often missing in large-scale program evaluation which focuses on outcomes and impacts, and so participants' own experiences are devalued in the discourse of reporting on a program at an abstract and generalized level. Commenting on this, he notes:

Our tendency to focus on the image of social organization as represented in programs has led to the loss of the image of the individual. What might program evaluation look like and involve were we to invert the conventional relationship between the individual and the program – that is, rather than document the program and 'read' the lives of individuals in that context; to document the lives and work of people and to use that as context within which to 'read' the significance and meaning of programs?

(Kushner, 2000: 11)

Nevertheless, Kushner is careful to explain that he is not arguing for a focus on the individual to replace the principal focus on the social program as the proper context for analysis and critique. 'We should seek to understand programs through experience – not displace them with it.'

Understanding more of the individual lives and values of program participants leads to understanding more about the program, the context in which it operates, and its potential. Of particular concern to evaluation is how such individuals form judgements about the program and whether these judgements are prejudiced or favoured by their relationship to power.

Stake argues that 'case content evolves in the act of writing itself' (Stake, 1998: 93). While it may be desirable to tell all, this is impossible to achieve, and choices are made by the researcher as writer. Asking how others can learn from case-study reports through reading them, Stake argues that researchers need to recognize that they pass on some of their knowledge of the meaning of events and relationships observed, but that readers too will bring to the report their own knowledge and experiences, reconstructing it in the light of their own circumstances. Transfer of knowledge is thus problematic, and the advice may be for the researcher to provide 'sufficient descriptive narrative so that readers can vicariously experience these happenings and draw their own conclusions' (Stake, 1998: 100).

An extended example of a student working through some of these problems in moving from the generation of data through analysis to writing the report is given in Example 6.1.

Example 6.1

A postgraduate student reflected as follows on the conflicts she felt about editing out information and detail to produce the report.

At the end of the data collection phase I had ended up with tape recordings of twenty-five individual interviews (each of which lasted between thirty and sixty minutes), and three one-hour focus groups. I now remembered a comment made by a researcher I had worked with in the past, who preferred note taking to audio-taping interviews because he resented interviewing interviews, and then having to interview his tape recorder!

I was advised by my supervisor to use a data matrix. However as with previous research I thought it would be difficult to transfer my rich data into this type of structure. In so doing the uniqueness and richness of my research would be fragmented and lost. I can sympathise with Denise Farran's experiences and feelings concerning her analysis of data collected for a British Sports Council research project. Denise describes her concern with fragmentation. During the coding process a 'sociological vanishing trick' occurs, debasing the uniqueness of the individual response (Farran, 1990: 100).

I wanted to capture the 'essence' of my interviews and focus groups. Therefore I worked my way through the beginnings of the analysis stage, by transcribing meticulously, although I produced 'summary' rather than word-for-word transcriptions. I produced 'horizontal' analyses. I would record the main themes and issues, and interesting quotes from interviewees, for each of my schedule questions. This method worked very well, although it was difficult to handle so much detailed information when it came to writing up my report and keeping within the required word count.

I employed two methods in my effort to capture some of my original data in the client report. Firstly I quoted 'typical' responses to each of the questions asked. For example the following extract (taken from my Full Report) typifies what my volunteers thought to be 'good' about volunteering:

> Other people focused more upon the day to day experience of working within their projects. Four respondents valued 'being involved' and 'feeling part of a team'; one of these making the further point that in her team there was no feeling of 'them and us'. Another four in the sample saw the importance of 'good reactions' or 'appreciation' or 'trust' gained from service users.

This tactic added some variety and interest but did not fully address the problem of fragmentation.

Secondly, I tried to make sure that all shades of opinion were included in my analysis, and subsequently in the writing up of the final report. However too much detailed data is not only difficult to actually incorporate into a client report, but as my supervisor commented, makes the reader unable to 'see the wood for the trees' (Payler, 2000).

Presenting criticisms

Chapter 3 dealt at some length with how to present critical findings, and proposed various strategies. It was suggested that it was important to give the program organization manager the opportunity to make a response. Oral feedback makes it possible for findings to be discussed at an interim stage, and is less blunt than a black-and-white printed version hitting the manager's desk at the end of a project, where it could be construed as an 'ambush'. With oral feedback, the organizational response to the findings can be incorporated into the final written report in discussion and conclusions – or when recommendations are being considered. However, the clear duty of the evaluator is to be honest in presenting the results, including justified criticism. If successful outcomes and good practice have been found, this can be the context within which more critical findings can be presented. This gives the report balance, and also enables the reader to more readily accept that the negative results are 'fair comment'.

Readers are also likely to spot problem areas without them being overemphasized. Most of us are sensitive to criticism, and at first reading the negative findings of a report (even if they are minor) may well assume a significance beyond their importance. Collaborative and participatory evaluation does require tact, though fearlessness is also necessary if evaluators have uncovered practices which do need to be improved urgently.

Example 6.2 Quality of life evaluation

Two students were asked to conduct a 'quality of life' evaluation of services provided by an agency that placed adults with special needs with carers in a family-like situation. Altogether 11 carers and 19 service users were interviewed using semi-structured interviews accompanied by observations, based on an assessment schedule.

The students found that overall the program was extremely successful, with most service users reporting high levels of satisfaction with the way the service was operating, and with the supportive family environment within which they were currently living. However, one student interviewed two people who were not receiving the standard of care that was required by the program. She was very upset about conditions within which they were living, which were dirty and unpleasant.

Following a suggestion from the supervisor, the student (with her companion) raised the issue in a general feedback session with the manager, who subsequently decided that the matter had been exaggerated and described the student's views as 'value judgements'. But in her reflective account, the student reviewed her actions:

> In writing the report, however, we included the facts of what had been observed but were extremely careful to avoid value laden judgements. We also wished to record the data sensitively so that the negative issues did not detract from the many good points we had observed.

There was an interesting outcome to this report. Although the program manager dismissed the criticisms, the report was later read by the organization manager, the unit head, and immediate action was taken. Two neglected

and isolated individuals were subsequently rehoused and their lives sub-
stantially improved as a result. Straightforward reporting of the negative
facts, embedded in the context of positive findings, had had the desired
effect – the evaluation was judged worthy of being taken seriously and further
investigation by the organization showed that the student's judgement was
indeed fair and accurate.

Beginning the written report

Beginning the task of writing is universally admitted to be a
breakthrough experience. It is not unknown for researchers to continue fieldwork to delay the awful necessity of committing findings
to paper. Weiss (1998: 295) recognizes the anxiety that can be
engendered by this new stage of the research process. Finally,
however, the line has to be drawn and analysis of the data moved
towards dissemination. The deadline of a written report can be
what propels the committal of ideas and the shaping of evidence to
paper, and the writing task begins.

'The secret to writing is to keep on writing' (Weiss, 1998: 295).
So good advice to getting the writing process underway is just to
start, and not aim for perfection in the first draft. Get ideas down.
Work within a structure, use headings and remember the audience.
Aim for clarity – if the writing is not clear then maybe the ideas
are not clear either, and need to be rethought. So know what you
want to say – and say it. Don't worry about order – text can be cut
and pasted.

Accept that the report will have to be rewritten – maybe more
than once. Editing and re-editing is an essential part of the process
of report writing for a public audience. Other readers – academic
supervisor, colleagues, friends – can all feedback on whether the
report makes sense, and whether it flows.

At this point, it will be apparent that the stages of research do
not follow a neat linear pattern from design to fieldwork to analysis
to report writing. Research designs may have had to be revisited,
perhaps if some of the intended samples were unavailable. With
qualitative research in particular, the generation of data can change
the shape of the ideas which occur to the researcher to follow
up (this can grandly be referred to as 'emerging theory'). With
quantitative research also, there may be the opportunity to test a
fresh set of hypotheses with the addition of new sample groups.

Writing the report, in turn, will sometimes produce the need to reanalyse data, by returning to evidence to explore further possibilities which may have been overlooked, or to amplify a presentation which may have become too succinct, and missed out the 'voices' of those whose views have been gathered. In extreme cases, and if time permits, extra fieldwork may be required to fill a glaring gap.

Structure of the written report

As indicated at the start of this chapter, an outline structure is essential, to guide the reader through the orderly presentation of materials in appropriate sections. Different audiences will have different interests, some being more interested in the technical aspects of the evaluation, others being mostly interested in a short and punchy summary of the main findings. Some will look for evidence that that the evaluation has been done competently and fairly while others will look to recognize what they know about the program in the report.

So the amount of detail in the different sections might vary with the intended audience, but the structure is one that has a general application. A few of the suggested guidelines are aimed at students whose reports have academic criteria to satisfy, but most are relevant to small-scale evaluators generally.

Title

A good title will encourage readers to take up the report. It should be descriptive of the contents, and should also indicate the aim of the study, who conducted the evaluation and their affiliation, and the date of the report.

Contents list

Not only does a list of contents enable the reader quickly to locate any particular section they may be interested in; it also shows that care has been taken in putting the report together, and that all the pages are numbered and in order.

Acknowledgements

Acknowledgements and thanks are appropriate, given that a number of people will have participated in the study, and should be recognized. This might include not only the project management (though it is always politic to give them an early mention, particularly if they are the key recipients of a report which it is hoped they will implement) but also the other stakeholders in the organization, including service users and volunteers. It is also a good idea to thank an academic supervisor who has contributed support to the project – and who may be marking it! Supervisors do not usually get much recognition, and even some modest thanks is always appreciated by these underrated people.

This short section also offers the opportunity for a sense of the personal, however slight, to emerge – right at the start of a document, which will otherwise be written in more neutral and formal language. For instance, students have briefly thanked various people for cups of tea and coffee, shoulders to cry on and free taxi services – acknowledgements which paid professional evaluators would not be likely to make. A photograph to accompany this section can complete the page, and remind the reader who the evaluators were, perhaps showing them outside a program organization with a key worker, manager or stakeholder who is willing to give consent for their photograph to be used in the report.

Executive summary

The executive summary at the start of the report is a distinctive feature, marking a difference from academic writing. It is the distillation of the research process – aims, methods, main findings and recommendations – and may be the only part that some readers see. Think about it a lot, and write it last:

> By and large, the report for evaluation sponsors should be addressed directly to the questions underlying the evaluation. Give the main findings up front. An evaluation is not a mystery story where the reader is kept guessing until the denouement at the end.
>
> (Weiss, 1998: 295)

This is a good point. Program managers may be reading with some anxiety to see if they are going to be the body with the dagger in the back. The main findings should emphasize the most important points, good or bad, about the program, and with key recommendations also included. This summary is aimed at busy readers – who may not have the time to read any further, so it needs to be clear, precise and well expressed. The summary should ideally cover two pages maximum, sentences should be short and pointed and key issues can be bulleted.

In the following example, a team of three students present their findings from an evaluation of a volunteer scheme at a hospital, which compared the experiences of two groups of volunteers.

Example 6.3   Benington Hospital Nurse Volunteers study

Executive summary
Research was conducted into the Benington Hospital Volunteer Scheme (BHVS) to evaluate the benefits of volunteering for student nurses. Several areas were considered, namely the reasons that people had for entering volunteering, their experiences as volunteers and what they felt they had gained whilst being on the wards at the Hospital.

Fifteen ex-volunteer student nurses took part in in-depth interviews to ascertain the benefits of the Volunteer Scheme. A further six non-volunteer student nurses were interviewed for comparative purposes. Three members of the senior managerial staff were also interviewed to explore their views and to provide an overall context for the evaluation.

The benefits for the Volunteer Scheme for potential nurses were identified by both the ex-volunteers and senior staff as:

• Allowing the development of interpersonal skills through interacting with patients, relatives and nurses.
• Providing a general insight into nursing through the observation of nurses at work.
• Providing the experience of working within a hospital ward.

Furthermore, half of the ex-volunteers also stated that they had encountered particular experiences whilst volunteering, such as seeing blood, that they had found to be beneficial for their nurse training. However, whilst the benefits of the Scheme were clear, they were felt to be limited by the inevitably restricted nature of the volunteers' role, particularly by their working within one ward or department.

The Scheme was highly regarded, leaving few areas for improvement. However, several recommendations are suggested

• The Scheme may benefit from accredited training, possibly through N.V.Q. or other skills-related programmes.
• Volunteers may benefit from working on several wards, particularly those volunteers who are considering entering nursing.

- As none of the six non-volunteer student nurses had heard of the Volunteer Scheme, this may indicate the need to promote the Scheme across the region, particularly to places where nurses are recruited.
- On a national level, it is recommended that the Scheme be seen as a model for a national strategy to ensure people have the opportunity to carry out volunteering before entering nurse training.

(Arnold *et al.*, 2000)

Introduction and background information

A short summary of an *organization's activities* provides a necessary context within which to situate the particular program which is being evaluated. A thumbnail history of the organization may be appropriate, along with an indication of its ethos – all of which can be supplied from the organization's own literature, publicity materials, annual reports or website. It is important to reference such material and use quotations – it is, after all, a way of indicating that this is how the organization perceives itself.

Of course, the people within the organization know these things already (perhaps some more than others). But it is still useful to do this because:

- It demonstrates the evaluator's knowledge of the formal set-up of the organization.
- It presents an outsider's view of the main features of the organization.
- It can be helpful for other readers with less knowledge of the organization, if the report is more widely disseminated.

The way the organization and program is funded is also relevant. *Funding criteria* determine what a program can aim to do and it is important that the evaluator is able to show awareness of the constraints within which the program operates. These constraints also determine the aims and objectives of the project being evaluated – the standards against which the evaluator will be reviewing evidence, drawing conclusions and making recommendations.

Information about the program also needs to be supplied. For instance, Weiss notes:

Short sections can describe the participants and staff in the program. Readers will understand outcomes much more readily if they know how many people participated, what their characteristics were, how long they

received program service, how many dropped out (and if it is known, why they dropped out), and anything else that is relevant to outcomes.
(Weiss, 1998: 298)

Finally, the *origins of the evaluation activity* may also be of importance to the reader – who decided that an evaluation was needed, how the contact with the evaluator was made, and what the initial expectations were of these potential participants in this study? The initial contacts and discussions leading up to the negotiation of a research agreement can be summarized here.

Purpose of evaluation and methods chosen

The *aims of the evaluation* should be written about with reference to the *evaluation questions* and the *research design*. Any subsequent changes to the aims should also be noted – sometimes access to particular samples has proved impossible, or another line of enquiry has opened up. For instance, in the hospital volunteers study (Example 6.3), it was originally intended to interview ten student nurses who had been volunteers and ten who had not, but in the event the non-volunteering nurses proved difficult to access, and the volunteering nurses proved not only accessible, but provided a variety of experience which it was important to capture. Therefore the focus of the research was altered to concentrate on the ex-volunteers and how they had benefited from the scheme.

When the report is intended for a practitioner audience, discussion of *research methods* can be concise – readers are more interested in *what* has been found than in the *way* it was found. However, a short discussion of research methods is essential. It provides credibility for the findings – proof that it was conducted in a professional way, using appropriate techniques (some references are useful) and in accordance with ethical guidelines or standards.

Where sensitive issues were covered or vulnerable service users interviewed, some indication of how this was done should be given. Readers will also want to know how *samples* were arrived at – in terms both of numbers and of content – and the anonymity of participants should be stressed. In cases where there has been difficulty in gaining access to 'hard-to-reach' groups, the methods chosen (for example snowball sampling) and their limitations should be explained, as this may help the organization if it intends to follow up the information at a later date.

If it is felt necessary to expand on the methods, or provide details of statistical techniques used in analysis, then these can be supplied in the appendices. Where the evaluation was conducted according to an ethos of partnering and collaboration, then this should be followed through in the way the report is presented. Accessible information on research methods will help the organization develop its understanding of research and evaluation – providing increased capacity through knowledge.

Results and findings

This part of the report is a key one, expanding and providing evidence for the points made in the executive summary. The text should be presented in terms of *thematic sections* which have clear headings and sub-headings. These group the issues covered in the interviews, questionnaires or observations so that the themes become apparent. As indicated in Chapter 5 a blow-by-blow account of every question asked, in the order of asking, will not help in telling the interesting story of what has been found. Instead, the report needs to prioritize the most important findings, and link them together, comparing and contrasting information from different groups or from the use of different methods.

Presenting numerical information in *tables or graphs* is usually a good form of communication, but it should also include a written *explanation* or discussion underneath. This is because tables and graphs summarize information and it is the writer's job to make sense of the statistics and highlight items of interest rather than leave all the work to the reader (who may be unfamiliar with the way the data is presented). Relevant *quotations* can also be included which further reveal the depth of data, and give an indication of individual responses which would otherwise be lost were only quantified data displayed.

Example 6.4 Benington Hospital Volunteers Scheme: findings

Areas of volunteering beneficial for nurse training
As all the volunteers had entered the scheme with the belief that it would benefit their nurse training, it was important to find out exactly which *areas* of volunteering they felt were beneficial. Table 6.1 shows that

Table 6.1   Areas of volunteering beneficial for nurse training

Q: Which areas of volunteering did you find the most beneficial for your nurse training?	Number of responses
Experiencing a ward environment	10
Seeing hospital equipment in use	7
Teamwork	6
Observing nurses	6
Being around patients	6
None in particular	2
Total number of responses	37
Total sample	15

two-thirds (10) of the ex-volunteers felt that experiencing a ward environment was most beneficial for their nurse training.

The total number of responses (37) was particularly high because one-third (5) of the ex-volunteer student nurses highlighted a number of areas which they found to be beneficial to their nurse training. For instance, for one respondent there were many benefits:

> Probably most of it; working with people, talking to patients, communicating and being on a ward – generally the whole picture.

Another felt that

> All these skills have prepared me for nurse training: watching staff approach different people, dealing with personal things and feeling comfortable with the environment.

(Arnold *et al.*, 2000)

Conclusions and recommendations

These two sections flow naturally together in practice, and some reports tend to produce a mixture of conclusions and recommendations, with evidence and interpretation and ideas for possible response by the organization intermixed. However, there are strong arguments for separating conclusions from recommendations. *Conclusions* look back over the evidence and review its stronger and weaker points. *Recommendations* look forward to future action, and present the evaluator's judgement on what should be done next. Not all reports require recommendations, as some would see this as part of the policy-makers' responsibility, with the evaluator just producing the evidence. But organizations may expect the evaluator to make recommendations, where the view of an additional person knowledgeable about the program, and without a personal axe to grind, may be helpful in initiating change (Weiss, 1998: 280–1).

Conclusions

The main conclusions from the study will already have been presented in the executive summary. Further discussion of these findings should be provided along with items which were not prioritized for the summary. This is a section in which the organization will be particularly interested, and negative as well as positive conclusions need to be presented. It is important to ensure that feedback is provided on the issues which the organization originally wanted the study to cover, as well as any new issues which may have emerged.

This section also allows the evaluator to comment. It can be made clear that although the views are the evaluator's, they are based on the evidence gathered. The task is not simply one of summarizing factual information but of interpreting the information. Weiss suggests that the report may also include interpretations from groups with whom the evaluator disagreed as an alternative perspective. In addition,

> [W]hatever limitations exist to the study's conclusions (short time period, low response rate, loss of cases, etc.) deserve an important place in the report as well.
>
> (Weiss, 1998: 299)

The conclusions are also an appropriate place for reflection on how the organization's aims or mission have led to the program, and how the outcomes of the program may have implications for the mission itself. Such consideration and interpretation provides an important link with the final section on recommendations for change.

Example 6.5 Conclusions on advocacy

One student project on an advocacy program concluded as follows:

> The first statement of the Basic Principles and Values (of the Mission Statement) states that the advocate will support people to speak for themselves. It also states that people who find it hard to speak for

themselves should be helped to get their voices heard. It is apparent from the client evaluation that this objective is not always met, therefore it has been recommended that it is considered again in advocate training sessions.

(Sullivan, 1998)

Recommendations

Recommendations are a decisive issue and yet Patton admits that he finds this issue is the hardest part of the process of teaching evaluation. The guidelines he gives to his student evaluators include the following:

Allow time to do a good job on recommendations, time to develop recommendations collaboratively with stakeholders, and time to pilot-test recommendations for clarity, understandability, practicality, utility, and meaningfulness.

(Patton, 1990: 326)

Students commonly worry that they are not qualified to make recommendations to people who are more experienced and expert in their field than they are. Recommendations are likely to have come from those who commented on the program – and these suggestions can be presented as feedback rather than as the evaluator's own views. However, if the process of interpretation outlined above is followed, then there is also room for the evaluator to make recommendations which are thoughtful and based on observation and evidence. Where student evaluations are conducted as part of an ongoing program of university–community partnerships, there may be a bank of knowledge available from previous evaluation research studies that can offer comparisons.

Recommendations should be practical, however, and be relevant for the resources to which the organization has access. If implementation would require further funding, then this needs to be noted along with any suggestions on how this could be secured. To miss out the resource implications is to produce a report which may appear to the reader naive and so risk them dismissing valuable findings.

The section on recommendations is likely to be improved if there has been good contact between the evaluator and the organization throughout the study – particularly with the key individuals who will be influential in acting on the final report. Discussion will help clarify whether there is a response which needs to be incorporated in the recommendations. It might be, for instance, that a proposed recommendation is one that the organization may have already considered – and rejected – in the past. If this is known, the report might further suggest why the time is now ripe for change, or why program stakeholders still want the change, or even raise the question of whether new funding opportunities could be found to make the recommendation practical.

Appendices

Appendices should be used to contain information which is referenced within the body of the report, including the evaluation agreement, questionnaires, interview schedules and any other research instruments. This is to show how the information has been generated, and it may also be of practical help in future studies. Tables, graphs and statistical information can also be supplied for the reader who wishes to dig deeper into the evidence which has been collected – including secondary as well as primary data. A sample interview transcript, with identifying details removed, is sometimes useful in permitting the reader to check how the information has been edited down in the analysis.

Sometimes it is useful to supply findings which have been cut from the main report because they detracted from the clarity of the argument being presented. The findings may be of interest to particular stakeholders, however, and the detail may be helpful if the report is to be used to support specific funding applications to develop a particular aspect of the service.

Presentation

Report presentation is very different from academic text presentation. To develop an appropriate style, it is helpful to analyse government reports and publications, or company and voluntary sector annual reports, in terms of style and layout. Contemporary and attractive ways of communicating are worth looking out for.

Some general guidelines are to break up text by the use of short paragraphs. Headings and sub-headings should be used to focus on the particular theme being discussed. This helps the report writer in organizing material coherently and effectively and directs the reader to the key themes.

With word processing, it is now possible to produce attractive and well-designed reports quite simply. Features such as changes of font between headings and text, indenting for emphasis, use of bullet points, numbering and colour all help to break up text, provide variety and make it more manageable to the reader – but this needs to be done well to an overall design, and not overdone, when it can be too irritating.

Visual data can be presented using graphs and tables, and photographs can help in bringing a report to life. But place them carefully on the page with an indication in the text of what these images are contributing to the evaluation 'story'.

For people who 'need to design pages but have no background or formal training in design', Williams (1994) provides a very usable introduction to the basic principles of:

- *Proximity*: similar items are placed together and clearly separated from dissimilar.
- *Alignment*: nothing is placed arbitrarily on a page, so tables and photos line up with text.
- *Repetition*: page design, headers, footers, numbering and so on are consistent throughout.
- *Contrast*: big contrast between different elements, such as headings and text, adds visual interest.

Once these design principles have been noted, they can be observed in government and organization reports, to a greater or lesser degree, and to a greater or lesser effect. So, see which reporting styles seem most pleasing or effective, and adapt the principles to the evaluation report.

Length

The length of an evaluation report is one of the first issues students raise, but unlike essays, reports need to be as long as they need to be. They should aim to be concise, to get to the point and to summarize the kind of information needed by busy readers (usually program staff). Writing of large-scale program evaluation, Weiss states:

> A comprehensive report is usually required by the study sponsor and is of interest to program managers. But it may be overkill for other

audiences. Staff, clients, policy makers, and the public are likely to toss aside a big heavy document that tells them too much, however brightly it is written.

(Weiss, 1998: 295)

Being concise can pose problems. The amount of data can be considerable, particularly if tape recordings of interviews have been made which have yielded what the evaluator regards as essential 'rich data'.

Example 6.6   The long and the short report

One student produced an immense amount of information, meticulously presented, but overwhelming for the reader to take in. The student justified her approach on the basis of good ethnographic practice and was reluctant to accept that this might need to be sacrificed for good evaluation practice – the production of a readable and digestible report.

In the event, a compromise was reached with the supervisor, and the student was willing to produce two reports – a short report for the university, which met the word length requirements and a longer report for the manager who might be interested in the detail. At the supervisor's suggestion, the organization received both reports so that the manager could decide which report was more useful – and for which members of the organization.

Example 6.6 shows that word length and therefore content are part of a tradeoff between what the evaluator wants to present but, crucially, what the audience needs to hear. A third element of the tradeoff is when the evaluation is for assessment, and a student has to conform with regulations on word length, with the additional audience of the examiners. The student needs to demonstrate to the examiners that they have produced a report based on substantial research, analysis and understanding. The reflective report, to be discussed in the next chapter, is useful in making this transparent.

Making the report accessible to readers and writers with dyslexia

The authors have been involved in a special project to make community based research accessible to people with dyslexia. In the published report it was noted that dyslexia is a syndrome affecting around 10 per cent of the population. Dyslexia is associated with a number of characteristics, the best known of which concerns literacy problems (which vary in severity). It also has positive aspects such as 'being highly aware of the environment, being highly intuitive and insightful, being creative and having good verbal skills' (Lockley *et al.*, 2000: 16).

These positive aspects mean that evaluators with dyslexia have a lot to offer, although problems with writing, planning and organization of time may be difficult, and for students, supervisors may have to work out strategies of support. Working in a group, for instance, can help resolve such problems, because a group can share tasks according to the members' strengths as well as offer support.

One student quoted in the dyslexia study, noted in an interview that:

> My report went in late. Because I was working on my own, I just got so stressed out about it all, I believe anyone working alone would have been in a similar situation but my dyslexia did not help matters – if you were in a group you could say 'I need help' but I had nowhere to take that – I would in the future, suggest anyone with dyslexia should work in a group.
>
> (Lockley *et al.*, 2000: 17)

As far as presentation of materials is concerned, the British Dyslexia Association (BDA, 2003) makes a number of suggestions (which can be accessed from their website). These are consistent with the design principles mentioned above, and include:

1. ragged right edges (left justification);
2. numbered bullet points rather than continuous prose;
3. boxed and indented sections to break up the text;
4. plenty of headings;
5. emboldening;
6. no capitalization or underlining;
7. coloured paper;
8. twelve-point or larger sans-serif fonts, with Arial preferred.

Dissemination

After the report has been produced, what next? Owen (1999: 128) sees one possibility as the evaluator changing role to becoming a consultant to help the organization put the evaluation into practice.

Where the opportunity for extended involvement with the specific program practitioners is not realistic, Weiss (1998: 307) suggests that presentations at professional conferences and workshops can extend the reach of the evaluation, even though much of the specific detail may be lost.

Reaching wider policy audiences means networking, some form of publication within the public domain where it may be picked up with internet searches, and use of intermediaries such as the media. For collaborative evaluation, this is not something the evaluator can achieve on their own but requires careful consultation with the partners in the evaluation.

CHAPTER 7

Reflecting on Evaluation

Summary

Reflection is an important part of the evaluation process. It allows the researcher to stand back and consider how the research is proceeding, and what personal as well as methodological issues need to be dealt with. Reflection is an aid to clear and critical thinking, and should improve the depth of the study which is produced. Reflection enables researchers to describe and analyse their feelings – and to take appropriate action as a result. All of this should contribute to maintaining, developing and focusing the study as it proceeds. A final reflective account may be valuable if the evaluation is part of an assessed program – and there may be scope for including some elements of this in the report to the organization.

Reflection is also required of the recipient and reader of the report. For dissemination purposes, if evaluation is concerned with research which can be implemented, then an understanding of how the evaluation process connects with the 'reflective practitioner' is going to be highly relevant. Usage does not automatically arise from reading a report, after all, but from reflecting upon the findings and their implications for organizational practice and resources before taking action. The reader will also have to deal with feelings as part of this process – a common response to negative findings is defensiveness. If a report is to be used, then it is helpful to consider how such a reaction might be avoided, or at least tempered.

Inevitably there is some overlap with the other chapters in the book as reflection is involved in all stages of evaluation – in formulating the project, in data collection and analysis, in resolving ethical dilemmas and in report writing. There is, however, value in discussing reflective issues together in one section – to deepen the understanding of what is involved and why reflection is such an important element of the model of evaluation being proposed in this book.

This chapter is really concerned with applying ideas about reflective practice to evaluation rather than with exploring the literature on reflection as an end in itself. Nevertheless, it is worth knowing that there is a substantial and well-developed body of work in this area which has come from diverse sources, such as psychology, education, sociology and philosophy. This literature has evolved mainly in response to issues of professional development and training, but it is now being extended to teaching and learning in higher education, to placements in the community and workplace, and to fieldwork research. An understanding of the debates and issues will clarify what reflection can (and cannot) contribute to producing effective evaluation.

THINKING ABOUT REFLEXIVITY AND REFLECTION

Reflection is thinking with a purpose or outcome, so all evaluation is a form of reflection: activities are thought about, and written about with the express purpose of deciding whether they have value or not, whether they need to be improved and how development might be devised. For the evaluator as researcher, reflection also has a purpose in increasing awareness of the 'self' in conducting research and constructing order on the data both in the analysis and the production of the report text. This allows for self-evaluation – for evaluators to be critically aware of the limitations of their work as well as the strengths. Reflection also provides an opportunity to consider not only what the evaluation can achieve in changing organisational activity but also to consider the wider context of the organization – and its role within societal structures. Here connection can be made with the approach of such writers as Habermas and critical researchers, including feminist writers, and a *reflexive* account can provide the opportunity to contextualize the findings both theoretically and in terms of policy and practice issues facing the organization.

Reflexivity

Habermas's interest in reflection came from a commitment to the ideals of empowerment and political emancipation, to truth, freedom and justice (Morrison, 1995). Habermas is particularly known for his advocacy of knowledge as potentially *emancipatory*, provided it is critical and questions oppressive structures. Knowledge which is instrumental, designed to gain control over the environment through the scientific empirical tradition, objectifies the world as a 'given'. By its impersonal nature and focus on technique, instrumental knowledge is alienative: it separates knowledge from the self and contributes to the oppressive use of knowledge in society.

In contrast, hermeneutics stresses the importance of understanding the meanings of human behaviour and communications through the interpretation of such knowledge by human beings, and this has historically been the task of the arts and humanities, and the social sciences. However, if knowledge is to be emancipatory, then it requires more than understanding or interpretation – it has to be a way of transforming society, and this is seen as the true task of the social sciences. Reflexivity is an essential part of producing emancipatory knowledge, because the acquisition of knowledge is aimed at producing a transformation not just of the social or world situation but of the self, or the personal. How knowledge is produced is as important as what is produced – both should be concerned with challenging oppression and creating a just and equal society. So, for Habermas,

> while the basic method of the social sciences can be interpretive, critical or evaluative processes of enquiry are necessary to create a critique that can foster self-understanding and the questioning of the processes by which interpretive inquiry can be subject to distortion.
>
> (Moon, 2000: 14)

Such ideas have been developed in *critical social research* which aims to dig beneath the surface of social relations, to the oppressive social structures which underlie them (for example emancipatory disabled research aims to locate disability problems not within the limitations of individuals but within societies which construct obstacles for disabled people).

Research is also produced through such relationships, and is therefore itself subject to structures which need to be challenged.

For critical researchers, the way research is conducted should be based on the recognition that there is dialogue, rather than a one-way transfer of information from an informant to a researcher. Reflexivity needs to express the opposition of critical research to a conventionally hierarchically structured relationship between the researcher and the researched which

> presupposes a one-way flow of information which leaves the respondent in exactly the same position after having shared knowledge and ignores the self-reflective process that the imparting of information involves... the direct corollary of the self-reflection is the inevitable engagement in dialogue where information is required or perspectives need to be discussed. The involvement of the researcher in this real dialogue involves her/him in the critical process.
>
> (Harvey, 1990: 12)

Position of the researcher

Researcher involvement also requires awareness of '*positionality*' – of the positioning of the researcher within a wider structure of how they come to understand knowledge as well as how they come to produce it (Rhoads, 1997: 17). Such reflexivity is often expressed by the researcher in a personal account which situates the research or evaluation in such epistemological issues, an account which forms part of the transformative nature of the work.

So Jenny Morris, for instance, explains her positioning as a feminist writer and disability researcher:

> My life as a feminist began with my recognition that women are excluded from the public sphere, ghettoised into the private world of the family, our standpoint excluded from cultural representations. When I became disabled I also realised that the public world does not take individual, particular needs into account... so people whose physical characteristics mean that they require help of some kind (whether this need is actually created by the physical environment or not) have no place in the public world.
>
> (Morris, 1992: 158)

Skeggs, however, points out that being 'positioned by structural relations (sexuality, gender, race, class) does not necessarily give access to ways of knowing (although some standpoint theorists would argue that it helps)' (Skeggs, 2002: 356). She quotes Haraway:

> Location is not a listing of adjectives or assigning of labels such as race, sex and class. Location is not the concrete to the abstract of decontextualisation. Location is the always partial, always finite, always fraught play of foreground and background. Text and context, that constitutes critical inquiry.
>
> (Haraway, 1997: 37)

Positioning which is used to give authority to the author's writing has raised many issues about the rights of authors to represent the voices of those they have studied, most of whom are less powerful than academic researchers, and who have been used as resources in the writing.

However, such inequality of power does not mean that the research necessarily lacks morality, and the argument can be made that without the writing (and use of resources the writer has), the voice of the researched would not be heard at all. Skeggs argues that rather than see reflexivity as reliant on a concept of the self, it should be about research methods and practice. Key issues in her reflection on her own research were not the recounting her own biography ('telling the self') but the attention to feminist concerns, to

> power relationships, attention to the representation of research participants and attention to issues such as ethics, reciprocity and responsibility.
>
> (2002: 367)

McKie, writing of her experience of evaluation, notes a further issue which the restriction of reflexivity to the self neglects:

> As researchers we may locate ourselves in terms of gender, race, class and status in relation to others. Yet we cannot anticipate how those involved in the research and evaluation may perceive the role authority and ultimately the power of the evaluator.
>
> (2002: 267)

For McKie, a reflexive approach was, therefore, one which encouraged participants to take an active part in the monitoring, reflection, draft stages and discussions. In this case, reflexivity was seen as an aspect of participation and as part of an action research methodology.

In relation to the small-scale evaluation model, elements of these reflexive approaches can be usefully developed. It is valuable for students to understand and clarify their value position, and to find a method of conducting research with which they are comfortable, intellectually, politically and emotionally. Evaluation can be designed to produce change which has emancipatory aspects, while awareness of evaluator involvement means eschewing an 'instrumental' or positivist model for one where the relationship between researcher and researched is an important issue.

Reflection

The literature on reflection, coming from a different tradition, is more concerned with how the self experiences learning processes. There are current debates about the value of *experiential learning* (such as learning through the experience of conducting an applied research project or an evaluation study). There are a number of key writers quoted in the literature as the essential sources of discussion about reflection – including John Dewey, Donald Schön and David Kolb.

Dewey was concerned with elucidating educational processes, with seeing learning as a wholehearted affair, linking emotions and intellect (Eyler and Giles, 1999: 8). For those developing a pedagogy for experiential learning, such as Schön, due reference is made to Dewey:

> In education for the fine arts, we find people learning to design, perform, and produce by engaging in design, performance, and production. Everything is practicum ... Emphasis is placed on *learning by doing*, which John Dewey described long ago as the 'primary or initial subject matter'. Recognition of the natural course of development ... always sets out with situations which involve learning by doing.
>
> (Schön, 1983: 16)

Schön (1983, 1987) studied *reflective practitioners* in a variety of disciplines such as engineering, architecture and town planning and found increasing evidence that professional groups were recognizing the need to be critically aware of how they actually practice, with a positivist model of theory application being replaced by one stressing the role of intuition, experience and feeling. This followed from what he terms a 'crisis of confidence in the professions', when professionals recognized that dealing with uncertainty and conflict required being able to understand (theorize about) their judgements or 'artistry' in a coherent and constructive way. Such practitioners had to transform theorizing from reflecting on past experience (*reflection on action*), to being able to improvise during the course of intervention (*reflection in action*) in an

> *action-present* – a period of time, variable with the context, during which we can still make a difference to the situation at hand – our thinking serves to reshape what we are doing while we are doing it.
>
> (Schön, 1987: 26)

Reflection in action is the process of social actors thinking about what they are doing, as the work progresses. For Schön, reflection in action provides a way of opening thought up to possibilities which might otherwise be blocked off. It helps produce flexibility in finding solutions when objectives are unclear or problematic, and so produces improvisation which is thoughtful rather than reactive. In addition, Schein (1999) notes the importance of recognizing the place of emotions in the decisions we take – we are not, after all, wholly rational beings. Emotional reaction is, in fact, often unrecognized and denied and its role in producing action is therefore ignored. For instance, sometimes we can react negatively to an issue because we feel threatened by it. The *feeling* of being threatened has produced the judgement, but we may not recognize this and believe we have moved directly from observation to judgement.

Schein proposes a reflective model with four stages – observation, reaction, judgement and intervention (ORJI) which pays due attention to such feelings. As Coghlan and Brannick explain:

> By identifying and attending to feelings (a) as initial reactions and (b) as influencing judgements, you may learn to deal with them and choose whether or not to act on them. Denial of feelings frequently means acting on them without adverting to the fact that you are acting on them.
>
> (2001: 34)

Reflection on action tends to be seen as a post hoc activity – 'stop and think' when the action is no longer current. Moon (2000: 44) points out, there is some ambiguity about this in Schön's writings, because all reflection is actually part of a continuing cycle. Even final-stage reflection – presented in an evaluation report or in a

separate reflective account – will be part of ongoing action, both for
the organization and for the evaluator who may use such reflection
for further activity, as part of subsequent career decisions, for
instance. Such reflection should arguably include political, social
and ethical issues to enable such professional development to
continue.

Reflection on action is also a valuable way of dealing with feelings, as it enables the researcher to analyse conflicts and difficulties
when emotions have settled, through a more distanced perspective.
For student evaluators, a reflective report is also an appropriate
place to discuss contextual, theoretical and methodological issues
as well as a place to discuss changes in personal learning and skills.

Schön's ideas have been developed by other professionals –
Gould, for instance, sees such reflective learning as a way of understanding how 'social workers make judgements and decisions in
domains which are uncertain and complex' (Gould, 1996: 1). He
argues that this reflective analysis is particularly important at
present, when employers are seeking to gain control over social
work education and impose a competency-based approach to
learning which would lead to severe educational reductionism and
downgrade critical analysis as an educational objective.

Experiential learning

Kolb has also developed theories about *experiential learning* using a
structural model derived from research in psychology, philosophy
and physiology, based on the works of Dewey, Lewin and Piaget.
Learning is defined as 'the process whereby knowledge is created
through the transformation of experience' (Kolb, 1984: 39). Kolb
has developed a four-stage cycle of:

* concrete experience;
* observation and reflection;
* abstract conceptualization and generalization;
* active experimentation.

These stages can be represented as forming a circular process,
each stage leading to the next, and so back to the beginning again.
Cowan (1998), who draws upon Schön's work, has adapted Kolb's
model, using slightly different terms for the four stages, but

essentially agreeing on the order and process involved. Cowan uses the verbs

- experience,
- reflect,
- generalize and
- test

to indicate his four stages. He views the cycle as an iterative process that can be repeated many times. Experience is reflected upon, generalized knowledge is acquired, and new actions are taken which form the basis for further reflection and analysis (Hall and Hall, 2000a).

Arguably, the process of experiential learning should contribute to producing a report which is more focused, in that decisions have been consciously thought through as the study proceeded, and ideas tested out. Reflection in action is particularly important in helping the evaluator understand and respond to feelings about the research, or emerging insights into the power relationship within which the work is situated. Reflection on action is valuable in developing critical insights into the evaluation process and in helping to judge what has been most successful or problematic. It also helps the evaluator develop professionally – to be able to move on, taking those skills into the next assignment.

DEVELOPING REFLEXIVITY AND REFLECTION IN EVALUATION PRACTICE

Both reflexivity and reflection can be aided through keeping a *research diary or journal*, a tradition long associated with ethnographic researchers in particular. This account is similar in many respects to a *learning log*, which is used in experiential learning programs for students to record actions and reflections. Such recording can contribute to producing good evaluation through *reflection in action*.

A reflective overview after the study is completed, *reflection on action*, can provide context for the findings, and can be produced as a separate *reflective account*. For students for whom the evaluation is part of their degree studies, this can form one element of their assessment. Discussion of issues of reflexivity in research practice can also be included in this account.

Research diary

Research diaries enable researchers to track the developments and decisions which occur in their research, to record their feelings and jot down ideas about conceptual insights and developing theory (reflection in action). Diaries also help reflection on action, because they provide a written record which can be consulted after the work is completed which will add to the accuracy of the account and provide an overview of the 'career' of the project.

For the evaluator, the structure of the diary is likely to relate to the model of evaluation that is being used – when the model is based on partnership, then the views of all the participants in the work are considered, not just the views of the program supervisor or manager. The entries should cover the activity which has happened, as well as any relationship issues which might have caused problems (or successes) and items to be thought through for the evaluation to progress. The evaluator's own role needs to be considered and feelings should certainly be recorded.

Emergent concepts too can be noted at the time, as this will make analysis clearer and will also provide a record of how theory has developed during the course of the study. In addition, reflexive issues can be discussed – such as how the structure within which the study is being produced is affecting relationships and knowledge.

Structure

Diaries can be free-form, but some structure is helpful, particularly when entries are being reviewed. For instance, the diary could have a simple format of three columns:

Date   Activity   Reflection

This has the advantage of being straightforward and relatively easy to complete (although it misses out an action phase – the outcome of the reflection).

To illustrate this, extracts from a student's diary are provided below. For this student, the diary was a way of recording some of the hassles in interviewing as well as a way of expressing feelings. In all the extracts which follow, care has been taken to remove or alter identifiable information, and consent from the students for publication has been granted.

Example 7.1   Diary: the family centre

Date	Activity	Reflection
30/11	Interview	My first interview. I'm not sure about the interview schedule, but I won't know until I try it on my first victim! Had to ring the Project to inform them I was interviewing and left name and address with a friend in case I went missing. The interview went OK, it took place in her home. I thought it was a bit short, but that may be how they all pan out. The respondent appeared a little nervous, but I hope I reassured her and tried to put her at ease. She has a [disabled] son who is very challenging and she was telling me how difficult it was since the Ferndown Centre had closed. I really felt for her, she's on her own and there's not much around for her since the closure. She said she enjoyed dropping in and chatting. I thought I might receive a negative response about the closure of the centre, which I did. Her answers were a bit brief but there was enough information to be going on with...
6/12	Interviews	Moved home over the weekend so a bit all over the place, with 3 interviews to do! First person was service user from outside the area. I was surprised by her responses. She had a lot to say, but all of them positive about the project moving. I think I was hoping all the responses would correlate, so it was easier, oh well the best laid plans! Second interview was in the church hall, with the Officer there. That interview lasted 40 minutes the longest so far. She had a lot to say, from the perspective of a worker during the move and as a user of

Date	Activity	Reflection
		services now. She thought the move was wrong, but contributed some interesting anecdotes and information. Feeling more relaxed about the whole interviewing process, and more in control. As I'm interviewing, more issues and questions pop into my head and the situation surrounding the closure is beginning to clarify. The third interview was with a worker at the project who was also an ex-volunteer and a local resident. I interviewed her in her home. She was very angry about the whole issue, and was very forthcoming with her views, despite being employed by the Project. She said she didn't mind her name being used either. At the moment, my respondents are weighted towards the relocation being a negative. I am collecting some really good data ...
23/01	Interview	Went to home of mum of 5 [I'd arranged to meet], but no reply. Waited a few minutes, but no show. Couldn't wait round so left it. Spoke to Anne in the office later in the day and she said that the mum of 5 had been held up at the school. If I get time I'll interview her. Not too upset though. Tutor said I need to be looking at starting my draft report. The thought of it is filling me with dread. I feel I want to go on holiday ...
21/02	Transcribing	Started transcribing, forgot how long winded and boring it is, it's taken me hours just to do one tape ...
27th March–3rd April	Analysis and writing	Started moving myself a bit now, it appears to be coming together. Things haven't appeared clear until now, just before the end. Themes are becoming apparent and I feel more confident in my writing and evaluating ...

(Anderson, 2002)

This simple diary structure could be developed by subdividing the reflective section, using Mezirow's model of reflection based on three categories, *content*, *process* and *premise*. Coghlan and Brannick summarize these as follows:

> *Content* reflection is where you think about the issues, what is happening, etc. *Process* reflection is where you think about strategies, procedures and how things are being done. *Premise* reflection is where you critique underlying assumptions and perspectives. All three forms of reflection are critical.
>
> (2001: 19)

Example 7.1 concentrated mainly on *process* issues, particularly the interview experiences. An example of *content* reflection is in the following extract. This postgraduate student was evaluating the services provided by a small neighbourhood organization which gives support to families of young people who have been accused or convicted of criminal offences. Part of her remit was to interview other agencies involved in dealing with young offenders. The extract shows her growing awareness of the structural issues defining the content of work with such families.

Example 7.2   Diary: the family support group

April 5th
Interview with police officer
This was an interesting interview, where I felt, at times, that the interviewee was being 'guarded' in what they said because of the fact that their employer is the Police. However, they did express some interesting ideas, and one of their theories relating to what factors may stop young people from offending was particularly interesting. This perspective differed in some respect to that of the two colleagues previously interviewed. [The respondent] was clearly *as aware* of the *victim* as of the *young person* who committed the offence. This seemed to relate back to their previous role as a regular police officer, as well as to the fact that they now have a remit to support the victim as well as the person who has carried out the offence.

Interview with 'Involve' member of staff
This interview was a very different experience to interviewing a person from the statutory sector. 'Involve' is a national voluntary organisation, and the focus of its work is to assist families that are under pressure. During the interview it came across that there is much more scope to work in an imaginative (autonomous?) way in the voluntary sector than there is in statutory organisations... Clearly the [statutory authority] is bound by the legislative framework of the Crime and Disorder Act 1998 that places all those working

within the youth justice system under a *statutory duty* to have regard to the principal aim of preventing offending by children and young people... The local authority, in co-operation with other agencies, has a *duty*... to produce a youth justice plan, stating how such services are to be provided and funded. 'Involve' is in a position of being able to respond to / be led by the needs of the local community. Preventing young people from offending may in part be a community need, but it is also driven by a political agenda.

(Molesworth, 2003)

Example 7.3   Diary: drug user treatment agency

5th February
Had supervision with John. This proved both useful and reassuring. We decided that it would be a good idea for me to contact the managers of other agencies in the area that use [the treatment] to see how they compare. They will have different client groups and also will have been trained by Brian – which will allow me to ask about the training they received. I told John that an issue that has arisen out of the data collected so far was that of expertise in delivering the treatment. There does seem to be a difference in the way treatments are administered and in the views and understandings of the volunteers. John thought it could be interesting to pursue this line of questioning in the interviews... He also thought it would be a good idea for me to examine the records to work out the proportion of clients who don't return for further treatments. Since the people I will speak to are those who *do* return, it would be useful to have some idea of the number of those who don't.

I left feeling as though I am on the right track with the research, although I do feel daunted about the amount of work I need to do...

Phoned [manager] this afternoon and updated him on the progress so far. He seemed pleased and it was good to establish contact with him – I was worried he might think I had given up on it as I hadn't seen or spoken to him for some time. I shall resume interview transcribing tomorrow – it is as time consuming as everybody says.

(Foster, 2003)

The third example (Example 7.3) is of *premise* reflection, or critiquing underlying assumptions and perspectives. This postgraduate student was evaluating how service users had experienced a pioneering treatment to help people successfully withdraw from drug usage. Following a supervision session with her tutor, John, she decided to widen her research to help gain a different perspective on the treatment from that being offered by her interviews within the organization.

The structure of the diary could also be extended to include a category which indicates what the outcome of an activity was – or what further action is needed. In the next example, a postgraduate student records the initial stages of setting up her project and adds a reflective section. She was conducting an evaluation of a program working with abusive men, which was organized by a women's group.

Example 7.4   Diary: women against abuse group

Date	Action	Outcome
24.01.02	Rang MW to confirm that she had received documents. This confirmed and MW advised she was happy with the documents. She pointed out that group sessions run on Wednesday and not Tuesday. I noted this. Confirmed meeting still okay for the 29th.	Advised MW looking forward to meeting with her next week.
29.01.02	Attended meeting with MW and KR of WAAG and MT to further discuss research agreement and research brief.	Notes of meeting written up (see Appendix). Need to contact MW on Friday 1 February as shown in meeting notes.

Reflection/personal:
Meeting very productive, so productive in fact my proposed research plan changed completely. No questionnaires. Definitely happy with this. Although not sure interviews with men only are enough. The program is run after all for the benefit of the abused women too. Think their stories need to be heard to corroborate anything the men might say about changes in their behaviour. Also need something to support/validate the usefulness or not of programs like WAAG (need more reading). Actually happier with new plan – seems more manageable.

Discussion now over and need to get down to the actual work. Quite anxious about the next few weeks and very aware of the importance of the project to Maureen in particular. Think I will feel much better once I have met the men next week at their WGP group session. Feel that I need to be myself but am very conscious that I need to gain their trust. I believe I can only be myself as I will be working with them for some time, so little point in trying to be anything else. Very anxious that they won't actually like me or trust me and am still worrying about what to wear! Just got to be myself and hope for the best.

(Sadler, 2003)

This diary format uses categories similar to those of Cowan's learning model – experience, reflect, generalize, test. If Cowan's categories were applied this would produce yet another way of recording diary information, in four main sections:

Date/Activity   Reflection   Concepts   Response

A practical word of caution, whatever system is used, is to keep the diary simple, otherwise it will become so laborious to complete that it may simply get avoided altogether, and that New Year Diary syndrome will kick in! Experience is that diaries are very individual – they need to fit with the needs of the researcher, and fulfil their therapeutic function of letting feelings 'hang out'. Holly (1984) notes that

> diary writing is interpretive, descriptive, on multiple dimensions, unstructured, sometimes factual and often all of these ... it is not easy to separate thoughts from feelings from facts.
>
> (Quoted in Bell, 1999: 150)

So, the evaluator as researcher needs to experiment with the structure and find the one which suits them personally (which may be a stream of consciousness, but written with awareness of the issues raised in this section).

There is one further consideration with diaries – and that is the audience. Even if the first audience is the writer, it is likely that there are other audiences in the background – this might include the examiner or tutor if the diary is required as part of assessment (at its basic level, a proof of the work completed). This will clearly affect the language and content of the diary. Even if the audience is not so explicit, there is often a 'virtual audience' beyond themselves that diarists are writing for, be it peers or posterity.

Reflective account

For students, a reflective account may be required for assessment, and will therefore be structured according to the academic criteria of their department. A suggested format is presented here, of a report whose audience is mainly private rather than public, restricted to the examiners, and not for the client organization. This reflective account stands alongside the client evaluation report, and both reports together constitute the 'dissertation' which is presented for assessment.

The reflective account is where contextual issues can be pursued, and these can be developed theoretically in ways which may not be of interest to the organization directly. It offers the opportunity to consider issues which arose during the fieldwork, and to develop analysis which is wider than the brief agreed with the organization. The account provides an opportunity to discuss the 'messiness' of real life research, which is often portrayed in a 'hygienic' form in textbooks and to provide *reflection on action* using the diaries as a source for comment. Finally, this account permits the researcher to reflect on personal learning and development, and to consider the career and life implications of the personal and social skills which have developed.

The reflective report should draw upon the research diary, including quotations from the diary as part of the content. The report can contain a discussion of all the issues so far covered in this chapter, and in the rest of the book; however, for clarity, a summary of such a report, with examples, is presented below. For coherence, the examples used have been largely taken from one study – the Family Centre Project.

Suggested format of a reflective account

- Context
- Theory
- Methodology
    Research design
    Role relationships and reflexivity
    Ethics
- Personal reflection
    Skills
    Would I do anything differently?
- References
- Appendices

Context

Context for the evaluation may be provided from material about the organization or about the wider environment within which the organization operates. Context can cover the issues related to the service users, the development of services to meet these needs and legislative and policy changes which affect the provision of services. Discussion can also be directed to current media issues, if

---

Example 7.5   Context: Family Centre project

The framework in which my research has been carried out is the change in philosophy by a national charity... Its emphasis has now changed [from providing services to families] to focusing on specific target issues through research and campaigning in order to raise awareness to influence government policy.... Three centre-based projects have been closed, resulting in staff redundancies and the loss of services to the communities they serve. The changes nationally by The Family Society have had far reaching implications on the local Community Development Project, its role, its service provision and the way it relates to the community it worked with. The Project found the whole process difficult to manage as the team did not support the move [into new premises], as it would adversely affect the community it worked with.

(Anderson, 2002)

Commenting on the move, the student evaluator added interview material which it would not have been appropriate to include in her report, but which really highlighted the intensity of feeling of staff:

[There was a loss of leadership at the crucial time of the move from the Ferndown Centre into] what has been described by one of the team as a 'big swanky building'... The worker summed it up: 'So we moved into this building and we left these poor bastards with no services and we should have left them with some services provided here before we left.'

(Anderson, 2002)

---

the research has dealt with a topical issue, and might explore stereotyping or moral panics.

As with the background section of the evaluation report (see Chapter 6), sources of information for context can be provided by the organization itself, either at the local or national level. Web-based materials can be extremely helpful, and the national organizational websites often provide useful links. As small scale-evaluation is necessarily locally based and finely focused, the object of this section is to set the organization into a wider context which helps make sense of the issues.

Another way to develop context is to treat the organization as a case-study, which exemplifies a certain key theme or issue. A collection of eight case-studies drawn from postgraduate research projects (Scott *et al.*, 2000), produced the following list of issues (each exemplified by one voluntary agency) – *infrastructure, values and identity, social entrepreneurs, stakeholders, managerialism, strategic planning, networking, external agendas.* The contextual analysis of 'London Ethnic Support Services', for instance, concentrated on managerialism and concluded:

> New public management approaches can improve organisational practice and service delivery, but they can also have deleterious consequences for voluntary organisations. New management systems, for example, can fragment organisational structure. Vertical demarcation is introduced between different tasks and areas of activity; horizontal demarcation is inserted between different levels of responsibility and power. Tighter individual management can mean looser individual commitment and the eventual development of a 'jobsworth' culture of bureaucracy and buck-passing. Such a loss of commitment and flexibility is not just a practical problem within voluntary organisations; it is a blow to their fundamental ethos – and once lost may not be easy to reclaim.
>
> (Scott *et al.*, 2000: 59)

Theory

A reflective report is the place to introduce relevant theoretical issues, and when reports are for assessment, it is the opportunity to show how the student is connecting learning in the classroom with the situated learning of the evaluation placement. Complex theoretical discussions can be disentangled through looking at specific applications of theory to an organization's activities. This also allows for analysis of how the organization's theorizing about its role (through its mission statement, for instance) actually matches up to the analysis by the evaluator of organizational practice.

Example 7.6 Theory: Family Centre project

The trust and strong relationship the community has with the project appears to have gone. Local people feel let down by the Project, which has led to less community participation and growing disillusionment about their power in the decision-making process... This has affected the delivery of one of the key aims of the Project, that of community capacity building, or social capital. Political scientist, Robert Putnam, describes social capital as:

The features of social life-networks, norms and trust – that enables participants to act together more effectively to pursue shared objectives.

> Social capital, in short, refers to social connections and the attendant norms and trust.
>
> (Putnam, 1995: 664–5)
>
> ...The area the Project operates in is one of the poorest in [the region], with associated problems such as high unemployment and low quality housing and poor educational attainment. Despite this, prior to relocation, there was a strong sense of social cohesion and trust within the community, trust being an important part in creating and maintaining the social capital within a community... Unless the balance is tipped more in favour of the community, the negative effects of this change in work practice will continue to adversely affect the social capital of the area,
>
> The more people work together, the more social capital is produced, and the less people work together, the more community stocks of social capital will deplete. (Putnam, 1995)
>
> (Anderson, 2002)

Theoretical discussion should also allow the student to critique the theory, in the light of the experience they have been researching. In the example above, for instance, social capital locally was reduced because of decisions made about funding by a nationally based organization, which was experiencing severe reductions in its income, and was being forced to use a community centre which had been created through a partnership of private and statutory agencies, including the local council. The Family Centre charity was therefore powerless in the decision to move to a 'swanky' building and forced to disrupt the community ties and relationships built up over many years. By concentrating on local networks and on the building of community trust, the application of social capital theory here could be criticized for minimizing the wider economic realities and structures within which local organizations work.

Methodology

Research design
It is unlikely that research will follow the original proposal without alterations or compromises being made. This will be reported in the evaluation report as part of the research methods section, but reflection also allows for an inside account of these changes and their reasons, and for consideration of the effects such changes make to the eventual evaluation which is produced. Sometimes

---

Example 7.7 Research design: Family Centre project

From the moment I met the client organization to negotiate my research agreement, I noted in my research diary that things felt 'as clear as mud'...I felt like a rabbit trapped in the headlights and noted that 'I am excited at the prospect of the project, but slightly apprehensive, as it feels too large and there are areas that need clarification.'

Eventually to my relief, the brief was narrowed and I was supplied with a list of 24 key informants that I could interview, in order to evaluate the Project's change in work practice.

(Anderson, 2002)

---

there are difficulties of access to the sample needed to provide the information the organization wants, and sometimes the organization is not clear about what the evaluation should cover. Evaluation goals tend to develop as the study continues to be negotiated.

The reflective report enables the researcher to show how the 'sanitized' version of the research presented in the evaluation report differed from the 'messy reality', and the initiative shown in revising research plans can also be demonstrated. Changes from design to practice should not be regarded as failures to be justified – they are part and parcel of what researching in the real world means. As Buchanan *et al.* note, 'the practice of field research is the art of the possible' (1988: 55).

How the researcher has experienced using the research methods should also be included, whether these are quantitative or qualitative. The departure from textbook recommendations is, again, almost inevitable, and the reflective account is the place to describe, explain and discuss decisions which had to be made.

Role relationships and reflexivity
De Laine notes that in fieldwork, 'role is not some fixed entity, negotiated in a one-off contract prior to fieldwork, like the role one fills when recruiting for paid employment' (de Laine, 2000: 95). Rather, roles differ according to researcher involvement, the degree of closeness or distance created with subjects, the state of harmony or tension in the group or community and the unrest or conflict which can arise when a group has an agenda different from that of the researcher. When time for evaluation is limited, it may be difficult to develop any close relationship with participants, and distance may therefore be inevitable, with implications for the way

data are gathered, and the depth of understanding the researcher can achieve.

Example 7.8   Role relationships: Family Centre project

In a perfect world, I would have wanted to build up some form of relationship with the children prior to interviewing, possibly observing them during Morris dancing. Greig and Taylor describe observing children as 'watching children individually, in relationships, in contexts, and asking: what do they see, what do they feel, what do they think, what do they do?' (Greig and Taylor, 1999: 83). I didn't have this luxury, which definitely affected the responses I received.

(Anderson, 2002)

However, having time to develop closer role relationships can also produce problems. An example is given in Chapter 4 where students have entered a setting as unobtrusively as possible, and participated with the service users to gain their confidence, then became identified with a volunteering role rather than a research role.

Reflecting on roles inevitably means engaging with the debates on reflexivity. The relationship between researcher and researched has traditionally been one based on unequal power, a relationship which critical researchers, and feminists in particular, have been keen to challenge. Sensitivity to the relationship, however defined, can be expressed in a reflective account. In the Family Centre project, the student had to conduct one-off interviews, rather than develop a long-term relationship with participants.

Example 7.9   Reflexivity: Family Centre project

I did not experience many problems during the course of my interviews. I wanted to establish a rapport with the person through open and honest exchange, which Maykut and Moorhouse describe as 'essential to indwelling and to achieving useful study outcomes' (Maykut and Moorhouse, 1994: 71), rather than being viewed as the person holding the power. It can be difficult eliciting information from a person you haven't met before. However, I think I managed to achieve this through a friendly yet respectful approach to each respondent, guaranteeing their confidentiality at all times.

(Anderson, 2002)

Reflexivity also involves considering the role of the researcher in producing the analytical framework for the report. This can relate to the *reflection in action* which is essential for the qualitative research process. *Reflection on action* – at the end of the process – can also help make sense of how the data were produced and conceptualized.

Example 7.10 Reflexivity: Family Centre project

The main failing of myself was having presumptions about the outcome of the findings at the beginning of the process. I found myself too eager to try and identify emerging themes before I had finished all my interviews ... Once I had stopped worrying so much about the outcome, I allowed themes to emerge, many of which did not make sense until the final days of writing the report.

(Anderson, 2002)

Ethics

Items for inclusion in this section have been discussed fully in Chapter 3, and include such basic issues as confidentiality of information and anonymity of informants. How was the consent of participants agreed? Was this procedure satisfactory or were there any problems? If the research was conducted with minors, how was parental consent given?

Ethical dilemmas go beyond these basic considerations and they also need to be discussed. Reference should be made to the diary where dilemmas are recorded in their rawness. The reflective account allows students to discuss the problem, and its resolution – in terms of the decision taken and its implications.

For the student evaluating the program working with abusive men (whose diary example was considered above), there was a sense of conflict between the rapport she developed with her respondents in interviews, and her feeling that she should be feeling more critical of them. Her diary entry noted her confused feelings as the research was being conducted.

This diary record became the basis of an ethical discussion in the reflective report, where the student was able to expand on how her feminist commitment produced methodological strategies appropriate to her research. Although she talks about being 'objective' in her diary, a feminist commitment means eschewing a detached

Example 7.11   Ethics: program with abusive men

Interviews so far: found myself enjoying the company of the men. Have laughed and shared their feelings with them. Seemed natural at the time. Listening back to the tapes started to question where my position in the field of domestic violence is. When started project assumed fiercely critical of the men and their behaviour but during my involvement with the group and in the interviews these feelings haven't evolved. I have got to know the men for who they are, and although they are abusive men, they are also people. Questioned own behaviour; should I take a more distant stance, should I be sharing a joke, sharing experiences, would other feminist researchers be appalled at my involvement/thoughts? Not sure where I am with any of this. One the one hand it seems important to have the trust and co-operation of the men while on the other, feel I should be more distant, although I'm not at the moment. Definitely a dilemma.

Not interviewing any women regarding their experiences of domestic violence, perhaps making it more difficult to grasp the affect of these men's behaviour on women, perhaps need to interview women to gain insight into this. Perhaps need to feel shocked and appalled.

So far don't feel shocked or weighed down. Men open about their behaviour though not specific. At the end of the day their specific behaviour is not what I'm investigating but feel this information could possible change my interaction with them, possibly less objective.

(Sadler, 2003)

stance and admitting to and dealing with emotions and feelings – which is what she was actually doing. This did not automatically or easily resolve issues in the field as her attitude to the male service users changed from being 'critical' to seeing them 'as people'.

When a report contains information critical of a program, the reflective report is the place to discuss what action was taken – whether through verbal feedback, tactful presentation of information in the evaluation report, incorporation of organizational response to the criticisms – or the decision to simply 'tell it as it is'. The reflective report can summarize the feelings which the student had to deal with, as well as the action taken, and whether *reflection in action* helped to produce a satisfactory outcome.

Personal reflection: skills and moving on
In the instance referred to in Example 7.12, the student recognized that the completion of an evaluation project had brought personal benefits which she expressed as empowerment and a

---

Example 7.12   Personal skills: Family Centre project

I enjoyed the role of researcher, as it allowed me to participate within an organisation, in a role I am unused to. I could come and go, listen, contribute, but knew that at the end of the process, that I was only a temporary fixture ... I feel empowered by the whole experience, and it has given me the motivation to seek employment in a different area to the one I already work in.

(Anderson, 2002)

---

clearer sense of direction for her future career. Other students have also mentioned that they have felt satisfaction in completing work to benefit others:

> The idea that something I have produced will help such a worthwhile organisation ... is something that fills me with pride and satisfaction. I cannot believe I have achieved such a feat, no other assignment in my academic career has produced such a feeling of pride within me. This alone has made all the hard work and stress worthwhile as well as boosting my self confidence dramatically.
>
> (Whitworth, 1999)

These comments are consistent with a survey of 30 former students, who had completed evaluation projects between two and nine years prior to being interviewed. They largely felt that their learning experience had been positive, and that it had had long-term benefits for them. Academic skills were mentioned including research skills (particularly in interviewing) and report writing, along with more general skills such as time management, problem-solving and the development of self-confidence. Personal satisfaction at doing a 'worthwhile' or 'useful' project was noted by about a quarter, while twelve mentioned that 'the people' in the program were the highlight of the experience. Two-thirds of the sample felt the project had influenced their career direction, and there was evidence that they felt their evaluation skills were still being applied and developed in their current work place (Hall and Hall, 2002).

One postgraduate student concluded his reflective account with an exuberant summary of what the experience had meant to him:

> For me the project has been the most fun packed roller coaster ride I have ever encountered. I know I have just done one project; I know that I'm just 'starting out', but I've learned so much from this experience.

Learned 'doing it' really, truly, madly and deeply isn't like anything
I expected, and I want to do it again. Please.

(Chamberlain, 1999)

Assessing the process of evaluation: the role of reflection

So far the reflective report has been considered as an outcome of
reflection at the conclusion of an evaluation. But can reflection also
be attested during the process of evaluation, and on that process?
For student evaluators, *reflection in action* can be formalized when
the process of evaluation is assessed not through a single report
but through a portfolio of documents. These can include the
evaluation agreement and brief along with a summary which
reflects on any changes which occurred during the negotiation of
these documents. An interim report can be included in the portfolio, again with an accompanying reflective discussion on progress to date, issues which need to be resolved and emerging
results which need further research.

As part of assessment, students can also be required to conduct
an oral presentation on their projects to the rest of the student
body. This can be helpful in establishing progress and developing
new themes and directions in the light of discussion. A reflective
account of the oral presentation can also be included in the portfolio. Where the evaluation spans the academic year, it can be
helpful to have presentations in both the first and the second
semesters, which allow students to report back and reflect on very
different stages of the evaluation. The second presentation is also
likely to reveal the student's growth in confidence as they develop
their knowledge of the specific field or organization they have
been evaluating. Such presentations are felt by students to be
helpful in focusing ideas, and in preparing material for the interim
and final program evaluation reports.

Reflection within the evaluation report?

Is there a role for reflection in an evaluation report? Traditionally,
the answer to this would be 'no'. Organizations with busy managers
are likely to want succinct reports, concentrating on issues where

they have specifically requested feedback. Academic research is more likely to be the place for in-depth self-reflection by the researcher on the research process and their role in producing the text.

It can be argued that readers of 'real life' evaluation research would prefer to concentrate on findings, with reference to their validity and reliability, and with anything personal relating to the researcher being kept very short. This is particularly true when reflection is seen as the 'telling of the self' of the evaluator. Such reflection could be criticized as a self-indulgent and narcissistic exercise which diverts attention away from the voices of the research participants, the voices which the program stakeholders want to hear.

However, it is possible to include something of the evaluator's reflection in the report, to indicate in a foreword what the evaluator's expectations were, or in a postscript, provide a personal note on what has been learned. For social welfare organizations, such reflection (admittedly short) is acceptable and often welcomed, as it connects with practitioner learning. For small organizations, working through networks and personal contacts, such statements are particularly appropriate – they show that the human side of their work has had resonance with the researcher. As a foreword or postscript (or perhaps, at greater length, an appendix), such statements can be kept separate from the formality of the report and from the findings which are intended to be implemented by the organization.

Reflection is also incorporated within the report, when it is concerned with research methodology, ethical issues and problems and changes that occurred. Again, such discussion should be kept short, because methodology *per se* is not likely to be of interest to the reader. It is included for two reasons. First, because it reminds the reader that the findings are the outcome of methodological decisions – and can be validated (or criticized) on the basis of the information given. Second, reflection on research methods issues can help with 'capacity building' for the reader – the evaluation may be the first time research has been commissioned, so the whole experience has been one of learning. Information in the report which helps explain the direction the research took, or how the report became shaped, is likely to help the reader understand it better, and be more likely to accept its results, even if they are not entirely what was expected.

CHAPTER 8

Case-studies of Small-Scale Evaluation

Summary

The two case studies in this chapter are reports of student projects with non-profit organizations. They supplement the argument of the previous chapters by giving an idea of the kind of projects that have been conducted using the model of small-scale evaluation, and of how the research has been used.

The information is derived from the students' client and reflexive reports, and follow-up interviews with the students and the organization managers conducted by the authors, and is used with permission. The names of the organizations have been changed. Only extracts from the reports are reproduced.

Charington Hostel

Charington Hostel is part of an evangelical Christian housing association, providing accommodation for single people aged 16–30 years, who have been referred from agencies providing emergency shelter. According to the mission statement, its aims are not to offer a specifically religious service but 'to provide accommodation that is secure, safe within a caring environment', while 'striving to meet the holistic needs of individuals, encouraging them to take a further step to independent housing'.

When the project was negotiated, it was agreed that evaluation of the services should be conducted 'by exploring the attitudes of clients (residents) and staff' and by documenting 'the residents' experiences of homelessness and by comparing Charington Hostel with other accommodation in which they have stayed.'

The hostel manager was also interested in understanding how individuals move through different forms of accommodation as part of the homeless 'career'. This interest related to a plan for future expansion of the service which was under discussion by his housing association – of providing 'move-on accommodation', supported apartments which would provide a 'half-way house' for residents between leaving the hostel and entering the mainstream housing market.

A student interviewed residents and staff members, using an interview guide which had been discussed with the program manager beforehand. The executive summary given at the beginning of the client report notes that the evaluation was broadly positive.

Executive summary

The evaluation study results strongly suggest that Charington Hostel is meeting the majority of its aims and objectives:

- Residents were, on the whole, satisfied with the service provided and compared Charington Hostel favourably with other hostels in which they had stayed.

Residents were generally positive about:

- their relationship and dealings with staff
- the activities provided
- the facilities available (such as the coffee bar and pool room)
- the prospect of move-on accommodation

Residents expressed grievances relating to:

- lack of privacy

The views of residents and staff on the aims of Charington Hostel and the presentation of the Christian ethos were largely the same.

Residents were able to define what a home is through being without one and talked about Charington Hostel in relation to these ideas.

In her account of the research methods used, the evaluator clearly indicated her ethical stance, that 'the interviews were conducted in a non-exploitative way', with a careful explanation of the research before the interviews, discussion of anonymity with respondents and the giving of an undertaking that identifiable information about them would be omitted. The evaluator also promised to avoid sensitive issues, which could occur with a vulnerable group of homeless people. Her approach was clearly summarized in these words:

'I wanted to treat the respondents as people, not as sources of data.'

The following extract from the report to the organization shows how references were made to methodological texts, as evidence of good academic practices to which the evaluator was working, to provide credibility to the client organization that the methodology was grounded in valid and approved practices, and to help the program manager (a practitioner) gain a deeper understanding of research methodology.

Research methods

My primary method of research for the project was the in-depth interview. This has proved an effective tool for collecting meaningful, detailed data and for preventing superficial and simplistic findings. Such interviews enable researchers to combine

> all the warmth and personality of a conversation with the clarity and guidelines of scientific searching.
>
> (Goode and Hatt, 1952)

Each interview was semi-structured and designed to facilitate the active participation of the respondent. As Acker, Barry and Esseveld (1983) explain, this will

> minimize the tendency ... to transform those researched into objects of scrutiny and manipulation

and

> create conditions in which the object of research enters into the process as an active subject.

I used an interview schedule (included in report as appendix 1) to create continuity of topics between interviews and to occasionally prompt respondents. I encouraged informants to express their opinions on issues which were important to them rather than imposing formalized and limiting questions upon them.

> The non-directive interviewer's function is primarily to serve as a catalyst to a comprehensive expression of the subject's feelings and beliefs.
>
> (Selltiz *et al.*, 1965)

Questions were open-ended to encourage respondents to take over the interview and to allow multiple responses. In conducting in-depth interviews it is essential to establish 'rapport' between interviewer and respondent. Ann Oakley (1981) defines rapport as

> the acceptance by the interviewee of the interviewer's research goals and the interviewee's active search to help the interviewer in providing the relevant information.

> I talked with each respondent prior to beginning the interview, explaining my research aims and methods and answering any questions they had about my work. The interviews were conducted in a non-exploitative way. I wanted to treat the respondents as people, not as sources of data.

Ten residents participated (20 per cent of the sample) of whom two were women, and there was a mix of employed and unemployed people who had been in the hostel for varying lengths of stay. Five staff members (25 per cent) were interviewed, drawn from management, project and domestic workers. The Report noted that the sample was, however, not necessarily 'representative', as there were difficulties in obtaining a sample of residents and the evaluator was primarily concerned with gathering depth data for understanding.

Limitations of the sample
My primary goal was to represent respondents' opinions and experiences of Charington Hostel, at length and in detail, rather than to obtain a representative sample.

The sample was to some extent self-selecting, residents had to volunteer and be willing to give up their time. I therefore faced the problem of non-response, which occurs in all social research (N. Gilbert, 1993). Non-responders may differ in significant ways from responders but as they do not participate in the research their views cannot be represented.

I endeavoured to counter this problem and maximize the response rate by

(a) approaching residents who did not participate in activities or use the coffee bar on their own landings or in reception.
(b) being persistent with (but not pressurizing) those residents who were sceptical or unenthusiastic about the research.

(c) following up those residents who agreed to take part but forgot
      about or pulled out of an arranged interview.

A particular problem arose in finding women willing to participate. Originally the evaluator had been keen to collect information
on women's experiences of homelessness. However, the coffee
bar was the main place where she met residents. Many of
the women in the hostel appeared unwilling to take part in the
social activities provided by the hostel, and tended to spend time
in their own (group) apartments. They also seemed to see hostel
residence as a 'temporary experience' which meant, as one woman
explained,

> If you knew you were gonna be here for three months – a year, it would
> change my attitude because then I'd really start getting involved. I'd do
> things I don't do now.

While the evaluation was being conducted, the coffee bar tended
to be a male-dominated domain. In the report it is recorded that
neither of the two women used the coffee bar and one is reported
as saying: 'I've poked my head round and they've been watching
football – and I've just stopped going any more.'
Women therefore restricted themselves to the private domain of
their own apartments, and it was more difficult for the evaluator to
gain access to them.

Negotiating the role of evaluator

The coffee bar caused other kinds of problems, too, for the way in
which the evaluator negotiated her role which she defined as
'student researcher'. Her physical location within the bar was
crucial in the acceptance she gained from the residents. If she sat
at the bar with them, she felt she was seen as 'one of them', and,
as her reflexive account notes, she felt 'this was the ideal basis for
an equal, friendly relationship' which she believed 'was essential
for the research to go beyond superficial, socially acceptable
answers'.
However, if she helped out on the other side of the bar she was
seen 'as a staff member, a figure of authority, as the "other"'.
Residents would not talk freely to her and viewed her research with
suspicion.

'This [is] for the management then, eh?' said one man. 'S'ppose they want to check up on us do they?'

There was also a more metaphorical 'bar' to be negotiated with some staff members as well. At the initial staff meeting where her project was introduced, staff seemed to be enthusiastic and welcoming. However, once she began meeting and interviewing residents, some staff members became uncomfortable with her interaction with residents – and became obstructive. She felt that she was

> perceived as undermining the hierarchical relationship between staff and residents. There were boundaries between staff and residents at Charington Hostel and expected norms of behaviour for each group. I discovered that, in relation to these boundaries and norms, my role as a researcher was fluid and disruptive.

These experiences caused the evaluator to redefine her role and to accept that her initial desire to be accepted as 'a friend' by the residents might have been naive. After discussion with her supervisor, and with the hostel manager, she told staff she was working to a professional code of practice (the British Sociology Association ethical guidelines). She also endeavoured to communicate more about her work, explaining to staff that non-hierarchical relationships with residents would be beneficial rather than detrimental to the interactive process of gathering in-depth data. Furthermore,

> as some of the staff were also prospective interviewees, I realized that I should be sensitive to their views and build relationships with them, too.

The findings

In the presentation of the findings, summary tables were provided together with a number of quotations to convey the depth of the data, both positive and negative. As far as staff–resident relations were concerned, there was a contrast between residents who emphasized the friendliness of staff while staff tended to be more likely to mention the authority which underpinned the relationship. (See Tables 8.1 and 8.2.)

Table 8.1   Residents' opinions of the staff: How would you describe the staff?

Response	No.	Percentage
Chatty	6	60
Friendly	5	50
Helpful	3	30
Supportive	3	30
Welcoming	2	20
Judgemental	2	20
Listeners	2	20
Figures of authority	2	20
Unsupportive	1	10
Sample	10	100
Total responses	26	

Table 8.2   Staff opinions of their relationship with residents: 'How would you describe your relationship with residents?'

Response	No.	Percentage
Friendly	5	100
Listeners	4	80
Service providers	4	50
Authoritative	4	80
Advisers	3	60
Supportive	2	40
Maternal	1	20
Counsellors	1	20
Sample	5	100
Total responses	24	

Staff–resident relations

Residents expressed overwhelmingly positive opinions of the staff. Most described staff as friendly and highlighted their willingness to get to know residents. One young man said:

> [T]hey're not like other places where they don't want to know anything and tell you to go away and stop complaining – you go downstairs and they start talking to you.

Another respondent described the relationship between residents and staff in terms of sameness rather than difference. He told me:

> They do their job but they're only human – we're all human and they'll sit down and have a chat with you.

One young resident said he saw the staff as figures of authority, 'they're like school teachers', he said. He went on to tell me that he respected them because:

> Even though we're kids they talk to you as if you were an adult.

Several respondents described staff as 'really helpful' in dealing with all sorts of queries and problems. One man said: 'They are helpful if you need anything really.'

Another respondent described how a member of staff approached him after something 'pretty traumatic' had happened:

> She wanted to know what had happened and afterwards we were talking for two hours.

On the whole, residents said the staff made them feel welcome at Charington Hostel. One woman highlighted 'being smiled at which really makes a difference'. She said that since she had become homeless, little things like that meant a lot to her.

All of the staff I spoke to emphasized the variety of role relationships which their job incorporates. Several respondents said that this meant relating to and interacting with residents in different ways. One staff member told me: 'This job is about being flexible – relating to people as individuals.'

Four of the staff referred to their position of authority but said that this role worked alongside a more equal staff–resident relationship. One respondent said:

> You have to have an authoritarian manner with them ... I always like to think I'm able to be their friend when there isn't the telling off to do.

Another member of staff commented: 'For the most part I would hope it's not an authority thing.'

Meaning of 'home'

Use of these in-depth interviews enabled the evaluator to explore the residents' definitions of 'home', in order to understand both what homelessness meant to them and to discover in what ways Charington was providing a home. This was an instance of the overlap between evaluation for enlightenment and evaluation for development.

An interesting division emerged between 'rooflessness' and 'homelessness', with one resident seeing a home as nothing more than a roof providing basic shelter:

> [T]he main thing is that you've got a roof over your head and somewhere warm to sleep at night.

Because he had these essentials, he did not see himself as homeless. But as the report notes:

> [M]ost other residents had broader definitions of a home and described athemselves as homeless though they lived in temporary accommodation.

For them, the key elements of a home were

- privacy;
- ownership;
- comfort;
- a roof;
- permanence;
- family;
- a place to identify with.

Privacy was the most frequently mentioned characteristic of a home. Respondents distinguished between private and public space. One man told me that being homeless meant having no private self, he said, 'my life is public property'.

Several residents told me how this affected their personal relationships. One man said that sustaining his relationship with his son was difficult, he told me:

> We can't do normal things together – watch TV and stuff – we end up just sitting in McDonald's or public places all the while.

Residents said that not having the privacy of a home had changed their behaviour. Three respondents saw a home as somewhere to be themselves and spoke of feeling 'on edge' without one. One respondent said, 'it doesn't feel as though you can relax'.

The interviews showed that Charington Hostel was not seen as a home by seven of the ten residents because of:

- A lack of privacy (5 residents):
  'There's always people wandering in and out.'

'You lock the door and you come back and you find someone's been in to fix a light and you think OK, they've done me a favour – but at the same time they could have let me know.'
- Temporary stay (3 residents):
  'Everyone is passing through.'
- Not being able to decorate (3 residents):
  'I can't change things – you know if it was mine I could paint and paper when I wanted and adjust things but I can't do that here'.

The remaining 3 residents, who did consider Charington a home, felt it was 'somewhere to live' – it did not have to be permanent, and provided a 'roof over my head'. Two people felt Charington was 'like' or 'almost as good as' sharing a flat or 'self-contained unit'.

Conclusions and recommendations

The evaluator concluded the report for the organization by noting the positive feedback she had received and the evidence that Charington was fulfilling the majority of its aims.

Conclusions
My research has found that Charington Hostel is providing a high level of service for its clients and is fulfilling the majority of its aims. Charington Hostel can continue to build on and extend the current provision for the future.

Proposals for move-on accommodation were received positively by residents and they felt that they would make use of and benefit from this scheme.

Recommendations
Residents said that steps could be taken to redefine their personal space and help them to regain the respect which the experience of being homeless had taken away.

They felt that communication between staff and residents could be improved, emphasizing the need for continuing work to ensure that residents are notified when maintenance work has to be carried out in their rooms.

Residents highlighted the problems of sharing certain facilities, such as fridges, and felt that this had a negative effect on their feeling of security and their relationship with other residents on their landing.

Changes could be made in order to enhance their environment and counter some of the negative effects of communal living.

Response of the client

The evaluator had aimed to provide feedback based on qualitative detail from in-depth interviews, and this had been negotiated with the manager at the initial stages of the evaluation. However, when the manager was interviewed by the supervisor some months after the completion of the project, he said he felt, when he read the report, that the research was unfocused:

> The project was open-ended. This was no-one's fault. If we did it again, we would try to pinpoint what it could lead to – the off-spills, and it would be more closed.

Later in the same interview, the manager somewhat contradicted this view and compared the student's evaluation report (and its depth data) with the type of 'tick the box' survey he was required to complete for the housing corporation. This type of survey research he felt was superficial and had little meaning, whereas 'the in-depth research of the report was more valuable'.

The report was being used in two ways. Firstly, it had high-lighted the importance of personal space in the hostel and the need for the provision of individual fridges in rooms, as residents had complained about food being stolen from communal fridges. He said his hostel had been pushing this issue for some time with the central management of the organization – at the national headquarters – and he felt the report gave weight to this, and he was using the report 'to put additional pressure on' for change.

The second use was to facilitate 'staff and personal development' within the hostel. The report was useful in making staff more aware of how they were perceived by service users, particularly through the quotations from residents which were included.

Comment

The evaluation research was undoubtedly small-scale, with a relatively small number of interviews, but the information gained and pre-sented in the report allowed the concerns of the residents to be heard, in their own voices, while providing reassurance that the program was in most respects meeting its objectives and satisfying its users.

The study required the researcher spending a considerable amount of time in the common area of the hostel where she could make observations of residents and staff activities. This pointed up some ambiguities and conflicts in the role of evaluator – where she could be perceived as taking sides with either the residents or staff, and creating distrust with either one or the other. This could only be resolved by open communication about her research and motives, and the commitment to independent and sensitive research.

The findings reported on the residents' experience of the hostel, and indeed produced some recommendations that could be taken forward as points for action, for example, regarding the provision of fridges. But also, the findings explored a much broader agenda, that of residents' experiences of homelessness. This might give the appearance of the report becoming 'unfocused', but opens up a wider agenda, which has value both for the evaluator and, as it happens, the program practitioners as well.

Oriel Day and Resource Centre

The Oriel Day and Resource Centre was opened in the late 1970s to meet the needs of adults with a physical disability by providing resource and day services. The current staff at the centre – rehabilitation officers, occupational therapy staff, care staff, domestic staff and driver – support service users in meeting their individual goals.

The evaluation research had its origin in a request from the centre for a study of service users, to find out what they thought of the services provided, and whether they had any suggestions for future provision. The project was therefore about the quality of service provision, but limited to consider the views of current service users only among all possible stakeholders. There would also be a prospective element in looking at unmet need, in terms of service users' wishes for additional or alternative activities.

It was apparent that there had been a substantial cut in funding which had reduced the number of staff. The possibilities were looming of even more cuts and possibly even the closure of the centre and the transfer of its functions elsewhere. In the negotiation for the agreement between the student and the centre manager, this issue had been identified as the reason why the research was needed, and the definition of the project in that document was as follows:

> To evaluate service users' views on the resources and activities in the Centre, with a view to discovering how the current situation is seen by

users, and in which directions they would like to see development taken. This will involve interviews with a cross-section of service users, and observation of the activities of the Centre.

Executive Summary

This report presents the views of service users at Oriel Day and Resource Centre. The Centre provides rehabilitation activities through educational and vocational classes for physically and sensory disabled people. The research was carried out to evaluate how service users perceive service provision, and whether they had any suggestions for further provision.

All the service users that were spoken to during the course of the research said they had benefited from the Centre; this included support and encouragement from the staff and the companionship of other service users as well the accessibility of the activities (pp. 17–18). However, many service users were concerned about the current policy of job freezing within Social Services, which has had the effect of reducing available activities, such as Arts and Crafts. There was also a great deal of concern expressed about the Centre being under the threat of closure and a strong feeling of banding together to fight any such threat (pp. 19–20).

Areas of improvement identified by service users were:

  i.   a need for introductory information for new service users
  ii. an increase in educational and vocational activities
  iii. a need for the building to undergo a 'facelift'
  iv. the introduction of a service contract on all the Information Technology equipment.

(pp. 21, 22, 25)

It was suggested that an introductory leaflet (item i) could be produced within the Centre as the facilities are available in the Computer and Information Technology Room.

There are cost implications for items ii–iv. Funding would be required from Social Services, local further education colleges outreach programs, or European grants.

As with Charington Hostel, the evaluator was concerned not to constrain the service users' replies by closed questions on a questionnaire, and chose to use semi-structured interviews, in part from a desire to prioritize depth and richness of information over sheer number of responses, and in part from a commitment to give voice to the service users, who as disabled people are generally not accorded status in our society but seen as passive and dependent. She explained her choices as follows:

Research methods

I used qualitative methods to enable the informants to be heard, with the idea that it was very much their 'voice' that would form the main body of the client report. As researchers are part of what is being researched, I agree with Abbott and Wallace (1990: 207–12) that involvement is not only necessary but that it is also inevitable.

Oakley (1981: 41) argues that the goal of finding out about people through interviewing is best achieved when the relationship of inter-viewer and interviewee is non-hierarchical, and when the interviewer is prepared to invest his or her personal identity in the relationship. I tried to achieve this, both within the interviews and in my more informal encounters with service users.

I used tape recording for the majority of the interviews, which had the advantage of gaining the full conversation and enabled me to check whether I had too much or too little input. And, as Gilbert has noted, using a recorder does put over the idea that responses are being taken seriously (Gilbert, 1993: 146). For two of the interviews I used note form because these informants had speech difficulties to the extent that I felt I would not be able to transcribe their responses from a tape.

There were twelve interviews in all, 5 women and 7 men whose ages ranged from 21 years to early 60s formed the sample of service users. This was about half of the current average of 25 daily users of the centre, and though care was taken to see that they included a mix of ages and gender, no claims for full representa-tiveness were made.

The interviews began only after a period of observation and familiarization within the setting of the centre, so activities at the centre were observed on a weekly basis (on various days of the week) over a three-month period, before the cross-section of 12 service users was interviewed in depth, while several other service users talked about the centre on a more informal basis during the observation of various activities, and also during recreation times.

The findings

The report for the organization provides some background information on the program users, and how they came to be at the centre, before going into details of their experience of the centre.

One of the consequences of the choice of interview research method and style of approach was to allow the program users space to comment on what was important to them, rather than being constrained by selecting from pre-chosen answers. This produced some rather unexpected findings. A number of people took the opportunity to give details of their life history before their physical impairment began, and to comment in particular on their first thoughts about coming to the centre.

One such quotation was as follows:

> When they first mooted that I would come here, I thought, there's no way I'm going to a funny farm. That was the first thought that went through my mind, but, as I say, it's completely changed my outlook. I am more my old self since I've come here.

The strong aversion to using a specialist centre for disabled people, and its impact on their identities, featured in these initial reactions – though their narrative resolved in appreciation of the acceptance and companionship encountered at the centre:

> The people, the company. You've got such a lot of people here with much more hardships, more than what I'm suffering from, and yet they've got such a spirit and I think that makes you realize, you know. We have a laugh and a joke, even about each other's complaints. The trouble is I go home from here and I'm hurting, but it's hurting from laughing.

Another person summed up the personal benefits from attending in this way:

> You don't feel disabled because we're all knackered to some degree or other. It's perfectly normal to be practically defunct! ... From everyone I've spoken to here we've all had the same feeling, we didn't want to come to a place like this because it's apartheid. We don't think it's morally correct. But by the time you've been alone and outside society several years, talking to the wallpaper, it sinks in, well, I'm cutting my nose off to spite my face here. At least there'd be somebody to talk to and see if I went there. It's a very, very hard thing to do, to come here. When I first came here, looking about tentatively, I thought, am I really reduced to this? But once you start doing things it helps being part of a group. You can get tired as you get older, but the group takes over.

What people liked about the activities at the centre had to do with

- the range of activities on offer, and the ability to learn new skills, particularly in computers and information technology, and in art;
- the flexibility that allowed service users to do what they want, choose which activity to do as the mood suits, or just read the newspaper;
- the staff, who were helpful without fussing, and arranged outings as well.

The evaluator summed up the program users' responses like this:

Many people said that they had been pleasantly surprised at how quickly they felt comfortable at the Centre. One described how he felt isolated at home and different outside. The Centre provided him with a focus and also a place to practise walking and talking without being stared at. Taking part in bowling and swimming, going to Spain, and working on the Lord Nelson (a sail training ship) has also helped to build his confidence, so much so that he plucked up courage to use public transport in order to get to the centre. For him the centre is a 'Godsend'.

Overall, the major benefit of the Oriel Centre as far as service users are concerned is the opportunity to get out and be with people in a place that is accessible. The most frequently used phrase was, 'everyone's in the same boat'.

Nevertheless, there were some areas where service users thought more could be done. While they valued the companionship and the activities, they were aware of the problems caused by funding cut-backs and how it impinged on what was possible. Four areas were identified for improvement.

1. Appearance of the centre
Many agreed it could do with a 'face-lift', or a 'lick of paint'.

2. Teaching at the centre
The courses put on in woodwork, arts and crafts, IT and computers, and French and local history were appreciated, but restricted because of the lack of additional tutors.

3. Information in the centre

Service users said they would like to have an information sheet with a daily timetable. They had the facilities to do this themselves.

4. Outreach from the centre

Creating greater awareness in the local community about what goes on at the centre would be helpful.

Conclusions and recommendations

The evaluator concluded the report by summarizing the points made by the service users, emphasizing that the recommendations were grounded in the experience of users themselves. This was backed up with extracts from actual interviews giving much more detail on users' feelings about the centre and its value to their lives.

There are two obvious difficulties for evaluations carried out under the circumstances facing the centre of recent funding cutbacks and future uncertainty. First, that service users' views may be almost entirely negative, given the réductions of activities and the remembrance of better times in the past. Second, that the evaluator may be over conscious of the weight hanging on the report in terms of the organization's survival, and searches to emphasize the good points of its activity at the expense of a rounded picture.

Neither of these concerns seemed to be borne out in practice. While service users did have suggestions for future activities that were not currently provided, or had been provided in the past, there was also satisfaction with the present stemming from the social organization and camaraderie of the centre, which had been unaffected. Regarding the possible cut-backs, centre users had already been active in lobbying their councillors and taking the political action open to them as citizens. The researcher mentioned in her reflective report that she did not join in these protests, on ethical grounds, as she felt it might have prejudiced the reception of her report. The report might help but would not determine the success of their ongoing campaign.

Response of the client

The centre manager was interviewed about six months after the client report had been completed and handed over. The manager felt the report had matched up to his original objectives, in allowing the service users to express their views on the services. Although the report contained no startling new information, its value for him was that it represented an external evaluation of the organization:

> The final report highlighted issues I was already aware of. It was useful for the research to be undertaken by a more independent body.

How had the report been used? It had been shared with the service users – all the service users interviewed had declined the evaluator's offer of anonymity, and insisted that their real names be used. Giving the report back to the program users, then, had given them a stake in the outcome and validated their experiences, and this was an important internal use. The centre manager had discussed it with his operational manager, who had found it 'interesting'. That is, it had a use both internal to the organization and external in terms of penetrating the managerial hierarchy.

The manager was pessimistic about more funding being found as a result of the report:

> In terms of highlighting the lack of resources, it was good. But there is little that can be done. [The borough council] is in a pretty poor state, so it is unlikely that things could change.

So in terms of actually having a direct effect on resource allocation, the evaluation was perceived to be of little influence. This was in part because of other funding priorities placed on the council at that time – a recent court ruling had shown that spending on older people was below what was required, and that would take priority for the time being.

Interestingly, the only reservation the centre manager had about the report was that it could have been even more critical, recognizing that it was

> less likely to be critical because of the interrelationships with staff and service users, and a desire to be positive. The student should not be too frightened of a critical analytical perspective. I am used to this from social work.

Comment

This evaluation research shared a number of common features with the preceding example of Charington Hostel. Again it was small-scale, with a small number of in-depth interviews, in which the service users wanted their own voices to be heard. The report showed that the program was meeting their objectives and satisfying the users, though there was still room for more to be provided.

As with Charington Hostel, it was also apparent that the study worked well because the researcher spent much time in the centre, just being there, seeing what was going on, making conversation with users, even joining in at times, before embarking on the semi-structured interviews. There was less conflict reported around the role of evaluator – perhaps because there was less distance between service users and staff. But other considerations also applied. The evaluator noted that her choice of the project was influenced by her local background and her family experience of disability:

> Having a close family member with a sensory disability I felt that I might have some insight into the prejudices that people with disabilities face and had no apprehension about spending time in their environment.

The most significant feature of the report turned out to be the validation it provided for the people using the program, because it enabled them to express their voice in a way which had not been done before. They wanted their names recorded, and they wanted to see themselves in the report.

APPENDIX 1
(UNIVERSITY TITLE)

Evaluation Agreement

The following is the outcome of a meeting on (date) between (academic supervisor's name, address, telephone and e-mail) and (student, university department) and (organization contact with name and title in the organization, address, telephone and e-mail.)

All parties may comment on the agreement and if any section needs to be altered a fresh agreement will be issued. Please contact the academic supervisor (name), with comments at the above address.

1. **Project Agreement**: between (parties as above)
2. **Duration of the Project**: the project will run from (start date to completion): fieldwork will be completed by (month).
3. **About the organization**: (short description of the organization, with information on the aspect of service to be evaluated. Use organization's own materials to source this section and reference accordingly e.g. Annual Report)
4. **Issues identified**: (short succinct statement).
5. **Proposed project**. (student) will evaluate the services provided by (organization), focusing particularly on (specific aspects of service). He/ she will (list methods to be used, sample[s] to be interviewed or surveyed or observed, and the stages involved).
   (State the access arrangements and how consent will be assured and whether data is to be recorded anonymously).
6. **Project outcome**: (student) will produce a written report which will be available in draft form by (month) and in its final form by (month) to (organization). He/she will also provide feedback to (organization) during the course of the project, as appropriate.
7. **Permission to reproduce the report**: (student) and (academic supervisor) will have the right to use the report for academic publication, provided (organization) is first consulted and has no objections.
8. **Attendance**: (student) will commit the equivalent of one day a week in the first semester for field work and a similar amount of time in the second semester for analysis and for writing reports.

9. **Expenses**: the payment of travel expenses will be paid by the (organization). (Student) will be responsible for providing a typed copy of his/her report to (University title) as part submission for his/her degree.
10. **Policy issues**: (Student) will abide by and be covered by the health and safety, equal opportunities and confidentiality procedures of (organization). Both he/she and (organization) will complete a risk assessment form as required by (University title).
11. **Supervision**: (academic supervisor) will be available for regular supervision throughout the study.
12. **Confidentiality**: (student) will work to the British Sociological Association guidelines on ethics and will respect the confidentiality of the information given. Due attention will be given to anonymity, and the research will be conducted in a sensitive manner.
13. **Assessment**: (student) will submit the client report and a separate reflective report to the (University / Department) and these together will comprise his/her dissertation.
14. **Acknowledgements**: At any time when the report or any part of it is used, proper acknowledgement should be made to (student), to the (department), (University title) and to (the academic supervisor).

Signed:

Dated:

(A completed example of the agreement can be found in Chapter 1.)

Risk Assessment

(MODULE TITLE)

This form should be completed by the tutor in consultation with the student for project work off campus.

1. **Department:**

   Supervisor:

   Name _____ phone number _____ e-mail _____

2. **Brief description of project:**

3. **Name(s) of those carrying out the fieldwork:**

4. **Hazard/Risk Analysis:**

   Is there felt to be any risk to personal safety? Yes / No

   Comments on the risk – points to raise with the placement provider:

   Will visits take place during hours of darkness? Yes / No

   If so, what extra precautions are required?

   Has the tutor covered issues concerning contact with members of the public during the placement? (e.g. on not touching, working with children)

5. **Precautions:**

What arrangements are in place for the student leaving an itinerary of movements and expected return times with a responsible person?

6. **Are the following precautions appropriate?**

	Yes	No	N/A	Notes
Pre-visit checks, eg on records				
Visiting in pairs with a companion in earshot				
Personal alarms				
Mobile phones				
Regular reporting to base and follow-up procedure				
Training in interpersonal communication skills				
Parking in appropriate well-lit areas				
Security locks on vehicles etc.				
Anti-theft devices and alarms				
Other precautions (state)				

7. *Provided the attached questionnaire to the placement provider has been completed satisfactorily, work may proceed subject to the conditions stated in this assessment*

Signed: _____ Status: _____

Date: _____

Health and Safety Questionnaire

(MODULE TITLE)

This form should be completed by the placement provider
Final Recipient: (University Title)

Part 1

Section 3 of the Health and Safety at Work Act 1974 (England and Wales) imposes a statutory duty on an employer in relation to risks to the health and safety of non-employees. This could be said to apply to the University for the benefit of the students in the sense that in arranging for an out-placement the University is "conducting its undertaking" and so far as is reasonably practicable, should take measures to protect students' health and safety. To enable the University to fulfil its "statutory and moral duty towards students" we request that community/voluntary groups complete the following questionnaire. Thank you for your cooperation.

Part 2

1. Name of organization (please print):

2. Address of organization

   Telephone

3. Please circle as appropriate

1. Do you have a written Health and Safety policy?	YES	NO
2. Have you carried out risk assessments to identify possible hazards as required by the Management of Health and Safety at Work Regulations 1999?	YES	NO
3. Do you have Employers' Liability insurance?	YES	NO
4. Do you have Public Liability insurance?	YES	NO
5. Do you have a fire certificate for your premises?	YES	NO
6. Do you have suitable and sufficient fire warning and evacuation systems?	YES	NO
7. Do you have suitable and sufficient fire extinguishing equipment and is this equipment maintained in a serviceable condition?	YES	NO
8. Do you have suitable and sufficient first aid equipment and assistance available?	YES	NO
9. Do you have competent persons trained to ensure the safe evacuation of all persons from buildings in the event of serious and imminent danger?	YES	NO

Part 3

Areas to be covered for student induction

Emergency procedures for serious and imminent danger

Fire precautions

First aid provisions

Accident reporting

Any other procedures or precautions which should be taken to be relevant to the type of work being undertaken and the work environment concerned.

Name of person completing questionnaire: _____

Position _____

Signature _____   Date _____

Thank you for taking the time to complete this questionnaire.

Please return to: (Tutor name, address, telephone number, e-mail)

Bibliography

Abbott, P. and Wallace, C. (1990) *An Introduction to Sociology: Feminist Perspectives*. London: Routledge.

Acker, J. Barry, K. and Esseveld, J. (1983) 'Objectivity and Truth: Problems in doing Feminist Research'. *Women's Studies International Forum*, **6**(4), pp. 423–35.

Alderman, G. (2001) 'Down the Drain', *The Guardian*, 10 July, p. 17.

Altheide, D. L. and Johnson, J. M. (1994). 'Criteria for assessing interpretive validity in qualitative research'. in N. K. Denzin and Y. S. Lincoln (eds), *Handbook of Qualitative Research*. London: Sage.

American Evaluation Association (AEA) (1994) 'Guiding Principles for Evaluators,' http://www.eval.org/EvaluationDocuments/aeaprin6.html

Anderson, J. (2002) 'Report for a Children's Charity'. Unpublished BA dissertation, Liverpool: Liverpool Hope University College.

Argyris, C. and Schön, D. A. (1978) *Organizational Learning*. Reading, MA: Addison-Wesley.

Arksey, H. and Knight, P. (1999) *Interviewing for Social Scientists*. London: Sage.

Arnold, J., Li, J. and Rice, J. (2000) 'Assessing the Benefits of the Volunteer Scheme for Student Nurses'. Unpublished BA Dissertation Report, Liverpool: Liverpool Hope University College.

Association for Research in the Voluntary and Community Centre ARVAC (2002) *Community Research: Getting Started*. London.

Atkinson, R. and Flint, J. (2003) 'Sampling, Snowball: accessing hidden and hard-to-reach populations'. In R. L. Miller and J. D. Brewer (eds), *The A–Z of Social Research*. London: Sage.

Babbie, E. (2004) *The Practice of Social Research*, 10th edn, Belmont, CA: Wadsworth/Thomson.

Balnaves, M. and Caputi, P. (2001) *Introduction to Quantitative Research Methods*, London: Sage.

Banks, M. (2001) *Visual Methods in Social Research*. London: Sage.

Barnes, C. (1992) 'Qualitative Research: Valuable or Irrelevant?' *Disability, Handicap and Society*, **7**(2) pp. 115–24.

Bartzokas, C. A., Williams, E. E. and Slade, P. D. (1995) *A Psychological Approach to Hospital-Acquired Infections*. London: Edwin Mellen.

Bazeley, P. and Richards, L. (2000) *The NVivo Qualitative Project Book*. London: Sage.

Bell, J. (1999) *Doing Your Research Project*, 3rd edn, Buckingham: Open University Press.

Black, T. R. (1994) *Evaluating Social Science Research*. London: Sage.

Blaikie, N. (1993) *Approaches to Social Enquiry*. Cambridge: Polity Press.

Blaikie, N. (2000) *Designing Social Research*. Cambridge: Polity Press.

Bloor, M., Frankland, J., Thomas, M. and Robson, K. (2001) *Focus Groups in Social Research*. London: Sage.

Bresnen, M. (1988) 'Insights On Site: Research into construction project organisations'. In Bryman, A. (ed.), *Doing Research in Organisations*. London: Routledge.

British Dyslexia Association (2003) *Dyslexia Style Guide*. Reading: British Dyslexia Association. http://www.bda-dyslexia.org.uk/main/information/extras/x09frend.asp

British Sociological Association (2002) Statement of Ethical Practice: www.britsoc.org.uk/inciex.php?link id=14&area=item1

Bryman, A. and Cramer, D. (2001) *Qualitative Data Analysis with SPSS Release 10 for Windows*. London: Routledge.

Bryman, A. (1998) *Quality and Quantity in Social Research*. London: Unwin Hyman.

Bryman, A. (2001) *Social Research Methods*. Oxford: Oxford University Press.

Buchanan, D., Boddy, D. and McCalman, J. (1988) 'Getting In, Getting On, Getting Out and Getting Back'. In A. Bryman (ed.), *Doing Research in Organisations*. London: Routledge.

Burgess, R. G. (1984) *In The Field: An Introduction to Field Research*. London: Allen & Unwin.

Chamberlain, J. M. (1999) *Mentally Disordered Offenders, The Care Progamme Approach: An Evaluation*. Unpublished MSc thesis, Liverpool: University of Liverpool.

Chaplin, E. (1994) *Sociology and Visual Representation*. London: Routledge.

Chelimsky, E. and Shadish, W. (1997) *Evaluation for the 21st Century: A Handbook*. Thousand Oaks, CA: Sage.

Chen, H.-T. (1990) *Theory-Driven Evaluations*. Newbury Park, CA: Sage.

Clarke, A. (1999) *Evaluation Research*. London: Sage.

Clegg, F. (1983) *Simple Statistics*. Cambridge: Cambridge University Press.

Coghlan, D. and Brannick, T. (2001) *Doing Action Research in Your Own Organization*. London: Sage.

Colman, A. and Corston, R. (2002) *A Crash Course in SPSS for Windows*. Oxford: Blackwell.

Converse, J. M. and Presser, S. (1986) *Survey Questions: Handcrafting the Standardized Questionnaire*. Newbury Park, CA: Sage.

Cook, T. D. (1997) 'Lessons Learned in Evaluation Over the Past'. In E. Chelimsky and W. R. Shadish (eds), *Evaluation for the 21st Century: A Handbook*, Thousand Oaks, CA: Sage.

Cook, J. A. and Fonow, M. M. (1990) 'Knowledge and Women's Interests: Issues of Epistemology and Methodology in Feminist Sociological Research'. In J. McC Nielson (ed.), *Feminist Research Methods: Exemplary Readings in the Social Sciences*. Boulder: Westview.

Corbetta, P. (2003) *Social Research: Theory, Methods and Techniques*. London: Sage.

Cousins, B. and Leithwood, K. (1986) 'The State-of-the-Art of Research on Evaluation Utilization'. *Review of Educational Research*, **56**(3), pp. 331–64.

Cowan, J. (1998) *On Becoming an Innovative University Teacher: Reflection in Action*. Buckingham: The Society for Research into Higher Education & Open University Press.

Darlington, Y. and Scott, S. (2002) *Qualitative Research in Practice: Stories from the Field*. Buckingham: Open University Press.

de Laine, M. (2000) *Fieldwork, Participation and Practice: Ethical Dilemmas in Qualitative Research*. London: Sage.

de Vaus, D. A. (2002) *Surveys in Social Research*, 5th edn. London: Routledge.

de Vaus, D. A. (2001) *Research Design in Social Research*. London: Sage.

Dillman, D. A. (1999) *Mail and Internet Surveys: The Tailored Design Method*, 2nd edn. New York: John Wiley.

Douglas, J. D. (1976) *Investigative Social Research: Individual and Team Field Research*. Beverly Hills, CA: Sage.

Duster, T., Matza, D. and Wellman, D. (1979) 'Fieldwork and the protection of human subjects'. *American Sociologist*, 14, pp. 136–42.

Eisner, E. (1991) *The Enlightened Eye: Qualitative inquiry and the enhancement of educational practice*. New York; Macmillan.

Etzioni, A. (1975) *Complex Organisations*. New York: Free Press.

Everitt, A. (1996) 'Developing Critical Evaluation'. *Evaluation*, **2**(2), pp. 173–88.

Eyler, J. and Giles, D. (1999) *Where's the Learning in Service-Learning?* San Francisco: Jossey-Bass.

Farran, D. (1990) 'Seeking Susan: Producing Statistical Information on Young People's Leisure'. In L. Stanley (ed.), *Feminist Praxis: Research, Theory and Epistemology in Feminist Sociology*. London: Routledge.

Fetterman, D. M. (2001) *Foundations of Empowerment Evaluation*. Thousand Oaks, CA: Sage.

Fetterman, D. M. Kaftarian, S. and Wandersman, A. (eds) (1996) *Empowerment Evaluation*. Thousand Oaks, CA: Sage.

Field, A. (2000) *Discovering Statistics using SPSS for Windows*. London: Sage.

Fielding, J. and Gilbert, N. (2000) *Understanding Social Statistics*. London: Sage.

Fielding, N. and Lee, R. (1991) *Using Computers in Qualitative Research*. London: Sage.

Finnegan, R. (1992) *Oral Traditions and the Verbal Arts: A Guide to Research Practices*. London: Routledge.

Flick, U. (1998) *An Introduction to Qualitative Research*. London: Sage.

Fong, S. (2001) 'Report for a Hospital Trust'. Unpublished BA dissertation. Liverpool: University of Liverpool.

Foster, V. (2003) 'Report for a Drug Treatment Agency'. Unpublished MSc dissertation. Liverpool: University of Liverpool.

Freeborn, D. (1986) *Varieties of English*. Basingstoke: Macmillan.

Freidson, E. (1988) *Profession of Medicine*. Chicago: University of Chicago Press.

Gabriel, Y., Fineman, S. and Sims, D. (2000) Organizing and Organizations, 2nd edn. London: Sage.

Gahan, C. (1998) *Doing Qualitative Research using QSR Nud.ist*. London: Sage.

Geertz, C. (1973) *The Interpretation of Cultures*. New York: Basic Books.

Gherardi, S. and Turner, B. (2002) 'Real Men Don't Collect Soft Data', in A.M. Huberman and M.B. Miles (eds), *The Qualitative Researcher's Companion*. Thousand Oaks, CA: Sage.

Gibbs, G. (2002) *Qualitative Data Analysis: Explorations with NVivo*. Buckingham: Open University Press.

Gilbert, N. (ed.) (1993) *Researching Social Life*. 1st edn. London: Sage.

Gilbert, N. (ed.) (2001) *Researching Social Life*. 2nd edn. London: Sage.

Glaser, B. and Strauss, A. (1967) *The Discovery of Grounded Theory*. Chicago: Aldine.

Goode, W. J. and Hatt, P. K. (1952) *Methods in Social Research*. New York: McGraw-Hill.

Gosling, L. with Edwards, M. (1995) *Toolkits: A Practical Guide to Assessment, Monitoring, Review and Evaluation*. London: Save the Children.

Gould, N. (1996) Introduction: social work education and the 'crisis of the professions'. In Gould, N. and Taylor, I. (eds), *Reflective Learning for Social Work*. Aldershot: Arena.

Greenbaum, T. L. (1998) *The Handbook for Focus Group Research*. Thousand Oaks, CA: Sage.

Greig, A. and Taylor, J. (1999) *Doing Research With Children*. London: Sage.

Guba, E. G. and Lincoln, Y. S. (1989) *Fourth Generation Evaluation*. Newbury Park, CA: Sage.

Habermas, Jürgen (1994) *The Past as Future*. Cambridge: Polity Press.

Hakim, C. (1983) *Secondary Analysis in Social Research: A Guide to Data Sources and Methods with Examples*. London: Allen & Unwin.

Hakim, C. (1987) *Research Design: Strategies and Choices in the Design of Social Research*. London: Allen & Unwin.

Hall, D. (2003) 'Images of the City'. In R. Munck (ed.), *Reinventing the City? Liverpool in Comparative Perspective*. Liverpool: Liverpool University Press.

Hall, I. and Hall, D. (1998) 'Applying Research to Practice in the Voluntary Sector in Merseyside'. Discussion paper, Department of Sociology, Social Policy and Social Work Studies, University of Liverpool.

Hall, D. and Hall, I. (2000a) 'Embedding Community Based Research in Academic Teaching and Learning through Evaluation', paper given to UK Evaluation Society Conference, London.

Hall, I. and Hall, D. (2000b) *Researching in the Community: A Positive Partnership*, Workbook 2, CoBaLT Project, Department of Sociology, University of Liverpool.

Hall, D., Hall, I. and Lockley, S. (2000) 'Third Sector/University Partnership: developing experiential research as community resource'. *International Society for Third Sector Research*, http://www.jhu.edu/~istr/conferences/dublin/workingpapers/hall.pdf

Hall, I. and Hall, D. (2002) 'Incorporating change through reflection: community based learning'. In R. Macdonald and J. Wisdom (eds), *Academic and Educational Development: Research, Evaluation and Changing Practice in Higher Education*. London: Kogan Page.

Hall, D. and Hall I. (2003) *UK Case Study Report*. Interacts Report No. 2f, Lyngby: The Science Shop, Technical University of Denmark.

Hall, D. and Hall, I. (1996) *Practical Social Research*. Basingstoke: Macmillan.

Hall, D., McDonald, J. and Andersen, H. (1999) *Streetscenes: Photoviews by Young People of Dingle and Speke/Garston*. Department of Sociology, Social Policy & Social Work Studies, University of Liverpool.

Hammersley, M. and Gomm, R. (2000) 'Introduction'. In R. Gomm, M. Hammersley and P. Foster (eds), *Case Study Method*. Sage: London.

Haraway, D. (1997) Modest_Witness@Second_Millennium.FemaleMan©_Meets_OncoMouse. London: Routledge.

Harvey, L. (1990) Critical Social Research. London: Unwin Hyman.

Harvey, L. and MacDonald, M. (1993) *Doing Sociology: A Practical Introduction*. Macmillan: Basingstoke.

Herman, J. L. (ed.) (1998) *The Program Evaluation Kit*, 2nd edn. Newbury Park, CA: Sage.

Holly, M. L. (1984) *Keeping a Personal Professional Journal*. Deakin, Melbourne: Deakin University Press.

House, E. R. (1993) *Professional Evaluation: Social Impact and Political Consequences*. Newbury Park, CA: Sage.

House, E. R. and Howe, K. R. (1999) *Values in Evaluation and Social Research*. Thousand Oaks, CA: Sage.

Jones, P. (1997) 'Report on an Adult Home Placement Project'. Unpublished BA Dissertation, Liverpool: Liverpool Hope University College.

Kavanagh, J. (1999) Report for a Victim Support Scheme, Unpublished BA Dissertation. Liverpool Hope University College.

Kinnear, P. R. and Gray, C. D. (2000) *SPSS for Windows Made Simple*. Brighton: Psychology Press.

Kirkcaldy, A. (2000) 'An Evaluation of Befrienders, Staff Support, and Trauma and Bereavement Services within a Hospital Accident and

Emergency Department'. Unpublished MSc dissertation. Liverpool Hope University College.

Kmietowicz, Z. (2000) 'Hospital Infection Rates Out of Control'. *British Medical Journal*, 29 July, 321 (7256), pp. 302–3.

Kolb, D. (1984) *Experiential Learning: Experience as the Source of Learning*. Englewood Cliffs, NJ: Prentice Hall.

Krueger, R. A. and Casey, M. A. (2000) *Focus Groups: A Practical Guide for Applied Research*. 3rd edn. Thousand Oaks, CA: Sage.

Kushner, S. (2000) *Personalizing Evaluation*. London: Sage.

Kvale, S. (1996) *Interviews: An Introduction to Qualitative Research Interviewing*. Thousand Oaks, CA: Sage.

Labov, W. (1972) *Language in the Inner City: Studies in the Black English Vernacular*. Philadelphia: University of Pennsylvania Press.

Layder, D. (1993) *New Strategies in Social Research*. Cambridge: Polity Press.

Ledwith, M. (1994) 'Listening as Emancipatory Research'. *Critical Public Health*, **5**(3), pp. 15–26.

Lee, R. M. (2000) *Unobtrusive Methods in Social Research*. Buckingham: Open University Press.

Lilley, S. (2002) *How to Deliver Negative Evaluation Results Constructively: Ten tips for evaluators*. Internet review, www.chebucto.ns.ca/~LilleyS/tips.html

Lincoln, Y. and Denzin, N. (1998) 'The Fifth Moment'. In N. Denzin and Y. Lincoln (eds), *The Landscape of Qualitative Research*. Thousand Oaks, CA: Sage.

Locke, L., Silverman, S. J. and Spiroduso, W. W. (1998) *Reading and Understanding Research*. Thousand Oaks, CA: Sage.

Lockley, S., Hall I. and Hall, D. (2000) *Accessible Learning and Course Materials for Students with Dyslexia: A Report Guide for Tutors*. CoBaLT/GNU Project, Liverpool Hope University College.

Lofland, J. (1976) *Doing Social Life*. New York: John Wiley.

Marsh, C. (1982) *The Survey Method: The Contribution of Surveys to Sociological Explanation*. London: George Allen & Unwin.

Mason, J. (2002) *Qualitative Researching*, 2nd edn. London: Sage.

Mayall, B. (2000) 'Conversations with Children: Working with Generational Issues'. In P. Christensen and A. James (eds), *Research with Children: Perspectives and Practices*. London: Falmer Press.

Maykut, P. and Moorhouse, R. (1994) *Beginning Qualitative Research, A Philosophic and Practical Guide*. London: Falmer Press.

McCall, G. J. (1984) 'Systematic Field Observation'. *Annual Review of Sociology*, **10**, pp. 263–82.

McCulloch, J. and Quarrie, F. (1998) 'More Care, Please'. Unpublished BA Dissertation. University of Liverpool.

McKie, L. (2002) 'Engagement and Evaluation in Qualitative Inquiry'. In T. May (ed.), *Qualitative Research in Action*. London: Sage.

Mezirow, J. (1991) *Transformative Dimensions of Adult Learning*. San Francisco: Jossey Bass.

Mies, M. (1993) 'Towards a Methodology for Feminist Research'. In M. Hammersley (ed.), *Social Research: Philosophy, Politics and Practice*. London: Sage.

Miller, R., Acton, C., Fullerton, D. and Maltby, J. (2002) *SPSS for Social Scientists*. Basingstoke: Palgrave.

Miller, R. L. and Brewer, J. D. (2003) *The A–Z of Social Research*. London: Sage.

Molesworth, S. (2003) 'Report for a Young Offender Family Support Agency'. Unpublished MSc dissertation. University of Liverpool.

Moon, J. (2000) *Reflection in Learning and Professional Development*. London: Kogan Page.

Morgan, G. (1986) *Images of Organisation*. London: Sage.

Morris, J. (1992) 'Personal as Political: A Feminist Perspective on Researching Physical Disability'. *Disability, Handicap & Society*, **7**(2), pp. 157–66.

Morrison, K. (1995) 'Dewey, Habermas and Reflective Practice'. *Curriculum*, **16**, pp. 82–94.

Moser, C. and Kalton, G. (1971) *Survey Methods in Social Investigation*. London: Heinemann.

Oakley, A. (1981) 'Interviewing Women: A Contradiction in Terms?' In H. Roberts (ed.), *Doing Feminist Research*. London: Routledge and Kegan Paul.

Ogden, D. (1997) 'The View From Here'. Unpublished BA Dissertation. University of Liverpool.

Olsen, W. (1994) 'Researcher as Enabler: An Alternative Model of Research for Public Health'. *Critical Public Health*, **5**(3), pp. 5–14.

Oppenheim, A. N. (2000) *Questionnaire Design, Interviewing and Attitude Measurement*. London: Continuum.

Owen, J. (1999) *Program Evaluation*. London: Sage.

Pallant, J. (2001) *SPSS Survival Manual*. Buckingham: Open University Press.

Parlett, M. and Hamilton, D. (1972) 'Evaluation as Illumination: A New Approach to the Study of Innovatory Programs'. *Occasional Paper 9*, Centre for Research in the Educational Sciences, University of Edinburgh.

Parlett, M. and Hamilton, D. (1976) 'Evaluation as Illumination: A New Approach to the Study of Innovatory Programs'. In G. V. Glass (ed.), *Evaluation Studies Review Annual*, vol. 1. Beverly Hills, CA: Sage.

Patton, M. Q. (1994) 'Developmental Evaluation'. *Evaluation Practice*, **15**(3), pp. 311–20.

Patton, M. Q. (1997) *Utilization-Focused Evaluation*. Thousand Oaks, CA: Sage.

Patton, M. Q. (1990) *Qualitative Evaluation and Research Methods*, 2nd edn. Newbury Park, CA: Sage.

Pawson, R. and Tilley, N. (1997) *Realistic Evaluation*. London: Sage.

Payler, A. (2000) 'A Study of Perceptions of Volunteering and Volunteers for a Voluntary Social Service Agency'. Unpublished MSc dissertation. University of Liverpool.

Plummer, K. (2001) *Documents of Life 2: An Invitation to Critical Humanism*. London: Sage.

Polanyi, M. (1959) *Personal Knowledge: Towards a Post-Critical Philosophy*. London: Routledge & Kegan Paul.

Porter, E. (1999) *Feminist Perspectives on Ethics*. London: Longman.

Posavac, E. J. and Carey, R. G. (1989) *Program Evaluation: Methods and Case Studies*, 3rd edn. Englewood Cliffs, NJ: Prentice-Hall.

Punch, K. F. (2003) *Survey Research: the basics*. London: Sage.

Putnam, R. D. (1995) 'Bowling Alone: America's Declining Social Capital'. *Journal of Democracy*, **6**(1), pp. 65–78.

Putnam, R. D. (2000) *Bowling Alone: The Collapse and Revival of American Community*. New York: Simon & Schuster.

Reason, P. (1998) 'Three Approaches to Participative Inquiry'. In N. Denzin and Y. Lincoln (eds), *Strategies of Qualitative Inquiry*. Thousand Oaks, CA: Sage.

Rhoads, R. A. (1997) *Community Service and Higher Learning: Explorations of the Caring Self*. New York: State University of New York Press.

Richards, L. (1999) *Using NVivo in Qualitative Research*. London: Sage.

Richardson, L. (1998) 'Writing: A Method of Inquiry'. In N. Denzin and Y. Lincoln (eds), *Collecting and Interpreting Qualitative Materials*. Thousand Oaks, CA: Sage.

Richardson, L., Fonow, M. M. and Cook, J. A. (1985) 'From Gender Seminar to Gender Community'. *Teaching Sociology*, **12**, pp. 313–24.

Richmond, J. (2001) 'Futures Coffee Shop'. Unpublished BA dissertation. University of Liverpool

Riessman, C. K. (1993) 'Narrative Analysis'. In *Qualitative Research Methods*, Vol. 30. Newbury Park, CA: Sage.

Roberts, H. (2000) 'Listening to Children: and Hearing Them'. In P. Christensen and A. James (eds), *Research with Children: Perspectives and Practice*. London: Falmer Press.

Robson, C. (2001) *Real World Research*, 2nd edn. Oxford: Blackwell.

Robson, C. (2000) *Small-Scale Evaluation*. London: Sage.

Rose, G. (1982) *Deciphering Sociological Research*. London: Macmillan.

Rose, G. (2001) *Visual Methodologies: An Introduction to the Interpretation of Visual Materials*. London: Sage.

Rose, D. and Sullivan, O. (1996) *Introducing Data Analysis for Social Scientists*, 2nd edn. Buckingham: Open University Press.

Rossi, P. H. and Freeman, H. E. (1995) *Evaluation: A Systematic Approach*, 5th edn. Newbury Park, CA: Sage.
Roth, J. (1990) 'Needs and the Needs Assessment Process'. *Evaluation Practice*, **11**(2), pp. 39–44.
Rubin, F. (1995) *A Basic Guide to Evaluation for Development Workers*. Oxford: Oxfam.
Sadler, T. (2003) 'Report for a Women's Aid Organisation'. Unpublished MSc dissertation. University of Liverpool.
Sainsbury, R., Ditch, J. and Hutton, S. (2003) 'CAPI (Computer Assisted Personal Interviewing)'. In R. Miller and J. Brewer (eds), *The A–Z of Social Research*. London: Sage.
Salkind, N. J. (2000) *Statistics for People Who (Think They) Hate Statistics*. Thousand Oaks, CA: Sage.
Sapsford, R. and Jupp, V. (eds) (1996) *Data Collection and Analysis*. London: Sage.
Schein, E. H. (1999) *Process Consultation Revisited: Building the Helpful Relationship*. Reading, MA: Addison-Wesley.
Schön, D. A. (1983) *The Reflective Practitioner: How Professionals Think in Action*. New York: Basic Books.
Schön, D. A. (1987) *Educating the Reflexive Practitioner*. San Francisco: Jossey Bass.
Scott, J. (1990) *A Matter of Record*. Cambridge: Polity Pres.
Scott, J. (2000) 'Children as Respondents: The Challenge for Quantitative Methods'. In P. Christensen and A. James (eds), *Research with Children: Perspectives and Practice*. London: Falmer Press.
Scott, D., Alcock, P. Russell, L. and Macmillan, R. (2000) *Moving Pictures: Realities of Voluntary Action*. Bristol: Policy Press.
Scriven, M. (1967) 'The Methodology of Evaluation'. In R. W. Tyler, R. M. Gagné and Scriven, M. (eds), *Perspectives of Curriculum Evaluation*. Chicago: Rand McNally.
Scriven (1972) 'Pros and Cons about Goal-Free Evaluation'. *Journal of Educational Evaluation* **3**(4), pp. 1–7.
Scriven, M. (1997) 'Truth and Objectivity in Evaluation'. In E. Chelimsky and W. R. Shadish (eds), *Evaluation for the 21st Century: A Handbook*. Thousand Oaks, CA: Sage.
Selltiz, C., Jahoda, M., Deutsch, M. and Cook, S. W. (1965) *Research Methods in Social Relations*. London: Methuen.
Senior, L. (1997) 'Report Evaluating a Hostel for Homeless People'. Unpublished BA Dissertation. Liverpool Hope University College.
Shadish, W., Newman, D., Scheirer, M. A. and Wye, C. (1994) *Guiding Principles for Evaluators*, see American Evaluation Association (1994).
Shaw, I. F. (1999) *Qualitative Evaluation*. London: Sage.
Silverman, D. (2001) *Interpreting Qualitative Data: Methods for Analysing Talk, Text and Interaction*, 2nd edn. London: Sage.

Skeggs, B. (2002) 'Techniques for Telling the Reflexive Self'. In T. May (ed.), *Qualitative Research in Action*. London: Sage.

Stake, R. (2000) 'The Case Study Method in Social Inquiry'. In R. Gomm, M. Hammersley and P. Foster, *Case Study Method*. Sage: London.

Stake, R. E. (1980) 'Program Evaluation, Particularly Responsive Evaluation'. In W. B. Dockrell and D. Hamilton (eds), *Rethinking Educational Research*. London: Hodder & Stoughton.

Stake, R. E. (1998) 'Case Studies'. In N. K. Denzin and Y. S. Lincoln (eds), *Strategies of Qualitative Inquiry*. Thousand Oaks, CA: Sage.

Stanley, L. and Wise, S. (1993) *Breaking Out Again: Feminist Ontology and Epistemology*, 2nd edn. London: Routledge.

Strauss, A. L. and Corbin, J. (1990) *Basics of Qualitative Research: Grounded Theory Procedures and Techniques*. Newbury Park, CA: Sage.

Stringer, E. T. (1999) *Action Research*, 2nd edn. Thousand Oaks, CA: Sage.

Stroebe, M. S., Stroebe, W. and Hansson, R. O. (eds) (1993) *Handbook of Bereavement*. Cambridge: Cambridge University Press.

Sullivan, K. (1998) 'An Evaluation of an Advocacy Project'. Upublished BA Dissertation. Liverpool Hope University College.

United States General Accounting Office (1991) Designing Evaluations, PEMD-10.1.4, Washington, DC: Program Evaluation and Methodology Division, USGAO, http://www.gao.gov/

Waheed, H. (2002) 'Report for a Hospital Volunteering Scheme'. Unpublished BA dissertation. Liverpool Hope University College.

Walsh, A. (1990) *Statistics for the Social Sciences*. New York: Harper & Row.

Webb, E., Campbell, D., Schwartz, R. and Sechrest, L. (1966) *Unobtrusive Measures: Nonreactive Research in the Social Sciences*. Chicago: Rand McNally.

Weedon, C. (1987) *Feminist Practice and Poststructuralist Theory*. Oxford: Blackwell.

Weiss, C. H. (1998) *Evaluation: Methods for Studying Programs and Policies*, 2nd edn. Upper Saddle River, NJ: Prentice-Hall.

Wengraf, T. (2001) *Qualitative Research Interviewing*. London: Sage.

Whitworth, C. (1999) Unpublished BA Dissertation. Liverpool Hope University College.

Williams, R. (1994) *The Non-Designer's Design Book*. Berkeley, CA: Peachpit Press.

Wolcott, F. (1999) *Ethnography: A Way of Seeing*. Walnut Creek, CA: Alta Mira Press.

Yow, V. R. (1994) *Recording Oral History: A Practical Guide for Social Scientists*. Thousand Oaks, CA: Sage.

Zeller, N. C. (1987) 'A Rhetoric for Naturalistic Inquiry'. Unpublished PhD dissertation. Bloomington, IN: Indiana University.

Index

Abbott, P. 229
access 18, 39–40, 82–3
Acker, J. 218
action research 50–1, 193
Alderman, G. 80–1
Altheide, D. L. 75
American Evaluation Association
  (AEA) 61, 64, 87
AEA Guiding Principles 28, 65,
  77–81, 86
American Psychological Association
  76
American Sociological Association 76
Anderson, J. 199–200, 206–13
archival research 103
Argyris, C. 23
Arksey, H. 135
Arnold, J. 178, 181
assessment 17
ARVAC 101
Atkinson, R. 133
audience 1–2, 164–5, 204

Babbie, E. 97, 103, 114, 116
Balnaves, M. 135
Banks, M. 108
Barnes, C. 126
Bartzokas, C. A. 70
Bazeley, P. 162
Bell, J. 204
Black, T. R. 127
'black box' 32–3, 46, 54–5
Blaikie, N. 56, 97, 130–1,
  133, 149
Bloor, M. 121
Bresnen, M. 73
British Dyslexia Association 187
British Psychological Society 76
British Sociological Association 76,
  107, 166–7

Bryman, A. 98–9, 114, 121–2, 127,
  134, 140, 144, 155–7, 162
Buchanan, D. 209
Burgess, R. G. 119

case studies 43, 67–71, 72–4, 169–70,
  206
census 126–7
Chamberlain, M. 83, 90, 214
Chaplin, E. 106–7
charts 143–4
checklist for research 101–2
Chelimsky, E. 32, 35, 93
Chen, H.T. 31, 46, 54–5
children 113, 120, 124–5
chi-square test 149–50
Clarke, A. 28, 31
Clegg, F. 162
codes see under ethics
coding 140–2, 155–6
Coghlan, D. 195, 201
collaborative evaluation 50, 57–9,
  131, 164, 173
Colman, A. 162
computers in data analysis 136, 142,
  154, 156–7, 162
confidentiality see under ethics
consent for research see under ethics
constructivism 53, 56, 78, 169
Converse, J. M. 135
Cook, T. D. 43, 119
costs of research 97
Cousins, B. 97
Cowan, J. 196–7, 204
credibility of research 97, 104
critical research 103, 119–20,
  191–2
criticisms, in findings 64–7, 81,
  172–3
cross-tabulations 147–9, 154

Darlington, Y. 83, 99, 123, 152
data generation 102–3
data matrix 139–40, 143, 154
de Laine, M. 75, 88, 209
de Vaus, D. A. 114, 116, 130, 139–41,
    143, 145
defining evaluation 28–9
descriptive analysis 143–5
Dillman, D. A. 135
disabilities 113, 125, 227
Duster, T. 91
dyslexia 186–7

Eisner, E. 76
emancipatory research 51, 125–6,
    161, 191
emotions, feelings 195, 204
empowerment and evaluation 53, 86,
    212
empowerment evaluation 50–2, 94
epistemology 98, 102–3
ethics 18, 76
    and access 39
    and harm 81, 86
    anonymity and confidentiality 85–6
    codes and guidelines 62, 76–7, 107
    confidentiality 112
    consent 76, 84–5, 122, 123
    democratic evaluation 62
    dilemmas 62, 75, 91
    evaluator's role 110, 116–20
    feminist perspectives 87
    in reflective reports 211–12
    natural justice 108
    small-scale evaluation 106
Etzioni, A. 82, 126
evaluation agreement 15–16
    as judgement 7, 27–8, 30, 53
    assessment 42
    brief history 30–1
    consultants 36
    definitions of 28
    for accountability 32–4, 37, 44–5, 93
    for development 9, 32–5, 37, 49,
        57, 59, 93, 223
    for empowerment 35, 50–1, 58
    for knowledge 32, 34, 37, 93, 223
    formative 29–30, 42, 46–7, 93

goal-free 45–6
guides 134–5
    profession of 79
    prospective 41
    questions 92–5, 113, 179
    report criteria 169–70
    report structure 164, 175–85
    responsive 48
    summative 29–30, 93
evaluator roles 34–6, 51, 57, 62
Everitt, A. 33
evidence-based findings 64
executive summary 176–7, 217–18,
    228
experiential learning 168, 194, 196–7
experimental designs 44–5
Eyler, J. 194

Farran, D. 172
feminist research 66, 119, 192, 211
Fetterman, D. M. 35, 36, 51, 57, 59
Field, A. 162
Fielding, J. 145, 162
Fielding, N. 156
Finnegan, R. 153
Flick, U. 135
focus groups 99, 120–3
Fong, S. 73–4
Foster, V. 202
fourth-generation evaluation 52–4,
    56, 169
Freeborn, D. 166
Freidson, E. 79
Freire, P. 125
frequency table 143–4

Gabriel, Y. 39
Gahan, C. 162
gatekeeper 38–9, 82, 112
Geertz, C. 170
generalization 129, 134
Gherardi, S. 6
Gibbs, G. 154–5, 162
Gilbert, N. 135, 145, 162, 219, 229
Glaser, B. 156
Goode, W. J. 218
Gosling, L. 164
Gould, N. 196

Greenbaum, T. L.   121
grounded theory   6, 156
Guba, E. G.   40, 48, 52, 54, 56, 78–9,
    169–70

Habermas, J.   190–1
Hakim, C.   127, 149
Hall, I. and Hall, D.   2, 12–13, 20, 22,
    25, 67, 72, 74, 108, 114, 123, 152,
    159, 164, 197, 213
Haraway, D.   193
Harvey, L.   192
health and safety   17, 237–41
Herman, J. L.   135
Holly, M. L.   204
House, E. R.   63, 76, 78–9
hypothesis testing   154

impact assessment and evaluation   31,
    44–5
independence, of research   59, 64, 71,
    75
interview guide or schedule   117–18,
    125, 153
interviews   99, 103
    as conversation   119
    face-to-face   118–19
    group   119–20
    personal   111, 117
    recording information   122–3
    semi-structured   100, 125
    telephone   111

Kinnear, P. R.   162
Kirkcaldy, A.   88–90
Kmietowicz, Z.   68
Kolb, D.   194, 196
Krueger, R. A.   121
Kushner, S.   61–3, 170
Kvale, S.   100, 103, 117, 128, 136, 139

Labov, W.   158–9
language   165–7
Layder, D.   6
learning log   197
    see also research diary
Ledwith, M.   103, 125
Lee, R. M.   107, 109, 156

Lilley, S.   67
Lincoln, Y.   161
Locke, L.   126, 165
Lockley, S.   187
Lofland, J.   91

Marsh, C.   139
Mason, J.   98, 104, 118–19, 133, 154
Mayall, B.   124
McCall, C. J.   104
McCulloch, J.   151
McKie, L.   193
Mezirow, J.   201
Mies, M.   119, 125
Miller, R.   162
mission statement   207, 216
Molesworth, S.   201–2
Moon, J.   191, 195
Morgan, G.   39
Morris, J.   192
Morrison, K.   191
Moser, C.   114
multiple methods   98–9

narratives   150, 157–9
natural justice   63–5
needs assessment   41
negotiation   13–17, 83
    agreement   65, 75, 105, 220–1
    checklist   14
    research design   95–7
non-response   140, 219

Oakley, A.   103, 219, 229
observation   104–10
Office for National Statistics   115
Olsen, W.   120
operationalize   94, 113, 137
Oppenheim, A. N.   135
oral feedback   163, 172
oral history   159–60
Owen, J.   187

Pallant, J.   162
paradigm wars   98, 103
Parlett, M.   47–8
participant observation   103–4, 108

participatory evaluation   36, 49–50, 94, 161, 173
Patton, M. Q.   22, 27, 36, 42–3, 46, 48–9, 56, 64, 94–5, 183
Pawson, R.   31, 42, 54–7, 98, 112
Payler, A.   172
photographs   105, 107, 108, 110
Piaget, J.   196
Plummer, K.   91, 123, 128, 150, 152, 155, 157–8
Polanyi, M.   6
policy decisions and evaluation   42–4
Porter, E.   60, 87
positionality   192–3
positivist approach   30, 56, 61, 98, 102, 167, 194
Posovac, E. J.   33
postmodernism   150
poststructuralism   167–8
power relationship   103, 193
process evaluation   46–7
pseudo-evaluation   43
Punch, K. F.   98, 113, 116, 135
Putnam, R. D.   207–8

qualitative evaluation   47, 94, 174
qualitative interviewing   98, 103, 117–22
qualitative methods   99–100
Quality Assurance Agency   17
Question Bank   115
questionnaires   99–100, 110
   design of   112–15
   length of   115
   pilot testing   115, 125, 139
   postal   111, 115–16
   response rates   115–16
   rules for design of   114–15
   third-party administration   112
questions
   closed   99, 138
   open-ended   99–100, 115, 141

realistic evaluation   42, 55–7
Reason, P.   168
recommendations   181, 183–4
records   127
reflection   91, 189–90, 194–204, 214–15

in action   195, 197–8, 211–12, 214
on action   195–8, 205, 211
reflective account   70, 88–90, 204–14
reflective learning   168
reflective practitioner   24, 189, 194
reflexive account   190, 196–7
reflexivity   191–4, 197–8, 210–11
relevance of research   97, 104
reliability   97–9
report, evaluation research   136, 147, 214
report, style   184, 185
representational crisis   161, 168, 193
research design   97–8
research diary or journal   69, 105, 128, 133, 197–204
Research Ethics Committee   69, 83, 89
research with disabled people   125–6
Rhoads, R. A.   192
Richards, L.   162
Richardson, L.   167–8
Richmond, J.   148
Riessman, C. K.   157–9, 161
Roberts, H.   125
Robson, C.   8, 20, 31, 60, 76–7, 135, 164–5
Rose, G.   6, 107, 137, 150
Rossi, P. H.   7, 34, 44–5
Roth, J.   41
Rubin, F.   35, 41–2, 164

Sadler, T.   203, 212
Salkind, N. J.   116, 145, 162
sample   97, 179
   non-probability   131–4
   probability   129–31
   size   130
sampling   128–34
   bias   129, 133
   frame   129
   convenience   133–4
   judgemental   132
   quota   131
   snowball   133
   stratified   130
   systematic   106, 130
   theoretical   132
Sapsford, R.   135

saturation, theoretical 132, 156
scales of measurement 137–8, 143–4
Schein, E. H. 195
Schön, D. A. 23–4, 29, 96, 194–6
science shop xiv–xv
Scott, J. 99, 127, 206–7
Scriven, M. 28–9, 35–6, 45–6
self-evaluation 190
Selltiz, C. 219
service learning xv
Shadish, W. 28
Shaw, I. F. 75–6
Silverman, D. 152, 154, 157
Skeggs, B. 192–3
small-scale evaluation model 7–13,
    62, 72, 194
  definition 8
  ethics 61, 66
  partnership and collaboration 9,
    58–9, 94
  principles 9–10
  resources 8, 18
  revisited 57–9
social capital 208
social exclusion 110
sponsors 38–9, 66, 82
Stake, R. 48, 171
stakeholder evaluation 50, 58
stakeholders 37, 39–41, 43, 48–9, 53,
    86, 99–100, 128, 164
Stanley, L. 66
stories 150–1, 157–8
Strauss, A. L. 132, 156
Stringer, E. T. 50–1
Stroebe, M. S. 89
students
  as evaluators 11–13, 58–9
  guidance for 175
Sullivan, K. 137, 150, 183
survey 19, 110, 139, 143, 159
  computer-assisted 112
  email or internet 111

tape recording 121, 123, 152, 157
text construction 167–72
thematic analysis 153–4
theorizing evaluation 52–7
theory of action 23, 96, 207
theory-driven evaluation 54–5
third mission (of universities) xiv
timing of evaluation 41, 97
transcription 151–3, 159
triangulation 98–9

unobtrusive measures 109–10
usage
  consultation and contact 22
  internal and external use 21
  managerial willingness to act 23
  small-scale evaluation 20–5, 226,
    233
  timing of evaluation 23
US General Accounting Office 31, 50
utilization-focused evaluation 49, 51,
    55, 94

validity 97, 99–100
variable 137, 139–42, 146–7, 149, 154

Waheed, H. 68–71
Walsh, A. 162
Webb, E. 109
Weedon, C. 168
Weiss, C. 18, 28, 34, 37, 43, 49, 57–9,
    60, 65–6, 174, 176, 178–9, 182,
    185–6, 188
Wengraf, T. 135
Whitworth, C. 213
Williams, R. 185

Yow, V. R. 159

Zeller, N. C. 169